Er. D.C. Gupta

Rotational Motion
for JEE Main & Advanced
(Study Package for Physics)

Fully Solved

disha
Nurturing Ambitions

Includes Past
JEE & KVPY Questions

Useful for Class 11,
KVPY & Olympiads

- **Head Office :** B-32, Shivalik Main Road, Malviya Nagar, New Delhi-110017
- **Sales Office :** B-48, Shivalik Main Road, Malviya Nagar, New Delhi-110017
  Tel. : 011-26691021 / 26691713

Page Layout : Prakash Chandra Sahoo

Typeset by Disha DTP Team

Printed at : Repro Knowledgecast Limited, Thane

DISHA PUBLICATION
ALL RIGHTS RESERVED

© Copyright Author

No part of this publication may be reproduced in any form without prior permission of the publisher. The author and the publisher do not take any legal responsibility for any errors or misrepresentations that might have crept in. We have tried and made our best efforts to provide accurate up-to-date information in this book.

For further information about the books from DISHA,
Log on to www.dishapublication.com or email to info@dishapublication.com

Booklet No.	Title	Chapter Nos.	Page Nos.
	STUDY PACKAGE IN PHYSICS FOR JEE MAIN & ADVANCED		
1	Units, Measurements & Motion	Ch 0. Mathematics Used in Physics Ch 1. Units and Measurements Ch 2. Vectors Ch 3. Motion in a Straight Line Ch 4. Motion in a Plane	1-202
2	Laws of Motion and Circular Motion	Ch 5. Laws of Motion and Equilibrium Ch 6. Circular Motion	203-318
3	Work Energy, Power & Gravitation	Ch 7. Work, Energy and Power Ch 8. Collisions and Centre of Mass Ch 9. Gravitation	319-480
4	Rotational Motion	Ch 1. Rotational Mechanics	1-120
5	Properties of Matter & SHM	Ch 2. Properties of Matter Ch 3. Fluid Mechanics Ch 4. Simple Harmonic Motion	121-364
6	Heat & Thermodynamics	Ch 5. Thermometry, Expansion & Calorimetry Ch 6. Kinetic Theory of Gases Ch 7. Laws of Thermodynamics Ch 8. Heat Transfer	365-570
7	Waves	Ch 9. Wave – I Ch 10. Wave –II	571-698
8	Electrostatics	Ch 0. Mathematics Used in Physics Ch 1. Electrostatics Ch 2. Capacitance & Capacitors	1-216
9	Current Electricity	Ch 3. DC and DC circuits Ch 4. Thermal and Chemical effects of Current"	217-338
10	Magnetism, EMI & AC	Ch 5. Magnetic Force on Moving Charges & Conductor Ch 6. Magnetic Effects of Current Ch 7. Permanent Magnet & Magnetic Properties of Substance Ch 8. Electromagnetic Induction Ch 9. AC and EM Waves	339-618
11	Ray & Wave Optics	Ch 1. Reflection of Light Ch 2. Refraction and Dispersion Ch 3. Refraction at Spherical Surface, Lenses and Photometry Ch 4. Wave optics	1-244
12	Modern Physics	Ch 5. Electron, Photon, Atoms, Photoelectric Effect and X-rays Ch 6. Nuclear Physics Ch 7. Electronics & Communication	245-384

Contents

Study Package Booklet 4 - Rotational Motion

1. Rotational Mechanics — 01-120

1.1	Some definition	01
1.2	Equations of motion of a rotating body	02
1.3	Instantaneous axis of rotation	06
1.4	Rotational dynamics	07
1.5	Couple	09
1.6	Moment of inertia or rotational inertia	09
1.7	Theorems of moment of inertia	10
1.8	Angular momentum	23
1.9	Rotational kinetic energy	27
1.10	Rotational work	28
1.11	Angular impulse	29
1.12	Rotation about a moving axis	34
1.13	Rolling motion	44
1.14	Accelerated pure rolling	52
	Review of formulae & important points	59
	Exercise 1.1 - Exercise 1.6	63-94
	Hints & solutions	95-120

CHAPTER 1

Rotational Mechanics

(1-120)

1.1	SOME DEFINITIONS
1.2	EQUATIONS OF MOTION OF A ROTATING BODY
1.3	INSTANTANEOUS AXIS OF ROTATION
1.4	ROTATIONAL DYNAMICS
1.5	COUPLE
1.6	MOMENT OF INERTIA OR ROTATIONAL INERTIA
1.7	THEOREMS OF MOMENT OF INERTIA
1.8	ANGULAR MOMENTUM
1.9	ROTATIONAL KINETIC ENERGY
1.10	ROTATIONAL WORK
1.11	ANGULAR IMPULSE
1.12	ROTATION ABOUT A MOVING AXIS
1.13	ROLLING MOTION
1.14	ACCELERATED PURE ROLLING

REVIEW OF FORMULAE & IMPORTANT POINTS

EXERCISE 1.1

EXERCISE 1.2

EXERCISE 1.3

EXERCISE 1.4

EXERCISE 1.5

EXERCISE 1.6

HINTS & SOLUTIONS

MECHANICS, THERMODYNAMICS & WAVES

1.1 Some definitions

Particle
A particle is defined as an object whose mass is finite but its size is negligible small.

Rigid body
A body is said to be rigid if it does not undergo any change in size and shape, however large external force act on it.

Translatory motion
When different particles of a body undergo same displacement, the motion of the body is called translatory motion.

Here $\quad AA' = BB' = CC'$

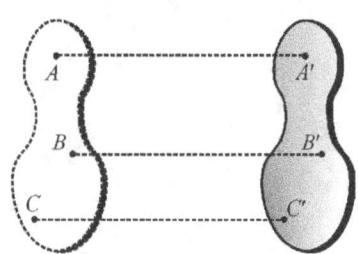

Fig. 1.1. Translatory motion.

Rotatory Motion
When different particles of a body undergo same angular displacement, the motion of the body is called rotatory motion. But different particles have different linear displacements.

If angular displacement traversed by the particles A, B and C on the body in time t is θ, then

$$\omega_A = \omega_B = \omega_C = \frac{\theta}{t}$$

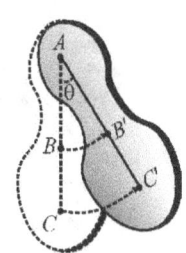

Fig. 1.2. Rotatory motion.

while linear velocity $\quad v_A = \frac{AA'}{t} = \frac{0}{t} = 0$

$$v_B = \frac{BB'}{t} = \frac{\theta r_B}{t} = \omega r_B$$

and $\quad v_C = \frac{CC'}{t} = \frac{\theta r_C}{t} = \omega r_C$

It is clear that, $\quad r_A < r_B < r_C$

so $\quad v_A < v_B < v_C$

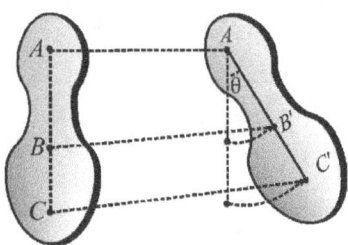

Fig. 1.3

Combined translation and rotation
The combination of above two motions results combined translation and rotation.

1.2 Equations of motion of a rotating body

First equation of motion
Let us consider a rigid body rotating about a fixed axis with constant angular acceleration α. By definition

$$\frac{d\omega}{dt} = \alpha$$

or $\quad d\omega = \alpha\, dt$

If at $t = 0$, $\omega = \omega_0$, then the angular velocity of the body at any time t is given by

$$\int_{\omega_0}^{\omega} d\omega = \int_0^t \alpha\, dt$$

$$|\omega|_{\omega_0}^{\omega} = \alpha |t|_0^t$$

or $\quad \omega - \omega_0 = \alpha(t - 0)$

or $\quad \omega = \omega_0 + \alpha t \qquad \ldots(1)$

Second equation of motion

By definition, we have

$$\frac{d\theta}{dt} = \omega$$

or

$$d\theta = \omega dt$$

If at $t = 0$, $\theta = 0$, then angular displacement in time t is given by

$$\int_0^\theta d\theta = \int_0^t \omega dt = \int_0^t (\omega_0 + \alpha t) dt$$

or

$$|\theta|_0^\theta = \left|\omega_0 t + \frac{1}{2}\alpha t^2\right|_0^t$$

or

$$\theta = \omega_0 t + \frac{1}{2}\alpha t^2 \qquad \ldots(2)$$

Third equation of motion

The angular acceleration can be expressed as

$$\alpha = \frac{d\omega}{dt} = \frac{d\omega}{d\theta} \cdot \frac{d\theta}{dt}$$

or

$$\alpha = \omega \frac{d\omega}{d\theta}$$

or

$$\omega d\omega = \alpha d\theta$$

Integrating above equation, we get

$$\int_{\omega_0}^{\omega} \omega d\omega = \int_0^\theta \alpha d\theta$$

or

$$\left|\frac{\omega^2}{2}\right|_{\omega_0}^{\omega} = \alpha|\theta|_0^\theta$$

or

$$\omega^2 - \omega_0^2 = 2\alpha\theta$$

or

$$\omega^2 = \omega_0^2 + 2\alpha\theta \qquad \ldots(3)$$

For uniformly retarded motion, these equations become;

$$\omega = \omega_0 - \alpha t$$

$$\theta = \omega_0 t - \frac{1}{2}\alpha t^2$$

and

$$\omega^2 = \omega_0^2 - 2\alpha\theta.$$

SI units :

SI unit of angular displacement is radian.
SI unit of angular velocity is rad/s.
SI unit of angular acceleration is rad/s².

Wheels rotate in contact

Consider two wheels of radii r_1 and r_2 are rotating in contact without slipping. If v_1 and v_2 are the linear velocities of their points of contact, then

$$v_1 = v_2$$

or

$$\omega_1 r_1 = \omega_2 r_2$$

If $r_1 = r$ and $r_2 = 2r$, then $\omega_1 = 2\omega$ and $\omega_2 = \omega$.

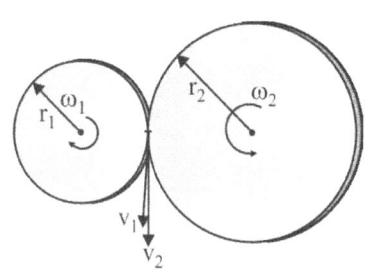

Fig. 1.4

4 MECHANICS, THERMODYNAMICS & WAVES

Ex. 1 The angular speed of a motor wheel is increased from 1200 rpm to 3120 rpm in 16 second.
(i) What is its angular acceleration, assuming the acceleration to be uniform?
(ii) How many revolutions does the wheel make during this time?

Sol.

Given, $\omega_0 = 2\pi n_0 = 2\pi \times \dfrac{1200}{60}$

$= 40\pi$ rad/s

$\omega = 2\pi n = 2\pi \times \dfrac{3120}{60}$

$= 104\pi$ rad/s

(i) Angular acceleration

$\alpha = \dfrac{\omega - \omega_0}{t} = \dfrac{104\pi - 40\pi}{16}$

$= 4\pi$ rad/s^2 **Ans.**

(ii) The angular displacement can be obtained as

$\theta = \omega_0 t + \dfrac{1}{2}\alpha t^2$

$= 40\pi \times 16 + \dfrac{1}{2} \times 4\pi \times (16)^2$

$= 1152\pi$ rad

Number of revolutions in 16 s

$= \dfrac{\theta}{2\pi} = \dfrac{1152\pi}{2\pi} = 576$ **Ans.**

Ex. 2 The angular acceleration of a flywheel is given by $\alpha = 12 - t$ where α is in rad/s^2 and t in second. If the angular velocity of the wheel is 60 rad/s at thwe end of 4 second, determine the angular velocity at the end of 6 second. How many revolutions take place in these 6 second ?

Sol.

Given that $\alpha = 12 - t$

i.e. $\dfrac{d\omega}{dt} = 12 - t$

or $d\omega = (12 - t)dt$

Integrating above equation, we get

$\int d\omega = \int (12 - t)dt$

or $\omega = 12t - \dfrac{t^2}{2} + C$

At $t = 4$ s, $\omega = 60$ rad/s

$\therefore$ $60 = 12 \times 4 - \dfrac{4^2}{2} + C$

or $C = 20$

$\therefore$ $\omega = 12t - \dfrac{t^2}{2} + 20$ ... (i)

At $t = 6$ s, $\omega = 12 \times 6 - \dfrac{6^2}{2} + 20$

$= 74$ rad/s   **Ans.**

Now we can write

$\dfrac{d\theta}{dt} = 12t - \dfrac{t^2}{2} + 20$

Integrating the above equation, we get

$\int d\theta = \int (12t - \dfrac{t^2}{2} + 20)dt$

or $\theta = \dfrac{12t^2}{2} - \dfrac{t^3}{6} + 20t + C'$

Let at $t = 0$, $\theta = \theta_0$, $\therefore$ $C' = \theta_0$

Thus we have $\theta = 6t^2 - \dfrac{t^3}{6} + 20t + \theta_0$

or $\theta - \theta_0 = 6t^2 - \dfrac{t^3}{6} + 20t$ ... (ii)

Angular displacement during 6 s

$\theta_6 - \theta_0 = 6 \times 6^2 - \dfrac{6^3}{6} + 20 \times 6$

$= 300$ rad

$\therefore$ Number of revolutions $= \dfrac{300}{2\pi} = 47.8$ **Ans.**

Ex. 3 The step pulley shown in *Fig. 1.5* starts from rest and accelerates at 2 rad/s^2. What time is required for block A to move 20 m ? Find also the velocity of A and B at that time.

Sol.

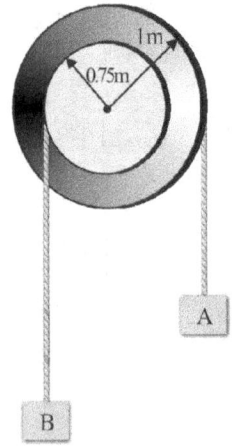

Fig. 1.5

When A moves 20 m, its angular displacement θ is given by

$s = r\theta$

or $\theta = \dfrac{s}{r} = \dfrac{20}{1} = 20$ rad

Given $\alpha = 2$ rad/s^2 and $\omega_0 = 0$.

By second equation of motion, we have

$\theta = \omega_0 t + \dfrac{1}{2}\alpha t^2$

$20 = 0 + \dfrac{1}{2} \times 2 \times t^2$

or $t = 4.47$ s   **Ans.**

Angular velocity of pulley at this time

$\omega = \omega_0 + \alpha t$

$= 0 + 2 \times 4.47 = 8.94$ rad/s   **Ans.**

Now velocity of A, $v_A = \omega r_A = 8.94 \times 1$
$= 8.94$ m/s
and $v_B = \omega r_B = 8.94 \times 0.75$
$= 6.70$ m/s **Ans.**

Ex. 4
The angular rotation in radians of an accelerated flywheel is given by $\theta = 9t^3/32$. Find the linear velocity and acceleration of a point at a distance of 0.75 m from the axis of rotation at the instant when its tangential acceleration and normal accelerations are equal.

Sol.
We have, $\theta = 9t^3/32$

Angular velocity $\omega = \dfrac{d\theta}{dt} = \left(\dfrac{9}{32}\right) 3t^2$
$= 27t^2/32$

and angular acceleration
$\alpha = \dfrac{d\omega}{dt}$
$= 27t/16$

Tangential acceleration of a point at a radius r is given by
$a_t = \alpha r$

and the normal acceleration is given by $a_n = \omega^2 r$
Since the tangential and normal accelerations at a distance r = 0.75 m are equal, so

$\alpha r = \omega^2 r$
or $\alpha = \omega^2$
or $\dfrac{27t}{16} = \left(\dfrac{27t^2}{32}\right)^2$

which gives $t = 4/3$ s

Linear velocity $= \omega r = \left(\dfrac{27t^2}{32}\right) r = \left(\dfrac{27}{32}\right)\left(\dfrac{4}{3}\right)^2 \times 0.75$
$= 9/8$ m/s **Ans.**

Tangential acceleration $= \omega^2 r = \left(\dfrac{27t^2}{32}\right)^2 r = \left[\dfrac{27}{32}\left(\dfrac{4}{3}\right)^2\right]^2 \times 0.75$
$= 7/16$ m/s² **Ans.**

Ex. 5
In a system of gears load A rotates a pulley of radius r and a gear wheel of radius r_1. This gear wheel is geared with a second gear wheel of radius r_2. If the load starts from rest and moves down with a constant acceleration, find the equation of second gear wheel.

Sol.

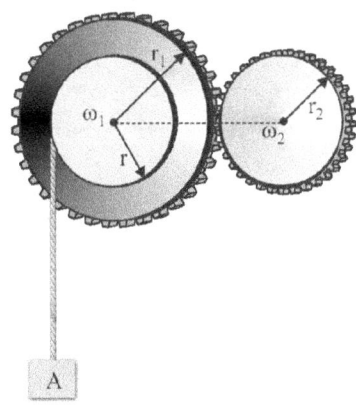

Fig. 1.6

Since the load A starts moving with constant acceleration a, its velocity at time t,
$v = at$.
Let ω_1 be the angular velocity of the pulley and the first gear wheel.
∴ Peripheral velocity of the pulley $= \omega_1 r = at$
$\omega_1 = at/r$
Peripheral speed of the first gear wheel $\omega_1 r_1$.
Since the two gear wheels have the same peripheral velocities, so
$\omega_2 r_2 = \omega_1 r_1$
or $\omega_2 = \omega_1 r_1 / r_2$
$= at\, r_1/(rr_2)$
Let θ be the angular displacement of the second gear at time t.
∴ $\omega_2 = d\theta/dt = at\, r_1/(rr_2)$
or $d\theta = at\, r_1/(rr_2) dt$
Integrating above equation, we get
$\theta = at^2 r_1/(2rr_2)$ **Ans.**

Ex. 6
Figure shows a compound wheel which rolls without slipping. If the velocity of the centre O is 1.25 m/s. Find the velocities of the points A, B and C.

Sol.

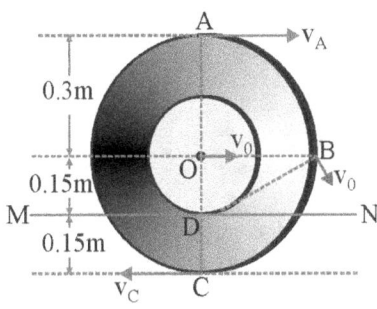

Fig. 1.7

Since the wheel rolls without slipping on the supporting surface MN, the point of contact D is the instantaneous centre of rotation. Let ω be the angular velocity about the instantaneous centre D.

Velocity of O $= v_0 = \omega \cdot DO$
Velocity of A $= v_A = \omega \cdot DA$
Velocity of B $= v_B = \omega \cdot DB$
Velocity of C $= v_C = \omega \cdot DC$

We have DO = 0.15 m, DA = 0.45 m

$DB = \sqrt{(0.3^2 + 0.15^2)} = 0.335$ m

and $DC = 0.15$ m
∴ $v_0 = 1.25$ m/s
$1.25 : v_A : v_B : v_C = (0.15) : (0.45) : (0.335) : (0.15)$
$v_A = 1.25 \times 0.45 / 0.15 = $ **3.75 m/s**
$v_B = 1.25 \times 0.335 / 0.15 = $ **2.80 m/s**
$v_C = 1.25 \times 0.15 / 0.15 = $ **1.25 m/s** **Ans.**

1.3 INSTANTANEOUS AXIS OF ROTATION

At any instant it is possible to locate a point in the plane which has zero velocity and hence plane motion of other points may be looked as pure rotation about this axis. Such point is called instantaneous centre and the axis passing through this point and right angles to the plane of motion is called instantaneous axis of rotation.

More about instantaneous axis of rotation

Motion of such an object may be looked as pure rotation about a point has zero velocity to simplify the study. Such a point is called **Instantaneous centre** and the axis passing through this point and perpendicular to the plane of motion is called Instantaneous Axis of Rotation (*IAOR*).

In the figure shown I_1 and I_2 are the instantaneous centres of rotation of rod at two different instants.

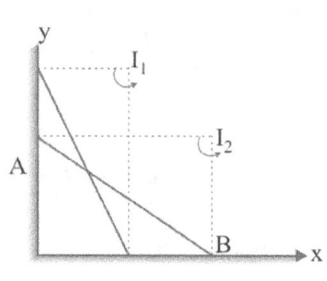

Fig. 1.8

To understand instantaneous centre consider a rigid body which has plane motion. Let A be a point having velocity v_A at the instant considered. Now locate a point I on perpendicular to the direction of v_A at A at a distance r_A. The motion of A can be split into translation of I and rotation about I. Thus we can write

$$v_A = v_I + \omega r_A,$$

if we take $r_A = \dfrac{v_A}{\omega}$, then $\quad v_A = v_I + \omega \times \dfrac{v_A}{\omega}$

$$\therefore \quad v_I = 0$$

Thus point 'I' is selected at a distance $\dfrac{v_A}{\omega}$ along the perpendicular to the direction of A, the plane motion of point A can be reduced to pure rotation about I. Hence I is the instantaneous centre.

If B is any other point on the rigid body then its velocity will be given by

$$v_B = v_I + \omega r_B$$

or $\quad v_B = \omega r_B \quad (v_I = 0)$

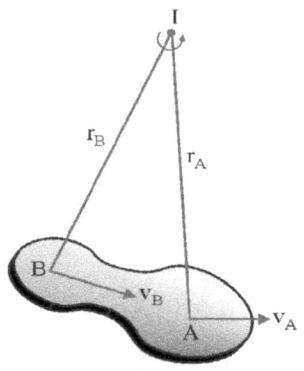

Fig. 1.9

Method of locating instantaneous centre

Instantaneous centre can be located by any of the following two methods:

(i) If the angular velocity ω and linear velocity v_A are known, instantaneous centre can be located at a distance v_A / ω along the perpendicular to the direction of v_A at A, as discussed earlier.

(ii) If the linear velocities of two points of rigid body are known, say v_A and v_B, drop perpendiculars to them at A and B. The intersection point is the instantaneous centre (see *Fig 1.8*).

Ex. 7

(a) A long rod AB rests over a fixed cylinder of radius r with its lower end B resting on a horizontal floor as shown in *Fig.1.10(a)*. If the end B moves with velocity v, find the angular velocity of the rod.

(b) Three links are hinged together to form a triangle ABC as shown in Fig 1.8 (b)

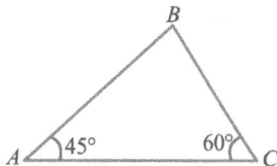

Fig. 1.10

At a certain instant, the point A is moving towards the mid-point of BC with a velocity of 5 m/s and B is moving at a perpendicular direction to AC. Find the velocity of C.

Sol. (a) By drawing lines perpendicular to the direction of motion of B and C, the point of intersection I obtained is the instantaneous centre of rotation.

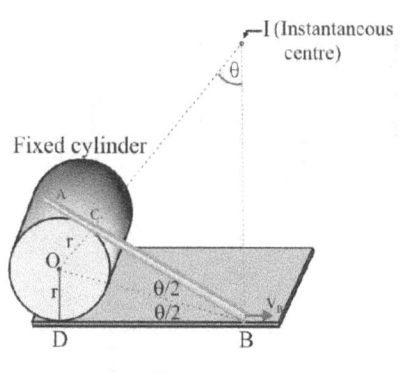

Fig. 1.10 (a)

Let the rod makes an angle θ with the horizontal.

$\angle OBD = \angle OBC = \theta/2$

$\angle CIB = \theta$

$BC = r \cot \dfrac{\theta}{2}$

$IB = BC \operatorname{cosec} \theta = r \cot \dfrac{\theta}{2} \operatorname{cosec} \theta$

Let the angular velocity of the rod be ω.
Velocity of end $B = v_B = v = \omega(IB)$

$\therefore \quad \omega = v/IB = v/(r \cot \dfrac{\theta}{2} \operatorname{cosec} \theta)$

$= 2\dfrac{v}{r} \sin^2 \dfrac{\theta}{2}$ **Ans.**

(b) Given : Velocity of A $(v_A) = 5$ m/s
First of all, let us locate the position of instantaneous centre of the point A and B graphically as shown in fig and as discussed below :
1. Draw the triangle ABC with the given data
2. Now draw the lines indicating the directions of motion of points A (towards mid-point of BC) and B (at right angles to AC)
3. Now draw perpendiculars at A and B on directions of motion of v_A and v_B.
4. Let these perpendicular meet at O, which is the instantaneous centre of the link AB and BC.
5. Now join OC and draw a line at right angle to OC indicating the direction of motion of the point C.

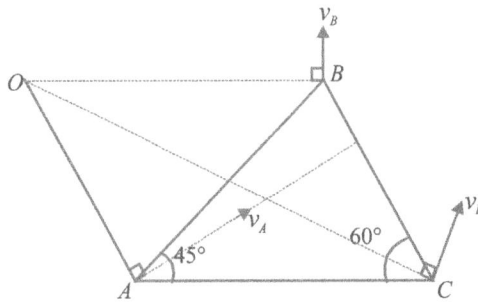

Fig. 1.10 (b)

Measuring the diagram to some scale, we find that $OA = 2.6$ cm and $OC = 5.4$ cm

We know that $\dfrac{v_C}{v_A} = \dfrac{OC}{OA} = \dfrac{5.4}{2.6} = 2.08$

$\therefore$ Velocity of C,

$v_C = v_A \times 2.08 = 5 \times 2.08 = 10.4$ m/s **Ans.**

1.4 Rotational Dynamics

Moment of force or torque (τ)

The torque is the turning effect of force about the axis passes away from line of action of the force. Its magnitude is equal to the product of the force and the perpendicular distance between the line of the force and the axis of rotation. It is a vector quantity and its direction can be obtained by right hand screw rule.

Consider a body is acted by a force $\vec{F}$ at a point whose position vector is $\vec{r}$ with reference to the origin of coordinate system, as shown in *Fig. 1.11*.

It is clear from the figure that $F \cos \theta$ can cause translation while $F \sin \theta$ causes rotation. Thus the moment of force is given by,

$\tau = F \sin \theta \times r$

$= Fr \sin \theta$

Here the direction of moment of force is along the positive z-axis. Thus we can write

$\vec{\tau} = Fr \sin \theta \hat{k}$

According to right hand screw rule, this can be written as

$\vec{\tau} = \vec{r} \times \vec{F}$

In the above treatment we have resolved the force perpendicular to the position vector $\vec{r}$. It is also possible to resolve $\vec{r}$ perpendicular to the line of action of force $\vec{F}$ (see *Fig. 1.12*).

Hence moment of force can be obtained as,

$\tau = F \times r \sin \theta$

In vector notation, we can write

$\vec{\tau} = \vec{r} \times \vec{F}$

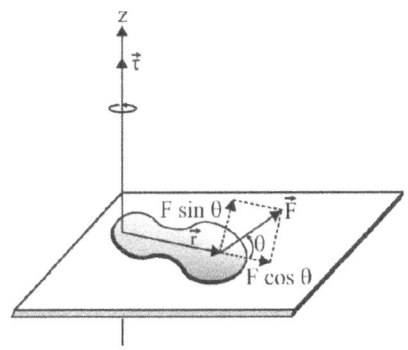

Fig. 1.11

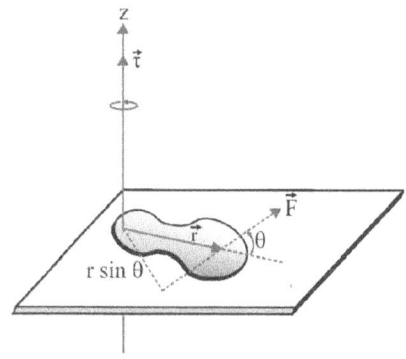

Fig. 1.12

MECHANICS, THERMODYNAMICS & WAVES

Moment arm

It is the perpendicular distance from axis of rotation to the line of action of the force. This is $r\sin\theta$.

Moment arm, $\qquad r\sin\theta = \dfrac{Fr\sin\theta}{F}$

or $\qquad$ Moment arm $= \dfrac{|\vec{r}\times\vec{F}|}{|\vec{F}|}$

Torque in terms of rectangular components

If $\vec{F}$ and $\vec{r}$ are given as;

$$\vec{F} = F_x\hat{i} + F_y\hat{j} + F_z\hat{k} \quad \text{and} \quad \vec{r} = x\hat{i} + y\hat{j} + z\hat{k}$$

then torque can be defined as:
$$\vec{\tau} = \vec{r}\times\vec{F}$$
$$= (x\hat{i}+y\hat{j}+z\hat{k})\times(F_x\hat{i}+F_y\hat{j}+F_z\hat{k})$$
$$= \begin{vmatrix} \hat{i} & \hat{j} & \hat{k} \\ x & y & z \\ F_x & F_y & F_z \end{vmatrix}$$

or $\quad \vec{\tau} = \tau_x\hat{i} + \tau_y\hat{j} + \tau_z\hat{k} = \hat{i}(yF_z - zF_y) + \hat{j}(zF_x - xF_z) + \hat{k}(xF_y - yF_x)$

Thus we have, $\quad \tau_x = yF_z - zF_y \;;\; \tau_y = zF_x - xF_z \;;\; \tau_z = xF_y - yF_x$.

Ex. 8 Find moment of force about the axis passing through origin and perpendicular to the plane of $\vec{F}$ and $\vec{r}$.

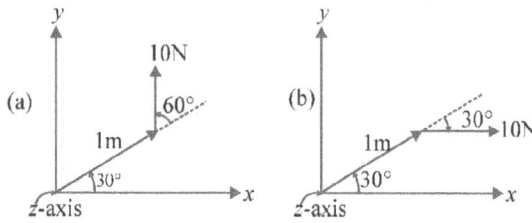

Sol. $\qquad$ *Fig. 1.13*

Method I:

(a) $\vec{\tau} = Fr\sin\theta\hat{k}$ $\qquad$ (b) $\vec{\tau} = Fr\sin\theta(-\hat{k})$
$= 10\times 1\times\sin 60°\hat{k}$ N-m $\qquad = 10\times 1\times\sin 30°(-\hat{k})$ N-m
$= 5\sqrt{3}\,\hat{k}$ N-m $\qquad\qquad = -5\hat{k}$ N-m

Method II:

$\vec{r} = 1\cos 30°\hat{i} + 1\sin 30°\hat{j} = \left(\dfrac{\sqrt{3}}{2}\hat{i} + \dfrac{1}{2}\hat{j}\right)$ m

$\vec{F} = 10\hat{j}$ N

$\vec{\tau} = \vec{r}\times\vec{F} = \left(\dfrac{\sqrt{3}}{2}\hat{i}+\dfrac{1}{2}\hat{j}\right)\times 10\hat{j} = 5\sqrt{3}\hat{k}$ N-m

Ex. 9 (a) A wheel of radius 1m is acted by the forces shown in *Fig. 1.14*. Find resultant moment of force about an axis passing through centre of the wheel.

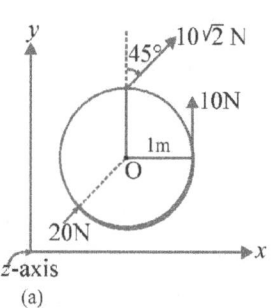

Fig. 1.14

(b) Calculate moment of system of forces about an axis passing through B and perpendicular to the plane of the forces.

Sol. (a) Moment of force of 20 N and 10 cos 45° N is zero about O because their moment arm is zero.

The net moment of force

$\vec{\tau} = 10\times 1\times\hat{k} + (10\sqrt{2}\sin 45°)\times 1\times(-\hat{k})$

$= 10\hat{k} - 10\hat{k} = 0 \quad$ **Ans.**

(b) Moment of forces about B,

$\tau_B = 20\times 0 + 40\times 0$
$\quad + 10\sqrt{2}\times 10 + 50\times 0 + 10\times 1$
$= 10$ N-m clockwise.

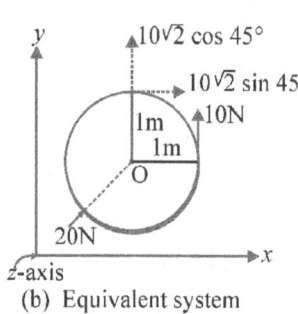

Fig. 1.15

1.5 Couple

Two equal and opposite forces whose lines of action are different constitutes a couple. The moment of couple can be found by taking moments of both the forces about any axis perpendicular to plane of forces and adding them algebraically. Thus moment of couple

$$\tau = F \times AO + F \times OB$$
$$= F(AO + OB)$$
$$= Fd$$

or τ = Force × perpendicular distance between the lines of action of forces

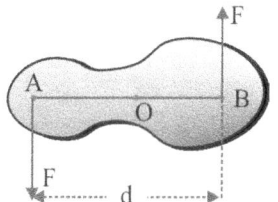

Fig. 1.16

1.6 Moment of Inertia or Rotational Inertia

Moment of inertia of a body is a measure of its ability to resist change in state of rotation. It plays the same role in rotational motion whatever inertia plays in translational motion. Mathematically moment of inertia of a particle of mass m about an axis is defined as;

$$I = mr^2$$

where r is the distance of particle from axis of rotation.
It is called a tensor quantity. Its SI unit is kg-m².

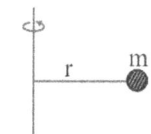

Fig. 1.17

Moment of inertia of system of particles

Consider a system of n particles as shown in *Fig. 1.18*. Its moment of inertia is given by

$$I = m_1 r_1^2 + m_2 r_2^2 + \ldots + m_n r_n^2$$

or $\quad I = \sum_{i=1}^{n} m_i r_i^2$

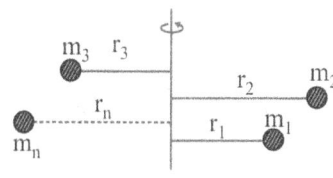

Fig. 1.18

Moment of inertia of a rigid body

Consider a body rotating about an axis as shown in *Fig. 1.18*. Choose small element of mass dm at a distance r from the axis, its moment of inertia about the axis of rotation (here z-axis)

$$dI = dm\, r^2$$

The moment of inertia of whole body can be obtained by

$$I = \int dm\, r^2$$

Limits of integration depends on the shape of the body.
The moment of inertia of a body depends on the following factors:
(i) Mass of the body.
(ii) Size and shape of the body.
(iii) Position and orientation of axis of rotation.

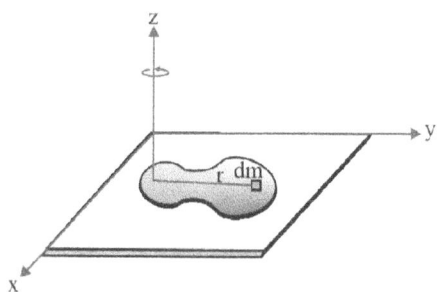

Fig. 1.19

Note:

1. Moment of inertia of a particle about an axis passing through the particle itself will be zero.
2. Any body can have infinite numbers of moment of inertia.

Radius of gyration

Consider a system of particles or a rigid body is rotating about an axis as shown in figure. Its moment of inertia about the axis is given by;

$$I = m_1 r_1^2 + m_2 r_2^2 + \ldots + m_n r_n^2$$

Now suppose the whole mass of the system M is concentrated at a point and placed at a distance k from the axis, then the moment of inertia of the equivalent system can be defined as, $I = Mk^2$

If $\quad Mk^2 = m_1 r_1^2 + m_2 r_2^2 + \ldots + m_n r_n^2 = I$,

then k is called radius of gyration and can be written as

$$k = \sqrt{\frac{I}{M}}$$

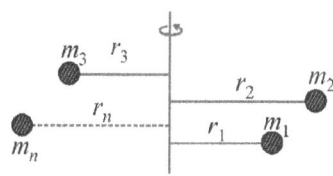

(a) Actual system

⇓

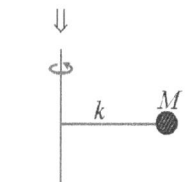

(b) Equivalent system

Fig. 1.20

10 MECHANICS, THERMODYNAMICS & WAVES

Thus radius of gyration of any system about its axis of rotation may be defined as the distance from the axis of rotation, if square of it multiplied by total mass of the system gives moment of inertia of the system about the axis.

1.7 THEOREMS OF MOMENT OF INERTIA

The value of moment of inertia depends on axis of rotation, so each time we requrie mathematical process to get moment of inertia. The calculation of getting moment of inertia can be made easier by deriving the following theorems of moment of inertia.

1. **Parallel axis theorem**

   Consider a body, whose moment of inertia about an axis passing through C.M. is I_{cm}. Let m is the mass of the particle at a distance x from the axis of rotation, then the moment of inertia of whole body about C. M. axis,

   $$I_{cm} = \sum mx^2 \quad ...(i)$$

   Choose an axis A parallel to the C.M. axis, and the separation between the axes is d. The moment of inertia of the body about axis A,

   $$I_A = \sum m(d+x)^2$$
   $$= \sum m(d^2 + x^2 + 2xd)$$
   $$= \sum md^2 + \sum mx^2 + 2\sum mxd \quad ...(ii)$$

   Here $\sum md^2 = Md^2$, $\sum mx^2 = I_{cm}$ and $\sum mx$ is the moment of total mass about the C.M. axis which will be zero, i.e., $\sum mx = 0$.

   $$\therefore \quad I_A = I_{cm} + Md^2 \quad ...(1)$$

   Thus the moment of inertia of a body about any axis is equal to its moment of inertia about a parallel axis through its centre of mass plus the product of the mass of the body and the square of the perpendicular distance between the two axes.

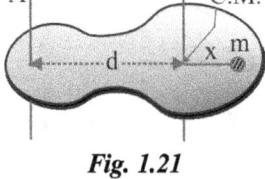

Fig. 1.21

Note: The parallel axis may lie inside or outside the body.

2. **Perpendicular axis theorem**

   Consider a body lying in the xy-plane. It can be assumed to made of large number of particles. Consider one such particle of mass m at a distance r from the origin of axis. In terms of cartesian coordinate,

   $$r^2 = x^2 + y^2 \quad ...(i)$$

   The moment of inertia of the particle about x-axis
   $$I_x = my^2$$
   The moment of inertia of the body about x-axis is
   $$I_x = \sum my^2 \quad ...(ii)$$
   Moment of inertia of the body about y-axis is
   $$I_y = \sum mx^2 \quad ...(iii)$$
   Moment of inertia of the body about z-axis
   $$I_z = \sum mr^2$$
   $$= \sum m(x^2 + y^2)$$
   $$= \sum mx^2 + \sum my^2$$

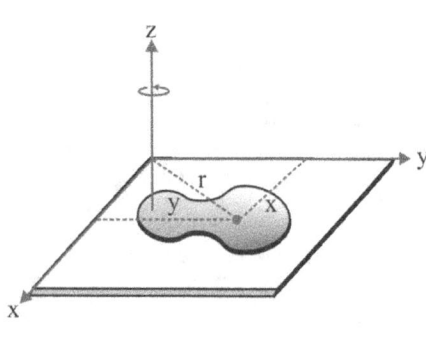

Fig. 1.22

From equations (ii) and (iii), we get

$$I_z = I_x + I_y \qquad \ldots(2)$$

Thus the moment of inertia of a body lying in a plane about an axis perpendicular to its plane is equal to the sum of the moment of inertia of the body about any two mutually perpendicular axes in its plane and intersecting each other at the point where the perpendicular axis passes through the body.

Note: Intersection of axes need not be the centre of mass of the body. Perpendicular axis theorem can be used for planar body but not for cone etc.

Moment of inertia of a thin uniform rod

Consider a thin uniform rod of mass m and length L, which is rotating about an axis passing through its C.M. and perpendicular to its length. For the thin rod its moment of inertia about an axis passing through its length will be zero.

Consider a small element of length dx at a distance x from its C.M. The mass of the element

$$dm = \frac{M}{L}dx$$

Moment of inertia of the element $dI = dm\, x^2$
Moment of inertia of whole rod

$$I = 2\int_0^{L/2} dm\, x^2$$

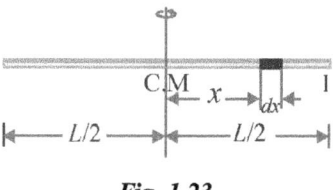

Fig. 1.23

$$= 2\int_0^{L/2} \left(\frac{M}{L}dx\right) x^2$$

$$= \frac{2M}{L}\left|\frac{x^3}{3}\right|_0^{L/2} = \frac{ML^2}{12}$$

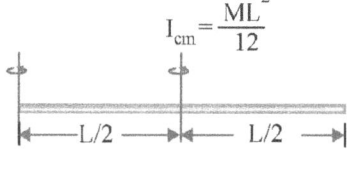

Fig. 1.24

Radius of gyration of thin rod about C.M. axis;

$$k = \sqrt{\frac{I}{M}} = \sqrt{\frac{ML^2}{12M}} = \frac{L}{\sqrt{12}}$$

Moment of inertia about any other axis can be obtained by using parallel axis theorem. Moment of inertia about end of the rod can be obtained as ;

$$I_{end} = I_{cm} + Md^2$$

$$= \frac{ML^2}{12} + M\left(\frac{L}{2}\right)^2$$

$$= \frac{ML^2}{3}$$

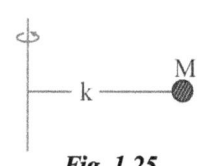

Fig. 1.25

Radius of gyration about the end of the rod,

$$k = \sqrt{\frac{I}{M}} = \sqrt{\frac{ML^2/3}{M}} = \frac{L}{\sqrt{3}}$$

Some special cases :

(i) M.I. of thin rod about an axis passing through end of rod, and it is inclined an angle θ with the axis.

The mass of the element
$$dm = \frac{M}{L}dx$$

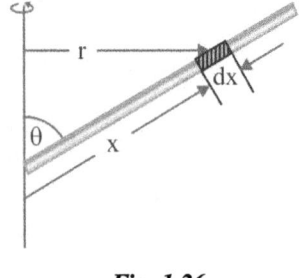

Fig. 1.26

The distance of the element from the axis
$$r = x\sin\theta.$$
The M.I. of the element about the axis
$$dI = (dm)r^2$$
The M.I. of the whole rod
$$I = \int_0^L dm\, r^2$$

$$= \int_0^L \left(\frac{M}{L}dx\right)(x\sin\theta)^2$$

$$= \frac{M}{L}\sin^2\theta \int_0^L x^2 dx$$

$$= \frac{ML^2}{3}\sin^2\theta$$

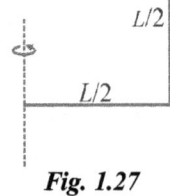

Fig. 1.27

(ii) The rod of mass M and length L is bent into L-shape. Its moment of inertia about the end

$$I_{end} = \frac{(M/2)(L/2)^2}{3} + \frac{M}{2}(L/2)^2$$

$$= \frac{ML^2}{6}$$

$$= \frac{ML^2}{6}$$

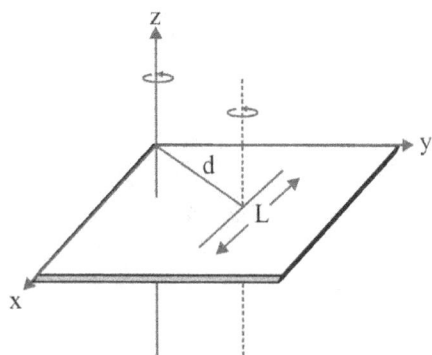

Fig. 1.28

(iii) $$I_z = \frac{ML^2}{12} + Md^2$$

(iv) $$I = 0 + \frac{ML^2}{3} + ML^2$$

$$= \frac{4}{3}ML^2$$

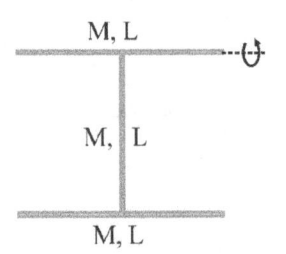

Fig. 1.29

Ex. 10 Consider a system of two particles of masses m_1 and m_2. The separation between them is r. Find M.I. of the system about an axis passing through their C.M. and perpendicular to the line joining them. Also find radius of gyration about centre of mass.

Sol.

Here $r_1 = \dfrac{m_1 \times 0 + m_2 r}{m_1 + m_2} = \dfrac{m_2 r}{m_1 + m_2}$ and $r_2 = r - r_1 = \dfrac{m_1 r}{m_1 + m_2}$

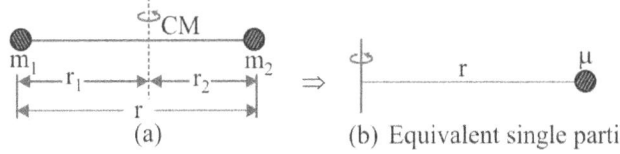

(a)   (b) Equivalent single particle system of mass μ.

Fig. 1.30

M.I of the system about C.M. axis

$$I_{cm} = m_1 r_1^2 + m_2 r_2^2$$

$$= m_1 \left(\dfrac{m_2 r}{m_1 + m_2}\right)^2 + m_2 \left(\dfrac{m_1 r}{m_1 + m_2}\right)^2$$

$$= \left(\dfrac{m_1 m_2}{m_1 + m_2}\right) r^2 = \mu r^2$$

where $\dfrac{m_1 m_2}{m_1 + m_2} = \mu$, is called reduced or effective mass of the system.

Radius of gyration

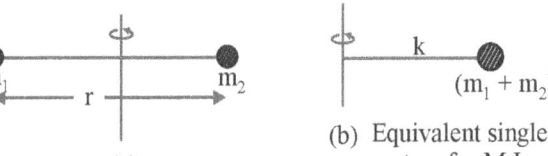

(a)

(b) Equivalent single particle system for M.I.

Fig. 1.31

$$k = \sqrt{\dfrac{I_{cm}}{M}} = \sqrt{\dfrac{\left(\dfrac{m_1 m_2}{m_1 + m_2}\right) r^2}{(m_1 + m_2)}}$$

$$= \dfrac{\sqrt{m_1 m_2}}{(m_1 + m_2)} r$$

Moment of inertia of thin rectangular lamina

Consider a rectangular lamina of mass m and length a and width b.
Choose a small element of width dy and length b at a distance y from the origin O. The mass of the element

$$dm = \dfrac{M}{ab} \times b\, dy = \dfrac{M}{a} \, dy$$

(i) Moment of inertia of the element about x-axis
$$dI_x = (dm) y^2$$
Moment of inertia of whole lamina about x-axis

$$I_x = 2 \int_0^{a/2} (dm) y^2 = 2 \int_0^{a/2} \left(\dfrac{M}{a} dy\right) y^2$$

$$= 2 \dfrac{M}{a} \left|\dfrac{y^3}{3}\right|_0^{a/2} = \dfrac{Ma^2}{12}$$

or $\quad I_x = \dfrac{Ma^2}{12}$

(ii) Similarly moment of inertia of lamina about y-axis

$$I_y = \dfrac{Mb^2}{12}$$

(iii) Moment of inertia of the lamina about z-axis: By using perpendicular axis theorem

$$I_z = I_x + I_y$$

or $\quad I_z = \dfrac{M}{12}(a^2 + b^2)$

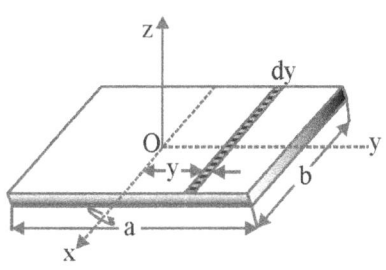

Fig. 1.32

Some special cases

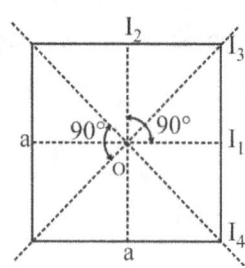

Fig. 1.33

(i) For square lamina, $a = b$

$$I_x = \frac{Ma^2}{12}, \quad I_y = \frac{Ma^2}{12}$$

$$\therefore \quad I_z = I_x + I_y$$

$$= \frac{M}{12}(a^2 + a^2) = \frac{Ma^2}{6}$$

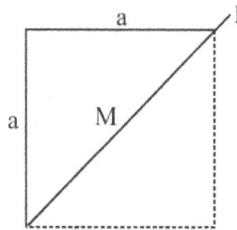

Fig. 1.34

(ii) From the figure *Fig. 1.30* shown,
$$I_0 = I_1 + I_2 \qquad \ldots (i)$$
here $I_1 = I_2$
Also $I_0 = I_3 + I_4 \qquad \ldots (ii)$
here $I_3 = I_4$
From equations (i) and (ii), we get
$$I_1 + I_2 = I_3 + I_4$$
or $\quad 2I_1 = 2I_3$

Thus we have $\boxed{I_1 = I_2 = I_3 = I_4 = \dfrac{Ma^2}{12}}$

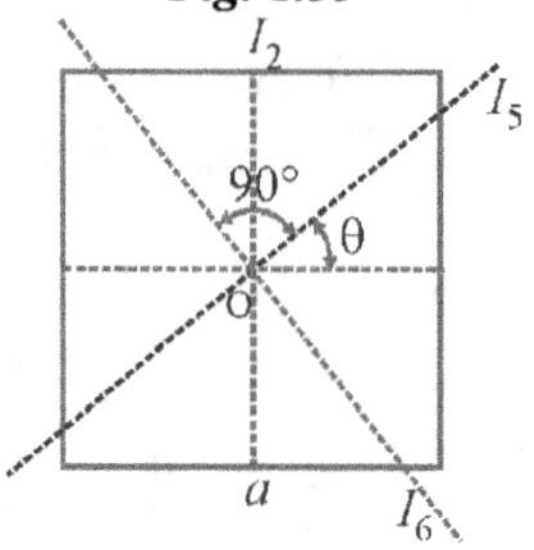

(iii) Now consider two perpendicular axes as shown in figure *Fig 1.34*
$$I_0 = I_5 + I_6 \qquad \ldots (iii)$$
As $I_5 = I_6$

$$\therefore \quad \boxed{I_1 = I_2 = I_3 = I_4 = I_5 = I_6 = \dfrac{Ma^2}{12}}$$

(iv) If we take isosceles triangle lamina of mass M, its M.I. about its diagonal

$$I = \frac{Ma^2}{12}$$

Fig. 1.35

Moment of inertia of ring or hoop

Consider a ring mass M and radius R, and take a small element, its mass

$$dm = \frac{M}{2\pi R} d\ell$$

Moment of inertia of this element about the axis (called geometrical axis) shown in Fig. 1.36

$$dI = (dm)R^2$$

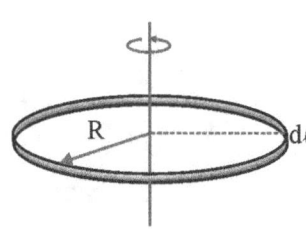

Fig. 1.36

Moment of inertia of whole ring

$$I = \int_0^{2\pi R} (dm) R^2$$

$$= \frac{MR^2}{2\pi R} \int_0^{2\pi R} d\ell$$

$$= \frac{MR^2}{2\pi R} |\ell|_0^{2\pi R} = \frac{MR^2}{2\pi R}(2\pi R - 0)$$

$$= MR^2$$

ROTATIONAL MECHANICS

Other cases:

(i) M.I. about the tangent parallel to the geometrical axis: By parallel axis theorem
$$I_T = I + Md^2$$
$$= MR^2 + MR^2 = 2MR^2$$

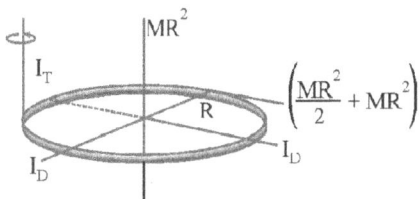

Fig. 1.37

(ii) M.I. about diameter: By perpendicular axis theorem
$$I_D + I_D = MR^2$$
∴ $$I_D = \frac{MR^2}{2}$$

(iii) M.I. about tangent parallel to the diameter: By parallel axis theorem,
$$I = \frac{MR^2}{2} + MR^2$$
$$= \frac{3}{2}MR^2$$

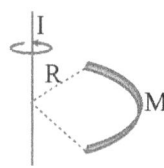

Fig. 1.38

(iv) A part of ring of mass M and radius R
$$I = MR^2$$

(v) M.I. of elliptical hoop:
$$I = \frac{M}{2}(a^2 + b^2)$$

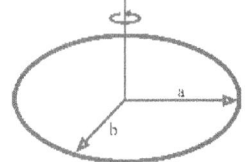

Fig. 1.39

Moment of inertia of disc

Consider a disc of mass M and radius R rotating about its geometrical axis.
Choose an element of radius r and width dr, its mass
$$dm = \frac{M}{\pi R^2} \times (2\pi r dr)$$

Moment of inertia of the ring element about the axis shown
$$dI = (dm) r^2$$
Moment of inertia of whole disc

$$I = \int_0^R (dm) r^2$$

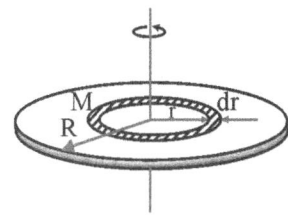

Fig. 1.40

$$= \int_0^R \frac{M}{\pi R^2}(2\pi r dr) r^2$$

$$= \frac{2M}{R^2} \left| \frac{r^4}{4} \right|_0^R$$

$$= \frac{MR^2}{2}$$

Other cases :

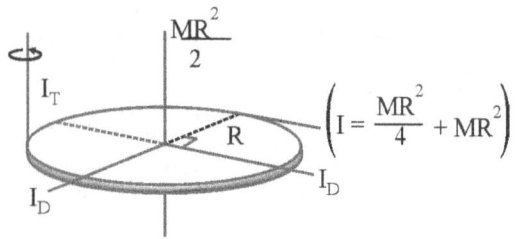

Fig. 1.41

(i) M.I. about the tangent parallel to geometrical axis : By parallel axis theorem

$$I_T = I + Md^2$$
$$= \frac{MR^2}{2} + MR^2$$
$$= \frac{3}{2}MR^2$$

(ii) M.I. about diameter of the disc ; By perpendicular axis theorem

$$I_D + I_D = \frac{MR^2}{2}$$

$$\therefore \quad I_D = \frac{MR^2}{4}$$

(iii) M.I. about the tangent parallel to diameter ; By parallel axis theorem

$$I = I_D + Md^2$$
$$= \frac{MR^2}{4} + MR^2 = \frac{5}{4}MR^2$$

(iv) M.I. of a small part of disc of mass M about the axis shown in *Fig. 1.42*

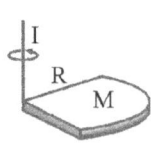

Fig. 1.42

$$I = \frac{MR^2}{2}$$

(v) M.I. of annular disc :
Choose an elemental ring of radius r and thickness dr, mass of the element

$$dm = \frac{M}{\pi(R_2^2 - R_1^2)} \times (2\pi r dr)$$

M.I. of the elemental ring

$$dI = (dm)r^2$$

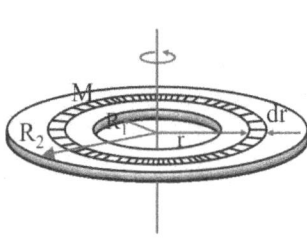

Fig. 1.43

M.I. of the annular disc about the axis shown

$$I = \int_{R_1}^{R_2} (dm)r^2$$

$$= \int_{R_1}^{R_2} \frac{M}{\pi(R_2^2 - R_1^2)} (2\pi r dr) r^2$$

$$= \frac{2M}{(R_2^2 - R_1^2)} \int_{R_1}^{R_2} r^3 dr$$

$$= \frac{2M}{(R_2^2 - R_1^2)} \left|\frac{r^4}{4}\right|_{R_1}^{R_2}$$

$$= \frac{M}{2(R_2^2 - R_1^2)} [R_2^4 - R_1^4]$$

$$= \frac{M}{2(R_2^2 - R_1^2)} (R_2^2 + R_1^2)(R_2^2 - R_1^2)$$

or $$\boxed{I = \frac{M(R_2^2 + R_1^2)}{2}}$$

Moment of inertia of a thick rod or cylinder

Consider a solid circular cylinder of mass M and cross-sectional radius R. The length of the cylinder is L.

(i) M.I. of the cylinder about geometrical axis. Choose an element of cylinder in the form of a pipe of length L and radius r and thickness dr.

The mass of the element

$$dm = \frac{M}{\pi R^2 L} \times (2\pi r dr)L = \frac{M}{\pi R^2} \times (2\pi r dr)$$

M.I. of the elemental pipe about the axis shown in figure *Fig. 1.44*

$$dI = (dm)r^2$$

M.I. of the whole cylinder

$$I = \int_0^R (dm) r^2$$

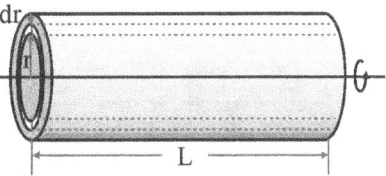

Fig. 1.44

$$= \int_0^R \left(\frac{M}{\pi R^2}\right)(2\pi r dr) r^2$$

$$= \frac{2M}{R^2} \int_0^R r^3 dr$$

$$= \frac{2M}{R^2} \times \frac{R^4}{4} = \frac{MR^2}{2}$$

(ii) M.I. of the cylinder about equitorial axis :

Choose an element disc of thickness dx at a distance x from axis of rotation.

The mass of the element

$$dm = \frac{M}{L} dx$$

The M.I. of the elemental disc about the axis of rotation

$$dI = \text{M.I. of disc about diameter} + (dm) x^2$$

$$= \left[\frac{(dm)R^2}{4} + (dm)x^2\right]$$

M.I of the cylinder

$$I = 2 \int_0^{L/2} \left[\frac{(dm)R^2}{4} + (dm)x^2\right]$$

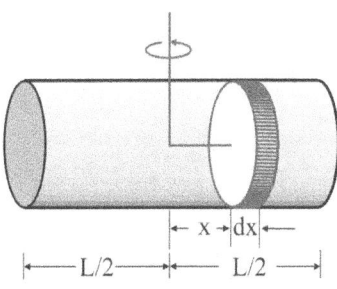

Fig. 1.45

$$= 2 \int_0^{L/2} \left[\frac{\left(\frac{Mdx}{L}\right)R^2}{4} + \left(\frac{M}{L}dx\right)x^2\right]$$

$$= 2 \times \frac{MR^2}{4L} \int_0^{L/2} dx + \frac{2M}{L} \int_0^{L/2} x^2 dx$$

$$= \frac{MR^2}{2L}|x|_0^{L/2} + \frac{2M}{L}\left|\frac{x^3}{3}\right|_0^{L/2}$$

$$= \left(\frac{MR^2}{4} + \frac{ML^2}{12}\right)$$

18 MECHANICS, THERMODYNAMICS & WAVES

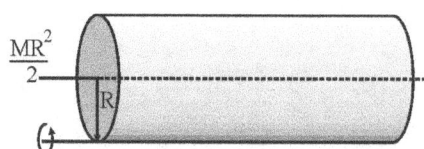

Fig. 1.46

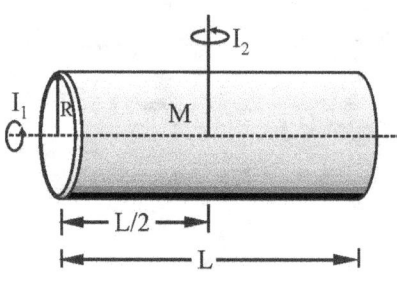

Fig. 1.47

Special cases :

(i) If M.I. of the cylinder about both the axes calculated are equal, then

$$\frac{MR^2}{2} = \frac{MR^2}{4} + \frac{ML^2}{12}$$

$$\Rightarrow \quad L = \sqrt{3}R$$

(ii) M. I. of cylinder about the tangent :
By parallel axis theorem

$$I_T = I + Md^2$$

$$= \frac{MR^2}{2} + MR^2$$

$$= \frac{3}{2}MR^2$$

M.I. of thin circular pipe

$$I_1 = MR^2$$

$$I_2 = \frac{ML^2}{12} + \frac{MR^2}{2}$$

Moment of inertia of sphere

Consider a sphere of mass M and radius R rotating about any of its diameter. Choose an element in the form of a disc of radius r and thickness dx. The mass of the element

$$dm = \frac{M}{\frac{4}{3}\pi R^3} \times \pi r^2 dx = \frac{3M}{4R^3}r^2 dx$$

Here $r^2 = (R^2 - x^2)$

M.I. of the element about the axis shown

$$dI = \frac{(dm)r^2}{2}$$

M.I. of the whole sphere

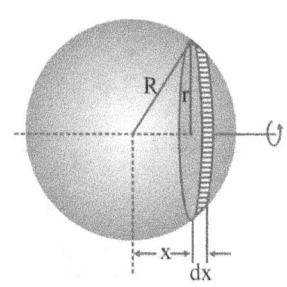

Fig. 1.48

$$I = 2\int_0^R \frac{(dm)r^2}{2} = 2\int_0^R \frac{\left(\frac{3M}{4R^3}r^2 dx\right)r^2}{2}$$

$$I = \frac{3M}{4R^3}\int_0^R r^4 dx$$

$$= \frac{3M}{4R^3}\int_0^R (R^2 - x^2)^2 dx$$

$$= \frac{3M}{4R^3}\int_0^R (R^4 + x^4 - 2R^2 x^2) dx$$

$$= \frac{3M}{4R^3}\left|R^4 x + \frac{x^5}{5} - \frac{2R^2 x^3}{3}\right|_0^R$$

$$= \frac{3M}{4R^3}\left(R^5 + \frac{R^5}{5} - \frac{2R^5}{3}\right)$$

$$= \frac{2}{5}MR^2$$

Rotational Mechanics

Other cases :

(i) M.I. about any tangent of the sphere :
By parallel axis theorem
$$I_T = I_{cm} + Md^2$$
$$= \frac{2}{5}MR^2 + MR^2$$
$$= \frac{7}{5}MR^2$$

(ii) Radius of gyration of the sphere about any tangent
$$Mk^2 = \frac{7}{5}MR^2$$
$$\Rightarrow k = \sqrt{\frac{7}{5}}R$$

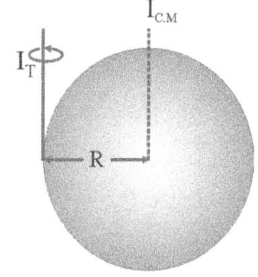

Fig. 1.49

Moment of inertia of thin circular shell

Consider a shell of mass M and radius R rotating about one of its diameter.
Choose an element in the form of ring of radius r and angular width $d\theta$.
Here $\quad r = R\sin\theta$.
The mass of the element
$$dm = \frac{M}{4\pi R^2} \times (2\pi r)(Rd\theta)$$

M.I. of the element about the axis shown in figure *Fig. 1.47*
$$dI = (dm)r^2$$

M.I. of the whole shell
$$I = 2\int_0^R (dm)r^2$$

$$= \int_{-R}^{R}\left[\frac{M}{4\pi R^2}(2\pi r)Rd\theta\right]r^2$$

$$= \frac{M}{2R}\int_0^\pi r^3 d\theta$$

$$= \frac{M}{2R}\int_0^\pi (R\sin\theta)^3 d\theta$$

$$= \frac{MR^2}{2}\int_0^\pi \sin^3\theta\, d\theta$$

$$= \frac{MR^2}{2}\int_0^\pi \sin^2\theta(\sin\theta\, d\theta)$$

$$= \frac{MR^2}{2}\int_0^\pi \sin^2\theta(-d\cos\theta)$$

$$= \frac{MR^2}{2}\int_0^\pi (1-\cos^2\theta)(d\cos\theta)$$

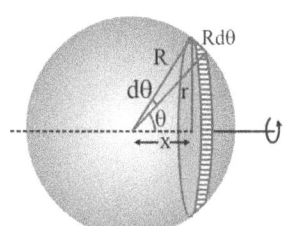

Fig. 1.50

$$= -\frac{MR^2}{2}\left|\cos\theta - \frac{\cos^3\theta}{3}\right|_0^\pi$$

$$= -\frac{MR^2}{2}\left[\left(\cos\pi - \frac{\cos^3\pi}{3}\right) - \left(\cos 0 - \frac{\cos^3 0}{3}\right)\right]$$

$$= \frac{2}{3}MR^2$$

Moment of inertia of a triangular plate

Consider a plate of uniform thickness t and base b and height h. If ρ is the density of material of plate, then mass of the plate

$$M = \rho \times \left[\frac{bh}{2}t\right] = \rho\frac{bht}{2}$$

Choose an element of plate of width b and thickness dy. From the similar triangles ABC and AB′C′

$$\frac{b}{h} = \frac{b'}{y}$$

or $$b' = \frac{b}{h}y$$

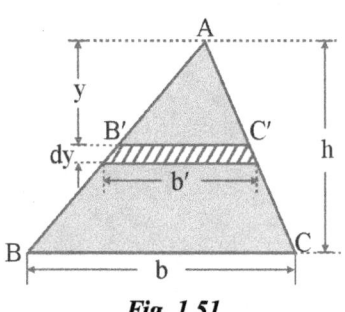

Fig. 1.51

The mass of the element
$$dM = \rho \times \text{volume of the element}$$
$$= \rho \times b'(dy)t$$
$$= \rho\left(\frac{by}{h}\right)(dy)t$$

Moment of inertia of the element about base of the plate (BC)
$$dI = (dM)(h-y)^2$$

Moment of inertia of whole plate about the base

$$I = \int dI = \int_0^h (dM)(h-y)^2$$

or $$I = \int_0^h \left(\frac{\rho by}{h}t\right)dy(h-y)^2$$

$$= \frac{\rho bt}{h}\int_0^h y(h-y)^2 dy = \frac{\rho bt}{h}\int_0^h (h^2 + y^2 - 2hy)y\,dy$$

$$= \frac{\rho bt}{h}\int_0^h (h^2 y + y^3 - 2hy^2)dy$$

$$= \frac{\rho bt}{h}\left[\frac{h^2 y^2}{2} + \frac{y^4}{4} - \frac{2hy^3}{3}\right]_0^h$$

$$= \frac{\rho bt}{h}\left(\frac{h^4}{2} + \frac{h^4}{4} - \frac{2h^4}{3}\right) = \frac{\rho bth^3}{12}$$

As $\frac{\rho bht}{2} = M$, so $I = \frac{Mh^2}{6}$

ROTATIONAL MECHANICS

Moment of inertia of a hollow sphere

Consider a hollow sphere of mass M and inner and outer radii R_1 and R_2 respectively. We can imagine the sphere to be made up of a number of thin, concentric spherical shells. Take one such shell of radius r and thickness dr. Its mass

$$dM = \rho(4\pi r^2 dr)$$

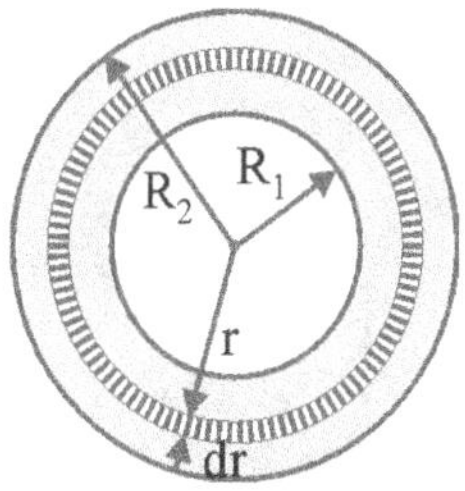

Moment of inertia of the shell about its diameter

$$dI = \frac{2}{3}(dM)r^2$$

$$= \frac{2}{3}(4\pi r^2 dr \rho)r^2$$

$$= \frac{8}{3}\pi \rho r^4 dr$$

Fig. 1.52

Moment of inertia of the sphere

$$I = \int_{R_1}^{R_2} dI$$

$$= \frac{8}{3}\pi\rho \int_{R_1}^{R_2} r^4 dr$$

$$= \frac{8}{3}\pi\rho \left[\frac{r^5}{5}\right]_{R_1}^{R_2}$$

$$= \frac{8}{15}\pi\rho(R_2^5 - R_1^5)$$

Mass of the hollow sphere

$$M = \rho \times \text{volume}$$

$$= \rho \times \frac{4}{3}\pi(R_2^3 - R_1^3)$$

$$\therefore \quad I = \frac{4}{3}\pi(R_2^3 - R_1^3)\rho \times \frac{2}{5}\frac{(R_2^5 - R_1^5)}{(R_2^3 - R_1^3)}$$

or $$I = \frac{2}{5}M\frac{(R_2^5 - R_1^5)}{(R_2^3 - R_1^3)}$$

Ex. 11 Calculate moment of inertia of a system of $(2N + 1)$ particles, separated by 'a' lying along a straight line about an axis passing through the centre.

Sol.

The total length, $L = 2Na \Rightarrow a = \frac{L}{2N}$

If m is the mass of each particle and M is the total mass of the system, then

$$M = (2N+1)m \Rightarrow m = \frac{M}{(2N+1)}$$

The moment of inertia of the system,

$$I = \sum_{n=1}^{N} 2ma^2 n^2 = 2ma^2 \sum_{n=1}^{N} n^2$$

$$\sum_{n=1}^{N} n^2 = \frac{N(N+1)(2N+1)}{6}$$

$$\therefore \quad I = 2ma^2 \frac{N(N+1)(2N+1)}{6}$$

After substituting values of a and m, we get

$$I = \frac{ML^2}{12}\left[1+\frac{1}{N}\right] \quad \textbf{Ans.}$$

For $N \to \infty$, $\quad I = \frac{ML^2}{12}$

Moment of inertia of a cone

Consider a cone of mass M and base radius R. Suppose the height of cone is h. Choose an element in the form of a disc of radius x and thickness dy as shown in *Fig. 1.53*. From the similar triangles, we have

$$\frac{x}{y} = \frac{R}{h} \Rightarrow x = \frac{Ry}{h}$$

The mass of the element

$$dm = \frac{M}{\frac{\pi R^2 h}{3}} \times (\pi x^2 dy) = \frac{3M}{R^2 h} x^2 dy$$

M.I. of the element about the axis shown

$$dI = \frac{(dm)x^2}{2}$$

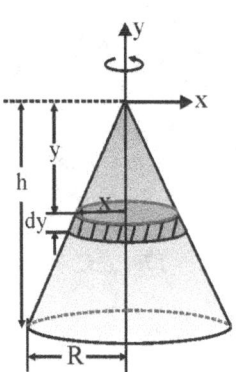

Fig. 1.53

M.I. of the whole cone $= \int_0^h \frac{(dm)x^2}{2}$

$$= \int_0^h \frac{\left(\frac{3M}{R^2 h} x^2 dy\right) x^2}{2}$$

$$= \int_0^h \frac{3M}{2R^2 h}\left(\frac{Ry}{h}\right)^4 dy$$

$$= \frac{3MR^2}{2h^5}\int_0^h y^4 dy$$

$$= \frac{3MR^2}{2h^5}\left|\frac{y^5}{5}\right|_0^h = \frac{3}{10}MR^2$$

Ex. 12 Three identical thin rods, each of mass m and length ℓ are joint to form an equilateral triangle. Find moment of inertia of the triangle about one of its sides.

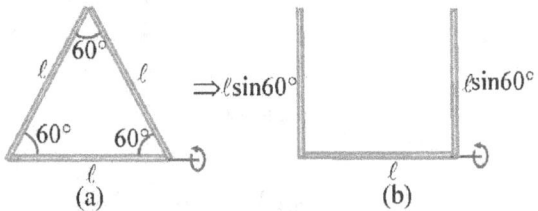

Fig. 1.54

Sol.
The given system of rods for its moment of inertia is equivalent to the system shown in *Fig.1.54(b)*. Thus the moment of inertia about the axis given

$$I = 0 + \frac{m(\ell \sin 60°)^2}{3} + \frac{m(\ell \sin 60°)^2}{3}$$

$$= 2\frac{m\ell^2}{3} \times \sin^2 60°$$

$$= \frac{2}{3}m\ell^2 \times \frac{3}{4} = \frac{m\ell^2}{2} \qquad \textit{Ans.}$$

Ex. 13 From a circular disc of radius R and mass $9M$, a small disc of radius R/3 is removed from the disc, as shown in *Fig. 1.55*. Find the moment of inertia of the remaining disc about an axis perpendicular to the plane of the disc and passing through the point O.

Sol. Given, total mass of the disc = 9M

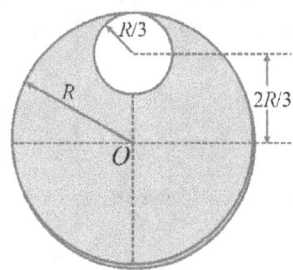

Fig. 1.55

M.I. of the disc about a perpendicular axis through O is

$$I = \frac{1}{2}(\text{mass}) \times R^2$$

$$= \frac{1}{2} \times 9M \times R^2 = \frac{9}{2}MR^2$$

ROTATIONAL MECHANICS

Mass of the small disc removed

$$m = \frac{9M}{\pi R^2} \times \pi (R/3)^2 = M$$

The M.I. of small disc about an axis perpendicular to O,

$$I' = I_{cm} + Md^2$$

$$= \frac{1}{2}M(R/3)^2 + M\left(\frac{2R}{3}\right)^2$$

$$= \frac{MR^2}{2}$$

M.I. of the remaining disc about an axis perpendicular to O

$$I_{net} = I - I'$$

$$= \frac{9}{2}MR^2 - \frac{MR^2}{2}$$

$$= 4MR^2 \quad \textbf{Ans.}$$

Ex. 14 A T-shaped object with dimensions shown in *Fig. 1.56*, is lying on a smooth floor. A force $\vec{F}$ is applied at the point P parallel to AB, such that the object has only the translational motion without rotation. Find the location of P with respect to C.

Sol.
Point P must be the centre of mass of the system. Let λ is the mass per unit length, then mass of AB, $m_1 = \lambda \ell$ and mass of CD, $m_2 = 2\lambda \ell$

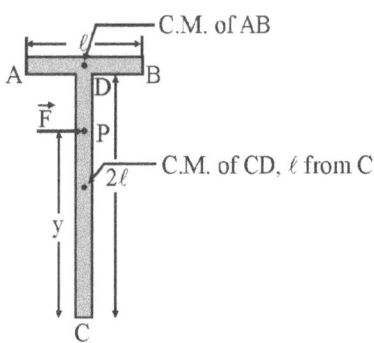

Fig. 1.56

Suppose y is the distance of C.M. from C,

$$y = \frac{m_1 y_1 + m_2 y_2}{m_1 + m_2}$$

$$= \frac{(\lambda \ell) \times 2\ell + (2\lambda \ell) \times \ell}{(\lambda \ell) + (2\lambda \ell)}$$

$$= \frac{4}{3}\ell \quad \textbf{Ans.}$$

1.8 ANGULAR MOMENTUM

In first part of mechanics, we have studied linear momentum. Here we will study its rotational effect.

Angular momentum of a particle about an axis is defined as the moment of the linear momentum of the particle about that axis. It is a vector quantity. Its SI unit is kg-m²/s.

(i) Angular momentum of a particle due to translational motion

Consider a particle of mass m, moving with a velocity $\vec{v}$. Its line of motion is at a distance $\vec{r}$ from the z-axis. Its linear momentum $\vec{p} = m\vec{v}$.

Angular momentum of the particle about z-axis is given by

$$L = (mv \sin \theta) \times r$$

and direction can be given by right hand screw rule.

In the case given, the direction of $\vec{L}$ is along positive z-axis.

Thus $\vec{L} = mvr \sin \theta \hat{k}$

or $\vec{L} = m(\vec{r} \times \vec{v}) = \vec{r} \times \vec{p}$

Here we have resolved momentum perpendicular to $\vec{r}$. The same thing can also be obtained by resolving $\vec{r}$ perpendicular to momentum $\vec{p}$. Thus we can write

$$L = r \sin \theta \times mv$$
$$= mvr \sin \theta$$

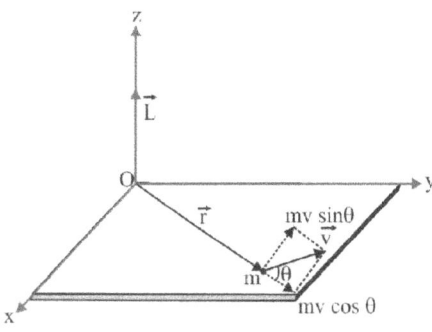

Fig. 1.57

(ii) Angular momentum due to rotation of the particle

Consider a particle of mass m is rotating about an axis with constant angular velocity ω. Its linear velocity

$$v = \omega r$$

The angular momentum of the particle about z-axis;

$$L = mv \times r \sin 90°$$
$$= m(\omega r)r = (mr^2)\omega = I\omega$$

The direction of $\vec{L}$ is along the direction of $\vec{\omega}$, so we can write

$$\vec{L} = I\vec{\omega}$$

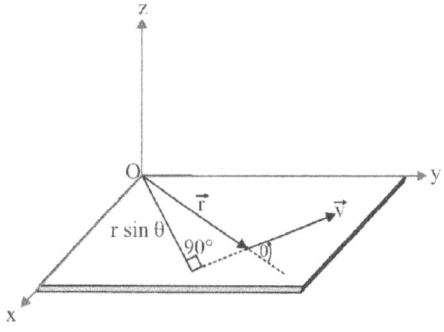

Fig. 1.58

(iii) Angular momentum of a rigid body due to rotation

Consider a body rotating about an axis shown in figure
Choose a small element whose M.I. about the axis is dI. Its angular momentum about the axis shown in *Fig. 159*.

$$dL = (dI)\omega$$

Angular momentum of whole body

$$L = \int (dI)\omega$$

As ω is same for each element of the body,

and $\int (dI)$ is the moment of inertia of whole body, say it is I,

so $\quad L = I\omega$

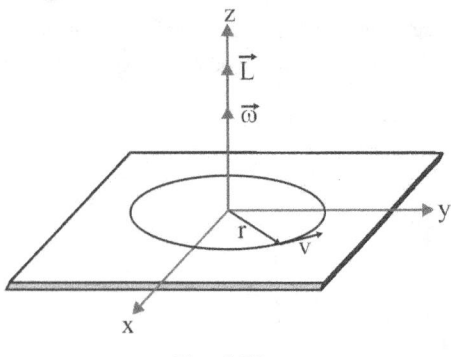

Fig. 1.59

(iv) Angular momentum of a rigid body due to translation and rotation both

Method I: Consider a body of mass m is rotating with angular velocity ω about C. M. axis and translating with a linear velocity $\vec{v}$ as shown in the *Fig. 1.61*.
The angular momentum of the body

$$\vec{L} = \vec{L}_{\text{translation}} + \vec{L}_{\text{rotation}}$$

or $\quad \vec{L} = mv_0 y(-\hat{k}) + I\omega(-\hat{k})$

$\quad\quad = -(mv_0 y + I\omega)\hat{k}$ kg-m²/s

where I is the moment of inertia of the body about the perpendicular axis through O'.

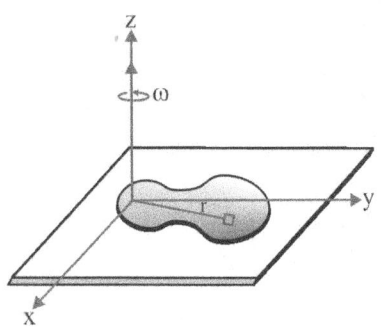

Fig. 1.60

Method II: Consider the situation described in method I. Choose a particle of mass m at position $\vec{r}$ having velcoity $\vec{v}$ in C.M. frame. Its position and velocity in ground frame at O will be $(\vec{r} + \vec{r}_0)$ and $(\vec{v} + \vec{v}_0)$ respectively.

Angular momentum of the whole body about O

$$\vec{L} = \Sigma m(\vec{r} + \vec{r}_0) \times (\vec{v} + \vec{v}_0)$$

Here, $\vec{r}_0$ and $\vec{v}_0$ are the positon vector and velocity vector of the C.M.

Thus $\quad \vec{L} = \Sigma m(\vec{r} \times \vec{v}) + \Sigma m(\vec{r}_0 \times \vec{v}) + \Sigma m(\vec{r} \times \vec{v}_0) + \Sigma m(\vec{r}_0 \times \vec{v}_0)$

$\quad\quad = \Sigma m(\vec{r} \times \vec{v}) + \vec{r}_0 \times (\Sigma m\vec{v}) + (\Sigma m\vec{r}) \times \vec{v}_0 + \Sigma m(\vec{r}_0 \times \vec{v}_0)$

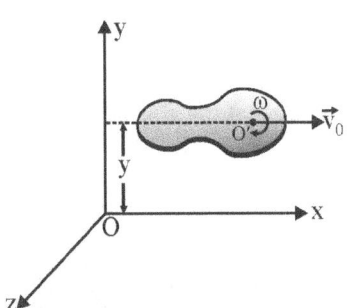

Fig. 1.61

As $\Sigma m\vec{v} = (M\vec{v}_0)_{cm} = 0$ and $\Sigma m\vec{r} = (Mr_0)_{cm} = 0$

$\therefore \quad \vec{L} = \Sigma m(\vec{r} \times \vec{v}) + \Sigma m(\vec{r}_0 \times \vec{v}_0)$

or $\quad \vec{L} = \vec{L}_{cm} + M(\vec{r}_0 \times \vec{v}_0)$

Here $\vec{L}_{cm}$ represents the angular momentum of the body about C.M. frame, and $M(\vec{r}_0 \times \vec{v}_0)$ equals the angular momentum of the body if it is assumed to be concentrated at C.M. translating with velocity $\vec{v}_0$. In figrue of method I,

$$\vec{r}_0 = (x\hat{i} + y\hat{j}), \quad \vec{v}_0 = v_0\hat{i}$$

$\therefore \quad \vec{L} = I\omega(-\hat{k}) + m(x\hat{i} + y\hat{j}) \times (v_0\hat{i})$

$\quad\quad = I\omega(-\hat{k}) + mvy(-\hat{k})$

$\quad\quad = (I\omega + mvy)(-\hat{k})$ kg $- m^2/s$

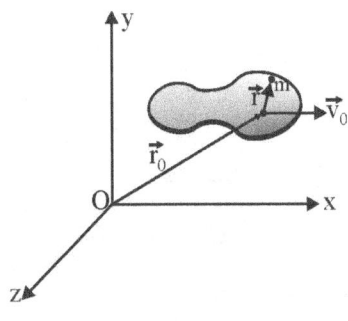

Fig. 1.62

ROTATIONAL MECHANICS

Ex. 15 Find angular momentum of a disc about the axis shown in *Fig. 1.63* and *Fig.1.64* in the following situations.

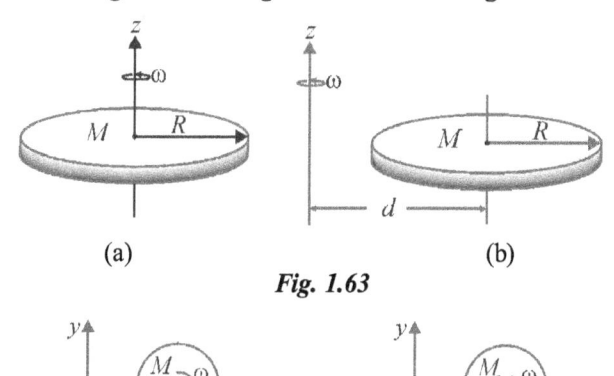

Fig. 1.63

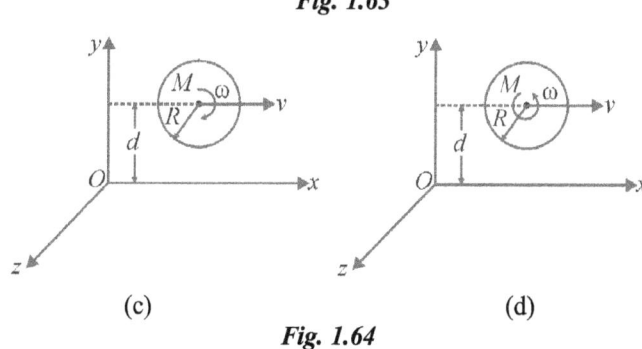

Fig. 1.64

Sol.

(a) $\vec{L} = I\vec{\omega} = \left(\dfrac{mR^2}{2}\right)\omega \hat{k}$ kg-m^2/s

(b) $\vec{L} = I\vec{\omega} = (I_{cm} + Md^2)\omega\hat{k}$

$= \left(\dfrac{mR^2}{2} + Md^2\right)\omega\hat{k}$ kg-m^2/s

(c) $\vec{L} = mvd(-\hat{k}) + I\omega(-\hat{k})$

$= \left(mvd + \dfrac{mR^2}{2}\omega\right)(-\hat{k})$ kg-m^2/s

(d) $\vec{L} = mvd(-\hat{k}) + I\omega(\hat{k})$

$= \left(mvd - \dfrac{mR^2}{2}\omega\right)(-\hat{k})$ kg-m^2/s

Angular momentum of earth motion

Fig.1.65 shows the earth rotation on its axis as it orbits the sun.

(i) Angular momentum due to rotation of earth about its axis

$L_{Rotation} = I_1\omega_1 = \left(\dfrac{2}{5}MR^2\right)\left(\dfrac{2\pi}{T}\right)$ [M = mass of earth]

$= \dfrac{2}{5} \times (5.98 \times 10^{24})(6.37 \times 10^6)^2 \times \dfrac{2\pi}{24 \times 60 \times 60}$

$= 7.1 \times 10^{23}$ kg-m^2/s

(ii) Angular momentum is associated with the orbital motion of earth about the sun

$L_{Orbital} = I_2\omega_2$

$= (Mr^2) \times \dfrac{2\pi}{T}$

[Assuming earth as point mass in comparision to the distance between earth and sun]

Here $M = 5.98 \times 10^{24}$ kg,

$r =$ mean earth-sun distance
$= 1.50 \times 10^{11}$ m

and $T =$ 1year $= 365 \times 24 \times 60 \times 60$ s

$\therefore$ $L_{orbital} = (5.98 \times 10^{24})(1.50 \times 10^{11})^2 \times \dfrac{2\pi}{365 \times 24 \times 60 \times 60}$

$= 2.7 \times 10^{40}$ kg-m^2/s

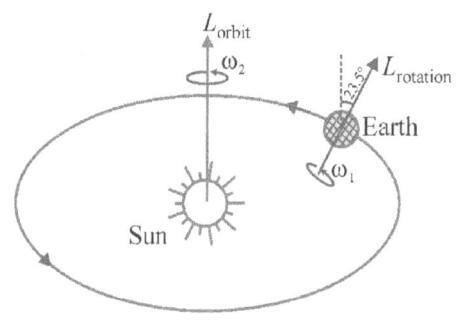

Fig. 1.65

The directions of $L_{rotation}$ and L_{orbit} are shown in *Fig. 1.65*. The resultant angular momentum of earth will be the vector sum of these two angular momentum.

Thus we can write $|\vec{L}_{net}| = \sqrt{L_{rotation}^2 + L_{orbital}^2 + 2L_{rotation}L_{orbital}\cos 23.5°}$

Geometrical meaning of angular momentum

Consider a particle of mass m moving with velocity $\vec{v}$ in x-y plane. Let $\vec{r}$ and $(\vec{r} + \Delta \vec{r})$ be the position vectors of the particle at instant t and $(t + \Delta t)$ respectively. The displacement of the particle in time Δt, $PQ = \Delta \vec{r} = \vec{v} \Delta t$

The area vector of the triangle OPQ,

$$\Delta \vec{A} = \frac{1}{2} (\vec{r} \times \Delta \vec{r})$$

or $\quad \Delta \vec{A} = \frac{1}{2} (\vec{r} \times \vec{v} \Delta t)$

or $\quad m \frac{\Delta \vec{A}}{\Delta t} = \frac{1}{2} (\vec{r} \times m\vec{v})$

or $\quad m \left(\frac{\Delta \vec{A}}{\Delta t} \right) = \frac{\vec{L}}{2}$

or $\quad \vec{L} = 2m \left(\frac{\Delta \vec{A}}{\Delta t} \right)$

The quantity $\frac{\Delta \vec{A}}{\Delta t}$ is the area covered by the position vector $\vec{r}$ per unit time and is called areal velocity.

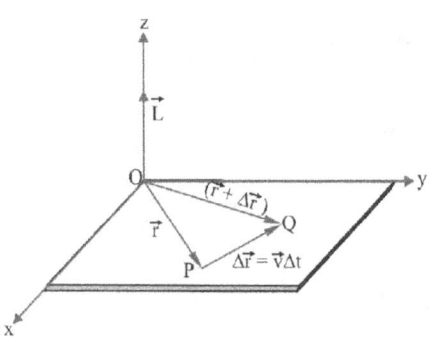

Fig. 1.66

Ex. 16
A particle of mass m is moving with velocity $\vec{v}$ along a line $y = x + 5$. Find the angular momentum of the particle about a perpendicular axis passing through origin O.

Sol.
The linear momentum of the particle $p = mv$. Compare given equation of the line of motion with $y = mx + c$, we have $m = 1$ or $\theta = 45°$ and $c = 5$ unit. It represents a particle moving as shown in figure. The angular momentum about O

$$L_O = mv \cos 45° \times 5$$

$$= \frac{5}{\sqrt{2}} mv \quad \text{unit}$$

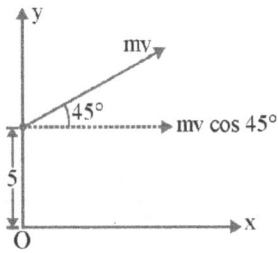

Fig. 1.67

Its direction is along negative z-axis. Thus

$$\vec{L}_O = -\frac{5}{\sqrt{2}} mv \hat{k} \quad \text{unit} \qquad \text{Ans.}$$

Ex. 17
Two particles, each of mass m and speed v, travel in opposite directions along parallel lines separated by a distance d, show that the vector angular momentum of the two particle system is the same whatever be the point about which the angular momentum is taken.

Sol.
Suppose the two particles are moving parallel to the y-axis as shown in Fig. 1.68

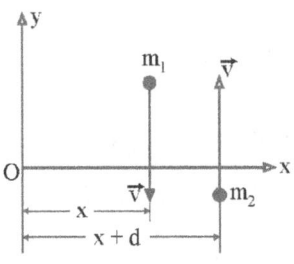

Fig. 1.68

Total angular momentum of the system

$$\vec{L} = \vec{L}_1 + \vec{L}_2$$

$$= \vec{r}_1 \times \vec{p}_1 + \vec{r}_2 \times \vec{p}_2$$

$$= (x\hat{i}) \times (-mv\hat{j}) + (x+d)\hat{i} \times (mv\hat{j})$$

$$= -mvx(\hat{i} \times \hat{j}) + (mvx + mvd)(\hat{i} \times \hat{j})$$

$$= -mvx\hat{k} + mvx\hat{k} + mvd\hat{k}$$

$$= mvd\hat{k}$$

It is clear from the result that angular momentum does not depend on x and hence on the origin. Thus the angular momentum of the two particle system is same whatever be point about which the angular momentum is taken.

Ex. 18 A particle of mass m is released from point P at $x = x_0$ on the x-axis from origin O and falls vertically along the y-axis, as shown in Fig. 1.66.

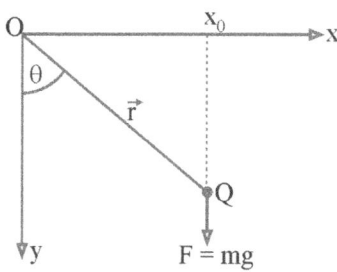

Fig. 1.69

(i) Find the torque τ acting on the particle at a time t when it is at point Q with respect to O.

(ii) Find the angular momentum $\vec{L}$ of the particle about O at this time t.

(iii) Show that $\tau = \dfrac{dL}{dt}$ in this example.

Sol.

(i) The gravitational force $F = mg$ produces the torque τ. If $\vec{r}$ be the position vector of Q, then the magnitude of the torque about an axis about O is given by

$$\tau = Fr\sin\theta$$
$$= mgx_0 \qquad (r\sin\theta = x_0) \quad \textbf{Ans.}$$

The direction of the torque will be along the negative z-axis which is perpendicular to the plane of $\vec{F}$ and $\vec{r}$.

(ii) The velocity v of the particle at time t is, $v = 0 + gt = gt$.
The magnitude of the angular momentum is given by,

$$L = pr\sin\theta$$
$$= mv(r\sin\theta)$$
$$= mgt(x_0)$$
$$= mgx_0 t \qquad \textbf{Ans.}$$

The direction of the angular momentum is also along the negative z-axis.

(iii) We have got $\quad L = mgx_0 t$

Differentiating above equation w.r.t. time, we get

$$\frac{dL}{dt} = \frac{d}{dt}(mgx_0 t)$$
$$= mgx_0 = \tau \qquad \textbf{Ans.}$$

Hence the relation $\tau = \dfrac{dL}{dt}$ holds in this example.

1.9 ROTATIONAL KINETIC ENERGY

Consider a body rotating about an axis shown in figure. Choose a particle of mass m at a distance r from the axis of rotation. Kinetic energy of the particle $= \dfrac{1}{2}mv^2$

As $v = \omega r$

$\therefore$ Kinetic energy of the particle $= \dfrac{1}{2}m(\omega r)^2 = \dfrac{1}{2}(mr^2)\omega^2$

Kinetic energy of whole body,

$$K = \sum \frac{1}{2}(mr^2)\omega^2 = \frac{\omega^2}{2}(\Sigma mr^2)$$

where Σmr^2 is the moment of inertia of the body about axis of rotation, say it is I.
Thus kinetic energy of rotating body

$$K_{Rot} = \frac{1}{2}I\omega^2$$

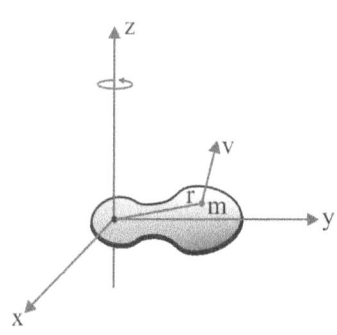

Fig. 1.70

Kinetic energy due to translation and rotation both

Consider a rotating body, which is translating with a velocity $\vec{v}$ as shown in *Fig. 1.71*.
The total K.E. of the body

$$K = K_{Translation} + K_{Rotation}$$
$$= \frac{1}{2}mv^2 + \frac{1}{2}I\omega^2$$

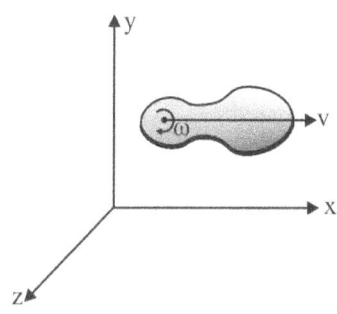

Fig. 1.71

1.10 Rotational Work

Consider a body subjected to a force F. Suppose body undergoes an angular displacement $\Delta\theta$ due to the torque of force F. The work done by the torque

$$\Delta W = F \times \text{displacement } PQ$$
$$= F \times \Delta s$$

Here, $\Delta s = r\Delta\theta$

$$\therefore \quad \Delta W = F \times r\Delta\theta$$
or $\quad \Delta W = \tau\Delta\theta$

In case of variable torque, we can write

$$W_{\text{Rotation}} = \int_{\theta_1}^{\theta_2} \tau d\theta$$

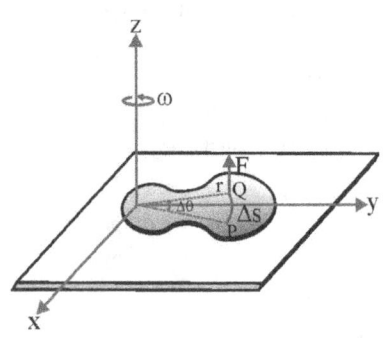

Fig. 1.72

Power delivered by torque

We know that $\quad \Delta W = \tau\Delta\theta$

Dividing both sides by Δt, we get

$$\frac{\Delta W}{\Delta t} = \tau \frac{\Delta\theta}{\Delta t}$$

or $\quad$ Power $P = \dfrac{\Delta W}{\Delta t} = \tau\omega$

Newton's second law for rotating rigid body

We have, torque $\quad \vec{\tau} = \vec{r} \times \vec{F} \quad \ldots\text{(i)}$

Angular momentum, $\vec{L} = \vec{r} \times \vec{p} \quad \ldots\text{(ii)}$

Differentiating both sides of equation (ii) w.r.t. time t, we get

$$\frac{d\vec{L}}{dt} = \frac{d(\vec{r} \times \vec{p})}{dt}$$

$$= \frac{d\vec{r}}{dt} \times \vec{p} + \vec{r} \times \frac{d\vec{p}}{dt}$$

$$= \vec{v} \times \vec{p} + \vec{r} \times \vec{F}$$

$$= (\vec{v} \times m\vec{v}) + \vec{\tau}$$

$$= 0 + \vec{\tau} \quad [\because \vec{v} \times \vec{v} = 0]$$

$$\therefore \quad \vec{\tau}_{\text{ext}} = \frac{d\vec{L}}{dt}$$

Thus the rate of change of angular momentum is equal to the external torque. This equation is the rotational analogue of Newton's second law for linear motion,

i.e., $\quad \vec{F}_{\text{ext}} = \dfrac{d\vec{p}}{dt}$

Also, we have $\quad \vec{L} = I\vec{\omega}$

$$\therefore \quad \vec{\tau}_{\text{ext}} = \frac{d\vec{L}}{dt} = \frac{d}{dt}(I\vec{\omega}) = I\frac{d\vec{\omega}}{dt}$$

or $\quad \vec{\tau}_{\text{ext}} = I\vec{\alpha}$

1.11 Angular Impulse

Consider a rod hinged at its one end. It is acted by an external force $\vec{F}$ for time Δt as shown in *Fig. 1.73*. The rod starts rotating about the hinge due to the torque $\tau = Fr$. The product of torque τ with the duration of its exertion is called angular impulse. Thus angular impulse

$$\vec{J} = \vec{\tau}\Delta t$$

Its direction is along the direction of $\vec{\tau}$. Here in the case discussed the direction of $\vec{J}$ is along positive z-axis. Its SI unit is kg-m²/s. By Newtons second law, we have

$$\vec{\tau}_{ext} = \frac{d\vec{L}}{dt}$$

or $\quad \vec{\tau}_{ext} dt = d\vec{L}$

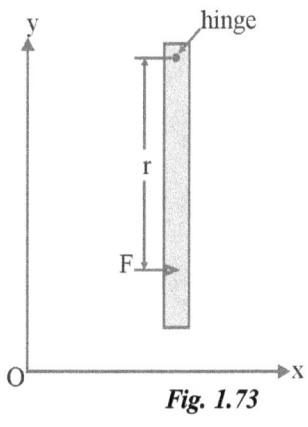

Fig. 1.73

The product $\vec{\tau}_{ext}(dt)$ is angular impulse and $d\vec{L}$ is the change in angular momentum. Thus we can write

Angular impulse = Change in angular momentum

Conservation of angular momentum

So far we have studied two powerful conservation laws, the conservation of linear momentum and conservation of energy. Now we meet a third law, the conservation of angular momentum. We can start from Newton's second law in angular form

$$\vec{\tau}_{ext} = \frac{d\vec{L}}{dt}.$$

If no net external torque acts on the system, this equation becomes

$$\frac{d\vec{L}}{dt} = 0$$

or $\quad \vec{L}$ = constant. (For isolated system)

This equation represents the law of conservation of angular momentum.

$$\tau = Fr\sin\theta$$

Examples based on conservation of angular momentum

1. Planetary motion around sun : (circular orbit)
   In planetary motion, the gravitational force (centripetal force) always passes through the axis of rotation, so its moment of force is zero. And therefore angular momentum of the orbiting planet remains constant. If v_1 and v_2 are the speeds of planet when it is at distances r_1 and r_2 respectively, then

   $$mv_1 r_1 = mv_2 r_2$$

   or $\quad v_1 r_1 = v_2 r_2$

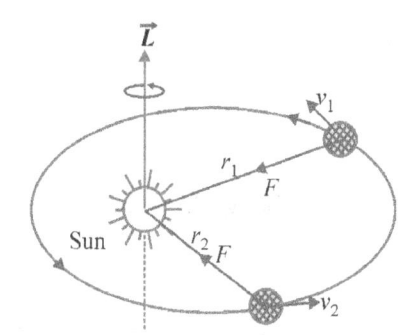

Fig. 1.74

2. *Fig1.75* shows a student sitting on a stool that can rotate freely about a vertical axis.

   The student, who is rotating initially with angular speed ω_i, holds his outstretched hands. His angular momentum vector $\vec{L}$ lies along the vertical axis as shown in figure (a). The student now pulls his arms; this decreases his moment of inertia from its initial value I_i to I_f ($I_f < I_i$). His angular speed increases from ω_i to ω_f. As no net external torque acts on the system along the axis of rotation, so the angular momentum of the system about axis remain constant. Thus we have

   $$I_i \omega_i = I_f \omega_f. \quad \text{As } I_f < I_i, \therefore \omega_f < \omega_i$$

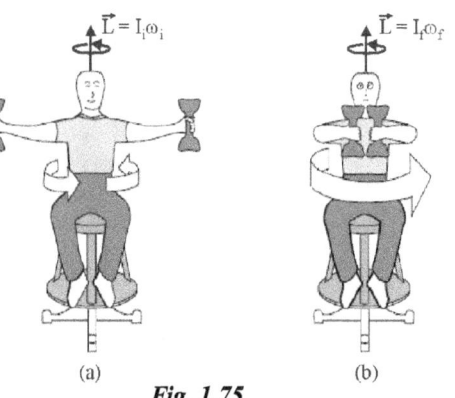

Fig. 1.75

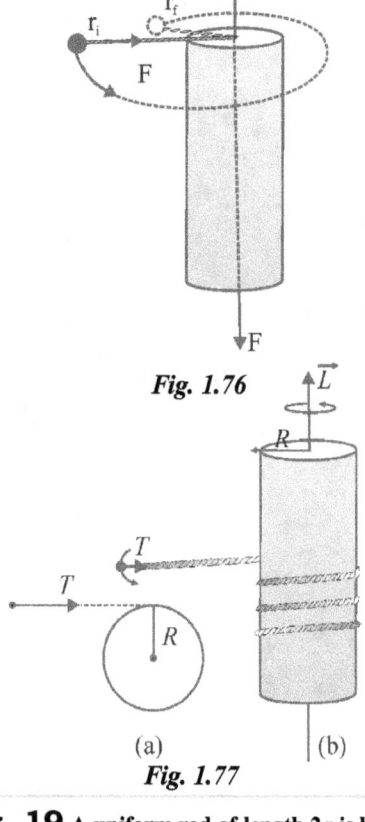

Fig. 1.76

Fig. 1.77

3. Consider a device shown in *Fig. 1.76* in which a small body attached with the string is rotating initially in a circle of radius r_i with angular speed ω_i. The free end of the string is pulled down and so body moves on a circle of smaller radius $r_f (r_f < r_i)$. As the torque of force F is zero about the axis of rotation, so the angular momentum of the rotating body remain constant. Therefore,

$$I_i \omega_i = I_f \omega_f.$$

The increase in K.E. of the body

$$= \frac{1}{2} I_f \omega_f^2 - \frac{1}{2} I_i \omega_i^2.$$

4. Consider another similar device in which the radius of path decreases by wrapping the string over the pipe as shown in *Fig 1.77*. Here the tension in the string T which is acting at a distance R (radius of pipe), constitutes a torque $\tau = TR$ along the axis of rotation (along the line of $\vec{L}$), so the angular momentum of the rotating body will change. Kinetic energy of the body remains constant.

Ex. 19 A uniform rod of length $2a$ is held with one end resting on a smooth horizontal table making an angle α with the vertical. Show that when the rod is released its angular velocity when it makes an angle θ with the vertical is given by

$$\omega = \left[\frac{6a(\cos\alpha - \cos\theta)}{a(1+3\sin^2\theta)}\right]^{1/2}.$$

Sol. If ω is the angular velocity about an axis through IAOR, then velocity of C.M. will be $\omega(a\sin\theta)$. In the process, loss in P.E. will equal to gain in K.E, therefore

$$mga(\cos\alpha - \cos\theta) = \frac{1}{2} I \omega^2 + \frac{1}{2} m(\omega a \sin\theta)^2$$

Since there is no force acting in the horizontal direction, therefore no translation of c.m. in that direction.

After simplifying, we get $\omega = \left[\dfrac{6a(\cos\alpha - \cos\theta)}{a(1+3\sin^{-1}\theta)}\right]^{1/2}.$

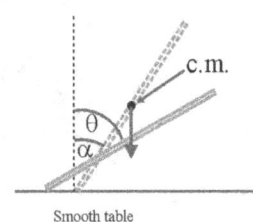 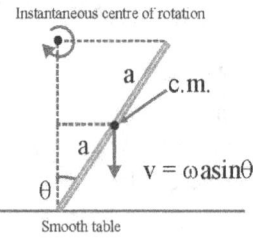

Fig. 1.78

Ex. 20 *Fig. 1.79* shows a student, sitting on a stool that can rotate freely about a vertical axis. The student, initially at rest, is holding a bicycle wheel whose rim is loaded with lead and whose moment of inertia is I about its central axis. The wheel is rotating at an angular speed ω_i from an overhead perspective, the rotation is counter clockwise. The axis of the wheel points vertical, and the angular momentum $\vec{L}_i$ of the wheel points vertically upward. The student now inverts the wheel; as a result, the student and stool rotate about the stool axis. With what angular speed and direction does the student then rotate ? (The moment of inertia of the student + stool + wheel system about the stool axis is I_0).

Sol.

There is no net torque acting on the system (student + stool + wheel), so the angular momentum of the system about vertical axis remains constant.

Let $\Delta \vec{L}_1$ and $\Delta \vec{L}_2$ are the change in angular momentum of (student + stool) and wheel respectively, then we have

$$\Delta \vec{L}_1 + \Delta \vec{L}_2 = 0$$

$$\therefore \quad \Delta \vec{L}_1 = -\Delta \vec{L}_2$$

ROTATIONAL MECHANICS

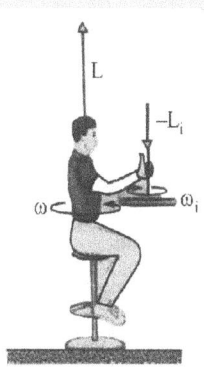

(a) A student holds a bicycle wheel rotating around the vertical.
(b) The student inverts the wheel, setting himself into rotation

Fig. 1.79

As $\quad \Delta \vec{L}_2 = -\vec{L}_i - \vec{L}_i$

$\quad\quad\quad\quad = -2\vec{L}_i$

$\therefore \quad \Delta \vec{L}_1 = 2\vec{L}_i$

As initial angular momentum of (student + stool) is zero, so

$\quad\quad 2\vec{L}_i = I_0 \vec{\omega}$

or $\quad\quad \vec{\omega} = \dfrac{2\vec{L}_i}{I_0}$

The positive result tells that the angular velocity of rotation is counterclockwise.

Ex. 21 Consider a disc of mass M and radius R is rotating with angular velocity ω about its geometrical axis as shown in *Fig. 1.80*. A small object of mass m falls gently on the edge of the disc and stick to it. Find then the angular velocity of the disc.

Sol.
Weight of the object constitutes a torque which is perpendicular to axis of rotation (or angular momentum), so angular momentum of the system remain constant along its initial direction. Thus we have

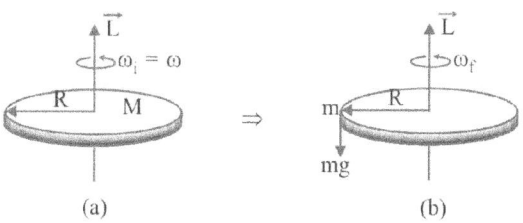

Fig. 1.80

$\quad\quad\quad \vec{L}_i = \vec{L}_f$

or $\quad\quad I_i \omega_i = I_f \omega_f$

or $\quad\quad \left(\dfrac{MR^2}{2}\right)\omega = \left(\dfrac{MR^2}{2} + mR^2\right)\omega_f$

$\therefore \quad\quad \omega_f = \left[\dfrac{M}{M+2m}\right]\omega \quad\quad$ **Ans.**

Analogy between translation and rotational motion

Translation	Rotation
Linear displacement $\vec{s}$	Angular displacement $\vec{\theta}$
Linear velocity $\vec{v} = \dfrac{d\vec{s}}{dt}$	Angular velocity $\vec{\omega} = \dfrac{d\vec{\theta}}{dt}$
Linear acceleration $\vec{a} = \dfrac{d\vec{v}}{dt}$	Angular acceleration $\vec{\alpha} = \dfrac{d\vec{\omega}}{dt}$
$\vec{s} = \vec{\theta} r \ ; \ \vec{v} = \vec{\omega} r \ ; \ \vec{a} = \vec{\alpha} r$	
Equations of Motion	
$v = u + at$	$\omega = \omega_0 + \alpha t$
$s = ut + \dfrac{1}{2}at^2$	$\theta = \omega_0 t + \dfrac{1}{2}\alpha t^2$
$v^2 = u^2 + 2as$	$\omega^2 = \omega_0^2 + 2\alpha\theta$
Mass $\quad m$	Moment of inertia $\quad I$
Force $\quad \vec{F} = m\vec{a}$	Torque $\quad \vec{\tau} = I\vec{\alpha}$
Linear momentum $\vec{P} = m\vec{v}$	Angular momentum $\vec{L} = I\vec{\omega}$
Newton's law $\vec{F}_{ext} = \dfrac{d\vec{P}}{dt}$	Newton's law $\vec{\tau}_{ext} = \dfrac{d\vec{L}}{dt}$
Linear impulse $\vec{J} = \vec{F}\Delta t$	Angular impulse $\vec{J} = \vec{\tau}\Delta t$
Translation K.E. $= \dfrac{1}{2}mv^2$	Rotational K.E. $= \dfrac{1}{2}I\omega^2$
Work done $= \int \vec{F}.d\vec{s}$	Work done $= \int \tau.d\theta$
Power $= \vec{F}\cdot\vec{v}$	Power $= \vec{\tau}\cdot\vec{\omega}$

Ex. 22 A flexible rope is wrapped several times around a solid cylinder of mass M and radius R, which rotates with no friction, about a fixed horizontal axis, as shown in *Fig. 1.81*. The free end of the rope is tied to a mass m which is released from rest a distance h above the floor. Find its speed and angular velocity of the cylinder just as mass m strikes the floor.

Sol.
Dynamical method:

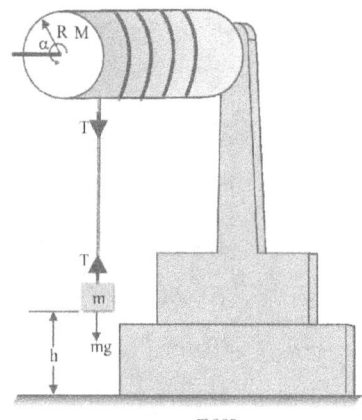

Fig. 1.81

Let acceleration of translation of mass m is a and angular acceleration of cylinder is α. As there is no slipping of rope over the cylinder, so

$$\alpha = \frac{a}{R}$$

For the translational motion of the block;
$$mg - T = ma \qquad \ldots(i)$$
For rotation of cylinder ;
$$TR = I\alpha$$
or $$TR = I\frac{a}{R}$$
or $$T = \frac{Ia}{R^2} \qquad \ldots(ii)$$

Solving equations (i) and (ii), we get
$$a = \frac{mg}{\left(m + \frac{I}{R^2}\right)}$$

Here m is the inertia of translation and $\frac{I}{R^2}$ is the inertia due to rotation. $\left(m + \frac{I}{R^2}\right)$ is called total inertia of motion.

As $$I = \frac{MR^2}{2}$$

∴ $$a = \frac{mg}{m + \frac{MR^2}{2R^2}} = \frac{g}{1 + \frac{M}{2m}}$$

The velocity of block when it strikes the floor : By using third equation of motion,
$$v^2 = 0 + 2ah$$
$$= 2\left[\frac{g}{1 + \frac{M}{2m}}\right]h$$

or $$v = \sqrt{\frac{2gh}{1 + \frac{M}{2m}}} \qquad \text{Ans.}$$

Angular velocity of cylinder
$$\omega = \frac{v}{R} = \frac{1}{R}\sqrt{\frac{2gh}{1 + \frac{M}{2m}}}$$

Energy method: Only conservative forces are acting on the system, so
loss in P.E. = gain in K.E.

or $$mgh = \frac{1}{2}mv^2 + \frac{1}{2}I\omega^2$$

The M.I. of the cylinder $I = \frac{MR^2}{2}$, and $\omega = \frac{v}{R}$.

Using these relations, we have
$$mgh = \frac{1}{2}mv^2 + \frac{1}{2}\left(\frac{MR^2}{2}\right)\left(\frac{v}{R}\right)^2$$

∴ $$v = \sqrt{\frac{2gh}{1 + \frac{M}{2m}}}$$

Note: In this type of problems when only velocity is asked, energy method is short and easy in calculation.

Ex. 23 A uniform rod AB is hinged at one end A. The rod is kept in the horizontal position by a massless string tied to point B as shown in *Fig. 1.82*. Find the reaction of the hinge on the end A of the rod at the instant when string is cut.

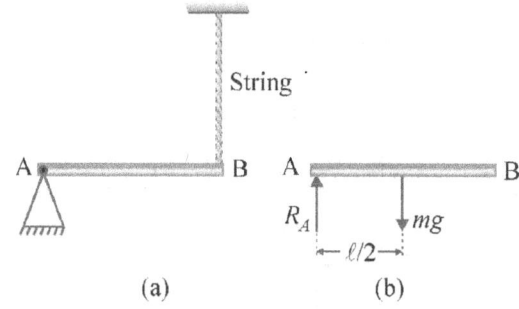

Fig. 1.82

Sol.
When string is cut, the weight of the rod constitutes torque about the hinge, so
$$\tau_A = mg\frac{\ell}{2} \qquad \ldots (i)$$

According to Newton's second law
$$\tau_A = I\alpha \qquad \ldots (ii)$$
where α is the angular acceleration of the rod about the end A.
From equations (i) and (ii)
$$I\alpha = mg\frac{\ell}{2}$$

or $$\alpha = \frac{mg\frac{\ell}{2}}{I}$$

Here $I = \dfrac{m\ell^2}{3}$

$\therefore \quad \alpha = \dfrac{mg\ell/2}{\dfrac{m\ell^2}{3}} = \dfrac{3}{2}\dfrac{g}{\ell}$

Acceleration of C.M. of the rod

$$a_{cm} = \alpha r = \dfrac{3}{2}\dfrac{g}{\ell} \times \dfrac{\ell}{2}$$

$$= \dfrac{3g}{4} = \dfrac{3g}{4}$$

Again by Newton's second law
$$mg - R_A = ma_{cm}$$
or $\quad mg - R_A = m \times \dfrac{3g}{4}$

$\therefore \quad R_A = \dfrac{mg}{4} \qquad$ **Ans.**

Ex. 24 A rod of length ℓ is pivoted about a horizontal, frictionless pin through one end. The rod is released from rest in a vertical position shown in *Fig. 1.83*. Find velocity of the C.M. of the rod, when rod is inclined at an angle θ from the vertical.

Sol. The fall in position of C.M. of the rod,

$$h = \dfrac{\ell}{2}(1 - \cos\theta)$$

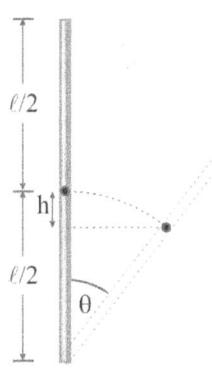

Fig. 1.83

In the process, decrease in P.E. is equal to the increase in rotational K.E. of the rod, so

$$mgh = \dfrac{1}{2}I\omega^2$$

or $\quad mg\dfrac{\ell}{2}(1 - \cos\theta) = \dfrac{1}{2}\left(\dfrac{m\ell^2}{3}\right)\omega^2$

$\therefore \quad \omega = \sqrt{\dfrac{3g}{\ell}(1 - \cos\theta)}$

The velocity of C.M. of the rod

$$v_{cm} = \omega r$$

$$= \sqrt{\dfrac{3g}{\ell}(1 - \cos\theta)} \times \dfrac{\ell}{2}$$

$$= \sqrt{\dfrac{3g\ell(1 - \cos\theta)}{4}} \qquad \textbf{Ans.}$$

Ex. 25 Two small blocks of masses m_1 and m_2 are attached to the ends of a cord which passes over the pulley of mass M and radius R. Calculate the acceleration of the blocks and tensions in the string.

Sol.

Due to inertia of the pulley, the tension in two sides of the cord are T_1 and T_2. Let acceleration magnitude of each block is a.
For the blocks, by Newton's second law

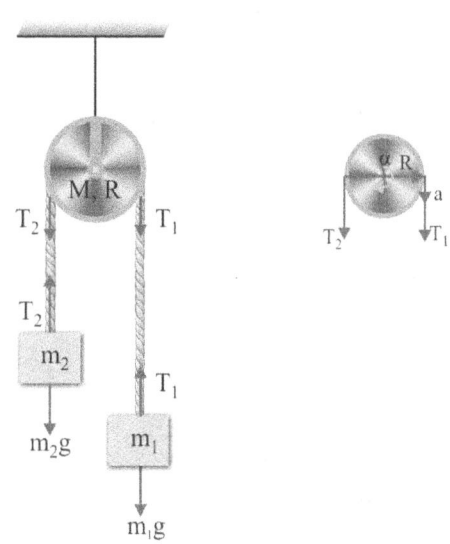

Fig. 1.84

$$m_1 g - T_1 = m_1 a \qquad \ldots (i)$$
and $\quad T_2 - m_2 g = m_2 a \qquad \ldots (ii)$

For the rotation of pulley :
$$T_1 R - T_2 R = I\alpha$$

For no slipping between pulley and cord

$$\alpha = \dfrac{a}{R}$$

$\therefore \quad T_1 R - T_2 R = I\dfrac{a}{R}$

or $\quad T_1 - T_2 = \dfrac{Ia}{R^2} \qquad \ldots (iii)$

Solving above equations, we get

$$a = \dfrac{(m_1 - m_2)g}{m_1 + m_2 + \dfrac{I}{R^2}}, \text{ here } I = \dfrac{MR^2}{2}$$

and $\quad T_1 = m_1(g - a) = \dfrac{m_1\left(2m_2 + \dfrac{I}{R^2}\right)g}{\left(m_1 + m_2 + \dfrac{I}{R^2}\right)}$

$T_2 = m_2(g + a) = \dfrac{m_2\left(2m_1 + \dfrac{I}{R^2}\right)g}{\left(m_1 + m_2 + \dfrac{I}{R^2}\right)} \quad$ **Ans.**

Note: In using the equation $\tau_{net} = I\alpha$, one should write

$$\tau_{greater} - \tau_{smaller} = I\alpha$$

Here α is along direction of greater torque.

Short cut : Student can use a short-cut method for those devices in which all the connected bodies have same acceleration magnitude.

$$\text{Acceleration,} \quad a = \frac{\text{Unbalanced load}}{\text{Total inertia}}$$

$$= \left[\frac{\text{Unbalanced load}}{\text{Inertia of translation + inertia of rotation}}\right]$$

For tension $\quad T = m_{down}(g-a)$

or $\quad T = m_{up}(g+a)$

Ex. 26 In the device shown in *Fig. 1.85*, find the acceleration of the blocks.

Sol.
Acceleration magnitude of the block

$$a = \left[\frac{\text{Unbalanced load}}{\text{Inertia of translation + inertia of rotation}}\right]$$

Here inertia of translation $= (m_1 + m_2)$,

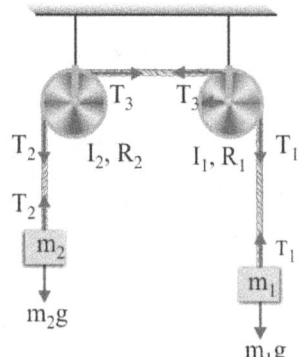

Fig. 1.85

and inertia of rotation $= \left(\frac{I_1}{R_1^2} + \frac{I_2}{R_2^2}\right)$

$$\therefore \quad a = \frac{(m_1 - m_2)g}{(m_1 + m_2) + \left(\frac{I_1}{R_1^2} + \frac{I_2}{R_2^2}\right)}$$

$$T_1 = m_1(g-a)$$
and $\quad T_2 = m_2(g+a)$

To get T_3: $\quad T_1 R_1 - T_3 R_1 = I_1\left(\frac{a}{R_1}\right)$ **Ans.**

Ex. 27 In *Fig. 1.86*(a) mass m_1 slides without friction on the horizontal surface, the frictionless pulley is in the form of a cylinder of mass M and radius R, and string turns the pulley without slipping. Find the acceleration of each mass, and tension in each part of the string.

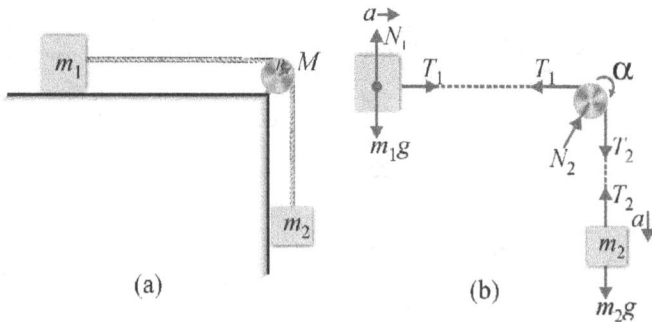

Fig. 1.86

Sol.
Positive direction of angular acceleration α is taken along the corresponding acceleration a_1 which is taken positive in the direction of net force. Also due to inertia of the pulley the tension in two parts of the string will be different. Let it is T_1 and T_2 as shown in *Fig. 1.85* (b). The equation of motion for masses m_1 and m_2 are

$$T_1 = m_1 a \quad \text{... (i)}$$
and $\quad m_2 g - T_2 = m_2 a \quad \text{... (ii)}$

The equation of motion of pulley is

$$T_2 R - T_1 R = I\alpha$$

(N_2 constitutes no torque about the axis of rotation)

As there is no slipping of string over pulley, so $\alpha = \frac{a}{R}$.

$$\therefore \quad T_2 R - T_1 R = I\frac{a}{R}$$

or $\quad T_2 - T_1 = \frac{Ia}{R^2} \quad \text{... (iii)}$

Solving above equations, we get

$$a = \frac{m_2 g}{\left(m_1 + m_2 + \frac{I}{R^2}\right)}, \quad \text{here } I = \frac{MR^2}{2}$$

and $\quad T_1 = \dfrac{m_1 m_2 g}{\left(m_1 + m_2 + \dfrac{I}{R^2}\right)}$

$$T_2 = \frac{\left(m_1 + \dfrac{M}{2}\right)m_2 g}{\left(m_1 + m_2 + \dfrac{I}{R^2}\right)} \quad \textbf{Ans.}$$

1.12 ROTATION ABOUT A MOVING AXIS

Analysis of motion which includes both translation and rotation of a body required two separate equations of motion for the body, one for translation, $\vec{F}_{net} = m\vec{a}$ and other for rotation, $\vec{\tau} = I\vec{\alpha}$. In addition to these equations it often requires the relation between these two motions i.e., $a = \alpha R$.

ROTATIONAL MECHANICS

Ex. 28 A string is wrapped around a solid cylinder and then the end of the string is held stationary while the cylinder is released from rest. Find the acceleration of the cylinder and tension in the string.

Sol.

Let M and R be the mass and radius of the cylinder. 'a' is the acceleration of C.M. of the cylinder.

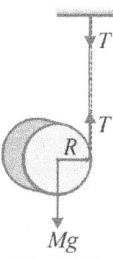

Fig. 1.87

For translation motion;

$$Mg - T = Ma \qquad \ldots (i)$$

For rotation motion;

$$TR = I\alpha$$

As $\quad \alpha = \dfrac{a}{R}$

$\therefore \quad TR = I\dfrac{a}{R}$

or $\quad T = \dfrac{Ia}{R^2} \qquad \ldots (ii)$

Solving equations (i) and (ii), we get

$$a = \dfrac{Mg}{\left(M + \dfrac{I}{R^2}\right)}$$

$$= \dfrac{Mg}{M + \dfrac{MR^2}{2R^2}} \qquad \left[I = \dfrac{MR^2}{2}\right]$$

$$= \dfrac{2g}{3} \qquad \textbf{Ans.}$$

and $\quad T = \dfrac{Ia}{R^2} = \dfrac{\left(\dfrac{MR^2}{2}\right) \times \dfrac{2g}{3}}{R^2}$

$$= \dfrac{Mg}{3} \qquad \textbf{Ans.}$$

Ex. 29 In figure the mirror of weight W is initially at the same level as a monkey of equal weight. The fixed pulley is massless and has a radius R. If the monkey starts running up the rope, can he get away from the mirror?

Sol.

Both sides of the pulley, the weight suspended are equal, so net torque acting on the centre of the pulley will be zero.

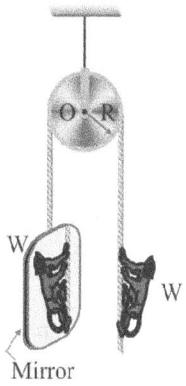

Fig. 1.88

Hence the angular momentum about this point is constant. Since the initial angular momentum of the system in equilibrium is zero, so it must remain same throughout. When the monkey starts running up the rope, let its velocity at any instant be v. This gives an angular momentum $(W/g) vR$ about O. Thus for the total angular momentum to be zero, the mirror must also have the same instantaneous velocity. In other words, the monkey cannot get away from his mirror image.

Ex. 30 A man of mass m stands on a horizontal platform in the shape of a disk of mass M and radius R, pivoted on a vertical axis through its centre about which it can freely rotate (*Fig. 1.88*). The man starts to move round the centre of the disk in a circle of radius r with a velocity v relative to the disk. Calculate the angular velocity of the disk.

Sol.

Since there is no torque acting about the axis of rotation of the disk, so the angular momentum of the system (disk + man) remain constant. Initially it is zero. Suppose ω is the angular velocity of the disk (take positive in the sense of motion of the man). The velocity of the man with respect to the ground observer will be :

$$[\vec{v}_{\text{man}}]_{\text{disk}} = [\vec{v}_{\text{man}}]_{\text{ground}} - [\vec{v}_{\text{disk}}]_{\text{ground}}$$

$\therefore \quad [\vec{v}_{\text{man}}]_{\text{ground}} = [\vec{v}_{\text{man}}]_{\text{disk}} + [\vec{v}_{\text{disk}}]_{\text{ground}}$

or $\quad [\vec{v}_{\text{man}}]_{\text{ground}} = v + \omega r$

Thus angular momentum of the man $= m(v + \omega r)r$.

Fig. 1.89

And angular momentum of the disk $= I_{\text{disk}}\omega = \dfrac{MR^2}{2}\omega$

By conservation of angular momentum, we have

$$0 = m(v + \omega r)r + \dfrac{MR^2}{2}\omega$$

After solving, we get

$$\omega = -\dfrac{mvr}{\left(mr^2 + \dfrac{MR^2}{2}\right)} \qquad \textbf{Ans.}$$

MECHANICS, THERMODYNAMICS & WAVES

Ex. 31 A thin rod is held resting on the ground with its length inclined at an angle α to the horizontal. The coefficient of friction between the rod and the ground is μ. Show that when the rod let go, it will start slipping on the ground, if

$$\mu < \frac{3\sin\alpha\cos\alpha}{1+3\sin\alpha}.$$

Sol. By Newton's second law

$$mg - R = ma\cos\alpha \qquad ...(i)$$

For not slipping, $\mu R > ma\sin\alpha$

Solving above equations, we get $\mu R > \dfrac{a\sin\alpha}{g - a\cos\alpha}$ ...(ii)

and for slipping, $\mu < \dfrac{a\sin\alpha}{g - a\cos\alpha}$ ...(iii)

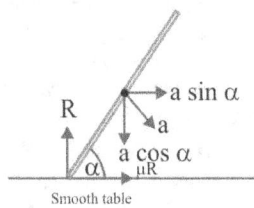

Fig. 1.90

a can be calculated as

$$I\alpha = mg \times L\cos\alpha \quad \text{where } \alpha = \frac{a}{L} \qquad ...(iv)$$

After solving equation, we get $\mu < \dfrac{3\sin\alpha\cos\alpha}{1+3\sin\alpha}$

Ex. 32 The composite pulley shown in *Fig. 1.91* weighs 800 N and has a radius of gyration of 0.6 m. The 2000 N and 4000 N blocks are attached to the pulley by inextensible strings as shown in figure. Determine the angular acceleration of the pulley and the tension in the strings. Neglecting the weight of the string.

Sol.

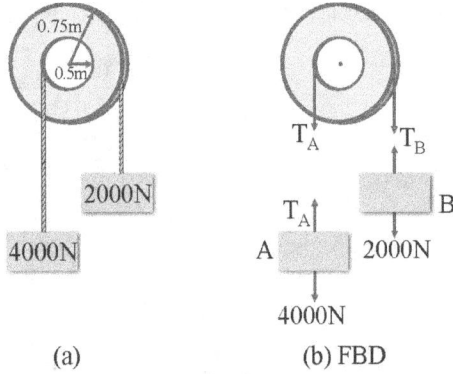

Fig. 1.91

Since the moment of 4000 N is more than that of 2000 N block about the axis of rotation of pulley, therefore pulley rotates in anticlockwise direction. Let a_A be the acceleration of block A, a_B that of B and α is the angular acceleration of the pulley, then

$$a_A = \alpha \times 0.5, \quad a_B = \alpha \times 0.75$$

Equations of motion are

$$4000 - T_A = (4000/9.81)a_A \qquad ...(i)$$
$$T_B - 2000 = (2000/9.81)a_B \qquad ...(ii)$$

and for pulley

$$4000 \times 0.5 - 2000 \times 0.75 = I\alpha \qquad ...(iii)$$

where
$$I = m_{pulley} \times k^2 = (800/9.81) \times 0.6^2 = 29.36 \text{ kg-m}^2$$

Solving above equations, we get

$$\alpha = 2.03 \text{ rad/s}^2, \ T_A = 3585.58 \text{ N}, \ T_B = 2310.82 \text{ N} \quad \textbf{Ans.}$$

Ex. 33 In *Fig. 1.92* the steel balls A and B have a mass of 500 g each, and are rotating about the vertical axis with an angular velocity of 4 rad/s at a distance of 15 cm from the axis. Collar C is now forced down until the balls are at a distance of 5 cm from the axis. How much work must be done to move the collar down?

Sol.

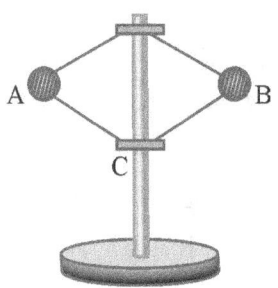

Fig. 1.92

In this process angular momentum remain constant

$$I_1\omega_1 = I_2\omega_2$$

where $I_1 = 2m(0.15)^2$, $\omega_1 = 4$ rad/s, $I_2 = 2m(0.05)^2$

Substituting these values in above equation, we get

$$\omega_2 = \frac{I_1\omega_1}{I_2} = 36 \text{ rad/s}$$

Work done on the collar

$$W = \frac{1}{2}I_2\omega_2^2 - \frac{1}{2}I_1\omega_1^2$$

or
$$W = \frac{1}{2}2m(0.05)^2 \times 36^2 - \frac{1}{2}2m(0.15)^2 \times 4$$

where $m = 500/1000 = 0.5$ kg

$$= 1.44 \text{ J} \qquad \textbf{Ans.}$$

Ex. 34 A small block of mass 4 kg is attached to a cord passing through a hole in a horizontal frictionless surface. The block is originally revolving in a circle of radius 0.5 m about the hole, with a tangential velocity of 4 m/s. The cord is then pulled slowly from below, shortening the radius of the circle in which the block revolves. The breaking strength of the cord is 600 N. What will be the radius of the circle when the cord breaks?

Sol.
Cord will break when centrifugal force exceeds breaking strength. Let r_2 be the radius of the circle at the instant of breaking, then

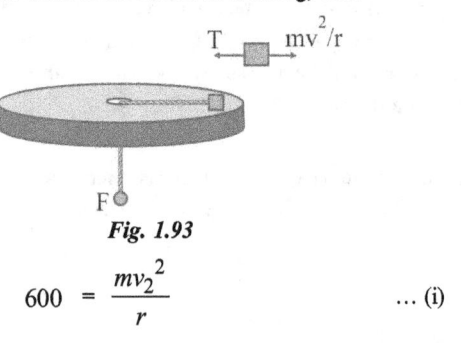

Fig. 1.93

$$600 = \frac{mv_2^2}{r} \qquad ...(i)$$

In the process of shorting of the cord, angular momentum remains constant.

$$mv_1 r = mv_2 r_2 \quad \ldots (ii)$$

or $\quad m \times 4 \times 0.5 = m \times v_2 \times r$

or $\quad v_2 = \dfrac{2}{r}$

Substituting the value of v_2 in equation (i), we get
$r = 0.2988$ m **Ans.**

Ex. 35 A block of mass M rests on a turntable that is rotating at constant angular velocity ω. A smooth cord runs from the block through a hole in the centre of the table down to a hanging block of mass m. The coefficient of friction between the first block and the turntable is μ. (see Fig. 195). Find the largest and the smallest values of the radius r for which the first block will remain at rest relative to the turntable.

Sol.

For minimum value of $r = r_1$, the tendency of motion of the block M is towards the centre, and therefore frictional force will act away from the centre.
For the equilibrium of M, we have

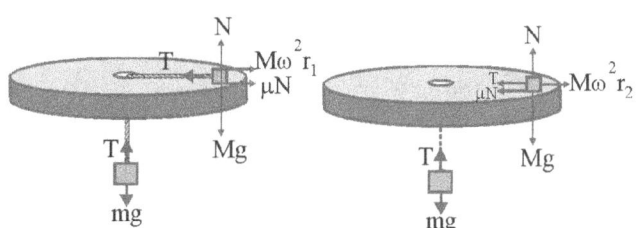

(a) FBD in rotating frame   (b) FBD in rotating frame

Fig. 1.94

$$T = M\omega^2 r_1 + \mu N \quad \ldots (i)$$

where $\quad N = Mg$

For the equilibrium of block m we have

$$T = mg \quad \ldots (ii)$$

From (i) and (ii), we get

$$mg = M\omega^2 r_1 + \mu Mg$$

or $\quad r_1 = (mg - \mu Mg)/(M\omega^2)$

For maximum value of $r = r_2$, the tendency of motion of block M will be away from the centre, therefore frictional force acts towards centre.
Doing the similar treatment for this case,

$$T + \mu Mg = M\omega^2 r_2$$

and $\quad T = mg$

After solving for r_2, we get

$$r_2 = (mg + \mu Mg)/(M\omega^2) \quad \textbf{Ans.}$$

Ex. 36 Disks A and B are mounted on a shaft SS and may be connected or disconnected by a clutch C, as in Fig. 1.95. The moment of inertia of disk A is one half that of disk B. With the clutch disconnected, A is brought upto an angular velocity ω_0. The accelerating torque is then removed from A and it is coupled to disk B by the clutch (Bearing friction may be neglected). It is found that 2000 J of heat are developed in the clutch when the connection is made. What are the original kinetic energy of disk A?

Sol. Let $I_A = I$ and $I_B = 2I$
In the connection of disk A with disk B, the angular momentum remain constant

or $\quad I\omega_0 + 0 = (I + 2I)\omega$

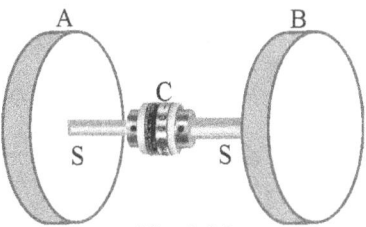

Fig. 1.95

which gives $\quad \omega = \dfrac{\omega_0}{3}$

The change in K.E. evolved as heat i.e.,

$$\dfrac{1}{2}I\omega_0^2 - \dfrac{1}{2}(3I)\omega^2 = 2000$$

Substituting the value of ω in the above equation, we get

$$\dfrac{1}{2}I\omega_0^2 - \dfrac{1}{2}3I\left(\dfrac{\omega_0}{3}\right)^2 = 2000$$

or $\quad \dfrac{1}{3}I\omega_0^2 = 2000$

∴ $\quad \dfrac{1}{2}I\omega_0^2 = 3000$ J

where $\dfrac{1}{2}I\omega_0^2$ in the initial energy of the disk A.

Ex. 37 A particle A moves along a circle of radius R = 50 cm so that its radius vector $\vec{r}$ relative to the point O rotates with the constant angular velocity ω = 0.40 rad/s. Find the modulus of the velocity of the particle, and the modulus and direction of its total acceleration.

Sol. In ΔOAB, by sine rule, we can write

$$\dfrac{R}{\sin\theta} = \dfrac{r}{\sin(180° - 2\theta)}$$

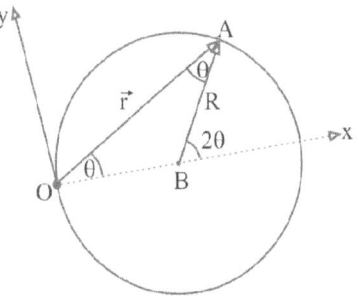

Fig. 1.96

or $\quad r = 2R\cos\theta \quad \ldots (i)$

38 MECHANICS, THERMODYNAMICS & WAVES

$\vec{r}$ can be written as ;

$$\vec{r} = r\cos\theta\hat{i} + r\sin\theta\hat{j}$$
$$= (2R\cos\theta)\cos\theta\hat{i} + (2R\cos\theta)\sin\theta\hat{j}$$
$$= 2R\cos^2\theta\hat{i} + R\sin 2\theta\hat{j} \quad \ldots (ii)$$

The velocity of the particle

$$\vec{v} = \frac{d\vec{r}}{dt} = \frac{d}{dt}\left[2R\cos^2\theta\hat{i} + R\sin 2\theta\hat{j}\right]$$
$$= \left[-2R\sin 2\theta\left(\frac{d\theta}{dt}\right)\hat{i} + 2R\cos 2\theta\left(\frac{d\theta}{dt}\right)\hat{j}\right]$$
$$= -2\omega R(\sin 2\theta\hat{i} - \cos 2\theta\hat{j})$$

$\therefore \quad |\vec{v}| = 2\omega R$
$$= 2 \times 0.40 \times (0.5) = 0.4 \text{ m/s}$$

Here ω is constant, so the tangential acceleration of the particle is zero. Thus the magnitude of total acceleration

$$a = \frac{v^2}{R} = \frac{(2\omega R)^2}{R} = 4\omega^2 R$$
$$= 4 \times (0.40)^2 \times 0.5 = 0.32 \text{ m/s}^2 \quad \textbf{Ans.}$$

Ex. 38 A cubical block of side a moves down on a rough inclined plane of inclination θ with constant velocity. Find the position of normal reaction.

Sol. As the block moves down with constant velocity, the net force on the block in the direction of motion is zero. Thus we have,

$$mg\sin\theta - f = 0$$
or $$f = mg\sin\theta \quad \ldots(i)$$

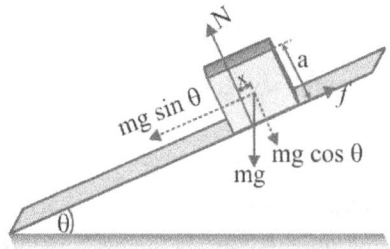

Fig. 1.97

Also, the block is not rotating, so net torque on it must be zero. The net torque can be zero only if normal reaction on the block will pass some distance away, from the C.M. (see figure). Thus for rotational equilibrium of the block,

$$f \times \frac{a}{2} - Nx = 0$$
or $$x = \frac{fa}{2N}$$

From equation (i), we have $f = mg\sin\theta$

$$\therefore \quad x = \frac{mg\sin\theta \times a}{2 \times mg\cos\theta}$$
$$= \frac{a\tan\theta}{2}$$

Thus normal reaction exerted by inclined plane on the block will pass through a distance $\frac{a\tan\theta}{2}$ from C.M. to keep the block in rotational equilibrium.

Ex. 39 A disc of mass M has a radius R can rotate freely about a horizontal shaft O which is located at a distance r from the centre of mass of the disc C. Assume that the disc is released from the position shown in the *Fig. 142*. Find minimum value of r for which the angular acceleration of the disc is maximum.

Sol. The moment of inertia of the disc about axis of rotation which passes through O;

$$I_o = I_{cm} + Mr^2$$
$$= \left(\frac{MR^2}{2} + Mr^2\right)$$

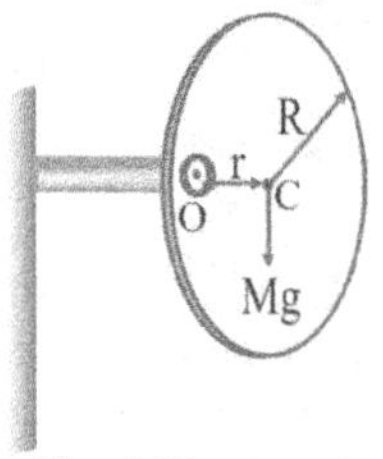

The angular acceleration of the disc is given by

$$\alpha = \frac{\tau}{I} = \frac{Mg \times r}{\left(\frac{MR^2}{2} + Mr^2\right)}$$

Fig. 1.98

$$= \left[\frac{2gr}{R^2 + 2r^2}\right]$$

The angular acceleration α to be maximum, $\frac{d\alpha}{dr} = 0$

or $$\frac{d}{dr}\left[\frac{2gr}{R^2 + 2r^2}\right] = 0$$

$$(R^2 + 2r^2) \times 2g - 2gr \times (0 + 2 \times 2r) = 0$$

$$\Rightarrow \quad r = \frac{R}{\sqrt{2}} \quad \textbf{Ans.}$$

Ex. 40 A stick of length L and mass M lies on a frictionless horizontal surface on which it is free to move in anyway. A ball of mass m moving with speed v as shown in *Fig. 1.146* collides elastically with stick. What must be the mass of ball so that it remains at rest immediately after collision?

Sol.
By conservation of linear momentum and angular momentum, we have
$$mv + 0 = m \times 0 + MV$$
$$\Rightarrow \quad V = \frac{mv}{M}$$
and $$mvd = I\omega$$
$$\Rightarrow \quad \omega = \frac{mvd}{I}$$

Since collision is elastic, therefore

$$\frac{1}{2}mv^2 = \frac{1}{2}MV^2 + \frac{1}{2}I\omega^2 \quad \textbf{Fig. 1.99}$$

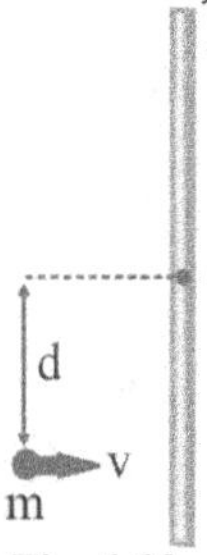

Substituting the values of v and ω in the above equation, we get

$$\frac{1}{2}mv^2 = \frac{1}{2}M\left(\frac{mv}{M}\right)^2 + \frac{1}{2}\left(\frac{ML^2}{12}\right)\left(\frac{mvd}{\frac{mL^2}{12}}\right)^2$$

$$\Rightarrow \quad m = \frac{ML^2}{L^2 + 12d^2} \quad \textbf{Ans.}$$

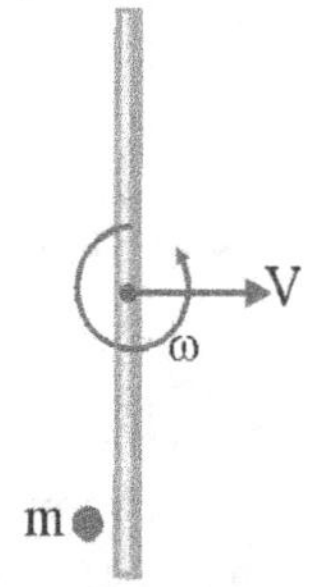

Fig. 1.100

Ex. 41 A thin uniform rod of length L is initially at rest with respect to an inertial frame of reference. The rod is tapped at one end perpendicular to its length. How far the centre of mass translate while the rod complete one revolution about its centre of mass. Neglect gravitational effect.

Sol.

Let Δt is the duration of impact, then

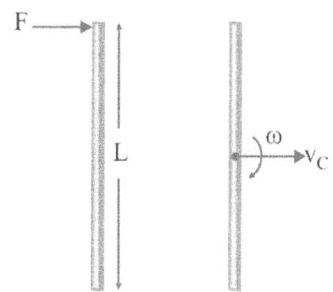

Fig. 1.101

$$\vec{F}\Delta t = \Delta \vec{P}$$

or $\quad F\Delta t = (Mv_c - 0) \quad \ldots (i)$

Also angular impulse is equal to change in angular momentum

or $\quad \left(\dfrac{F\ell}{2}\right)\Delta t = I\Delta\omega$

$$= I(\omega - 0) \quad \ldots (ii)$$

Dividing equation (i) by (ii), we get

$$\dfrac{v_c}{\omega} = \dfrac{\ell}{6}$$

Let t be the time in which rod rotates an angle 2π, then

$$\dfrac{v_c}{\omega} \times \dfrac{t}{t} = \dfrac{\ell}{6}$$

or $\quad \dfrac{x_c}{\theta} = \dfrac{\ell}{6}$

or $\quad \dfrac{x_c}{2\pi} = \dfrac{\ell}{6} \Rightarrow x_c = \dfrac{\ell\pi}{3}$ **Ans.**

Ex. 42 A rod AB of mass M and length L is lying on a horizontal frictionless surface. A particle of mass m travelling along the surface hits the end A of the rod with a velocity v_0 in a direction perpendicular to AB. The collision is completely elastic. After the collision the particle comes to rest.

(a) Find the ratio $\dfrac{m}{M}$.

(b) A point P on the rod is at rest immediately after the collision. Find the distance AP.

(c) Find the linear speed of a point P at time $\dfrac{\pi L}{3v_0}$ after the collision.

Sol.

(a) Let v_c and ω are the velocity of C.M. and angular velocity just after collision.

Using conservation of linear momentum, we have

$$mv_0 = 0 + Mv_c \quad \ldots (i)$$

and by conservation of angular momentum

$$mv_0 \dfrac{L}{2} = I\omega$$

or $\quad mv_0 \dfrac{L}{2} = \left(\dfrac{ML^2}{12}\right)\omega \quad \ldots (ii)$

From equations (i) and (ii)

$$v_c = \dfrac{mv_0}{M} \text{ and } \omega = \dfrac{6mv_0}{ML}$$

Since collision is completely elastic, therefore K.E. before collision is equal to after collision

or $\quad \dfrac{1}{2}mv_0^2 + 0 = \dfrac{1}{2}Mv_c^2 + \dfrac{1}{2}I\omega^2$

or $\quad \dfrac{1}{2}mv_0^2 = \dfrac{1}{2}M\left(\dfrac{mv_0}{M}\right)v_c^2 + \dfrac{1}{2}\left(\dfrac{ML^2}{12}\right)\left(\dfrac{6mv_0}{ML}\right)^2$

which gives $\quad \dfrac{m}{M} = \dfrac{1}{4}$ and $v_c = \dfrac{v_0}{4}$ **Ans.**

(b)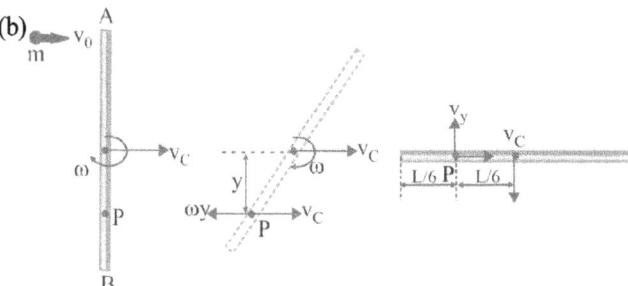

Fig. 1.102

Velocity of point P immediately after collision be zero, let it is at a distance y from C.M.

$$\therefore \quad v_c - \omega y = 0$$

or $\quad \dfrac{mv_0}{M} - \left(\dfrac{6mv_0}{ML}\right)y = 0$

which gives $\quad y = \dfrac{L}{6}$

$\therefore \quad AP = \dfrac{L}{2} + \dfrac{L}{6} = \dfrac{2L}{3}$

(c) Angle rotated by rod in time $\dfrac{\pi L}{3v_0}$

$$\theta = \omega t = \dfrac{6mv_0}{ML} \times \dfrac{\pi L}{3v_0}$$

$$= \dfrac{\pi}{2} \quad \textbf{Ans.}$$

The rod turns through $\frac{\pi}{2}$, in this interval of time. The velocity of point P in y-direction will be

$$v_y = \omega y = \frac{6mv_0}{ML} \times \frac{L}{6}$$

$$= \frac{v_0}{4}$$

The resultant velocity of point P

$$v = \sqrt{v_c^2 + v_y^2}$$

$$= \sqrt{\left(\frac{v_0}{4}\right)^2 + \left(\frac{v_0}{4}\right)^2}$$

$$= \frac{v_0}{2\sqrt{2}} \quad \text{Ans.}$$

Ex. 43 A constant force P is exerted on a rod of mass M. The rod is supported by frictionless wall. If the rod starts from a position of rest when $\theta = 45°$, as shown in Fig 1.154, what is its angular speed when the end A has moved a distance 1.5 m?

Sol.

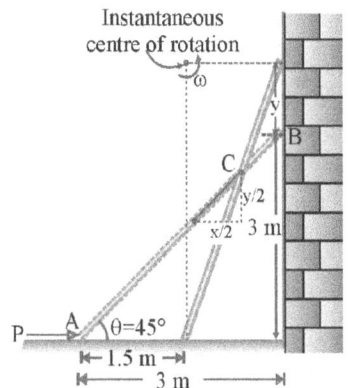

Fig. 1.103

The length of the rod $= \sqrt{3^2 + 3^2} = \sqrt{18}$ m

When the end A moves a distance $x = 1.5$ m, let end B moves distance y, which can be obtained as:

$$(3 - x)^2 + (3 + y)^2 = 18$$

Substituting $x = 1.5$ m, y will be equal to 0.97 m. Thus the distances of ends A and B from axis of rotation are 1.5 m and 3.97 m respectively. Let v_A and v_B are the velocities of the ends A and B respectively, then

$$v_B = 1.5\omega \quad \text{and} \quad v_A = 3.97\omega$$

The velocity of the centre C,

$$v_C^2 = \left(\frac{v_A}{2}\right)^2 + \left(\frac{v_B}{2}\right)^2$$

or $\quad v_C^2 = 4.52\omega^2$

In this process centre will rise $= y/2 = 0.97/2 = 0.485$ m
Using work-energy theorem, we have
Work done by the force = increase in P.E. of the rod + gain in translational K.E. + gain in rotational K.E.

or $\quad P \times 1.5 = Mg(0.485) + \frac{1}{2}Mv_C^2 + \frac{1}{2}I\omega^2 \quad$ where

$$I = \frac{ML^2}{12} = M \times \frac{18}{12} = \frac{3M}{2}$$

Substituting the all known values in above equation, we get

$$\omega = \left(\frac{0.498P}{Mg} - 0.16\right)^{1/2} \quad \text{Ans.}$$

Ex. 44 A uniform bar of length 6a and mass 8m lies on a smooth horizontal table. Two point masses m and 2m moving in the same horizontal plane with speed 2v and v respectively strike the bar and stick to the bar after collision. Calculate
(a) the velocity of centre of mass after collision,
(b) angular velocity of rotation about the centre of mass,
(c) total energy.

Sol.
(a) In the process of collision the linear momentum remains constant

$$2mv - m2v + 0 = (2m + m + 8m)v_{cm}$$

or $\quad v_{cm} = 0 \quad$ Ans.

(b) Angular momentum of the system also remain constant

$$\therefore \quad 2mv.a + (2mv).2a + 0 = I\omega \quad \ldots \text{(i)}$$

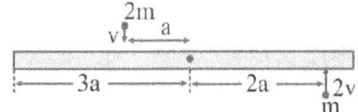

Fig. 1.104

where I is the moment of inertia of the system after collision.
I = M.I. of the rod + M.I. of the mass $2m$ + M.I. of the mass m

or $\quad I = \frac{(8m)(6a)^2}{12} + 2m \cdot a^2 + m \cdot (2a)^2$

$$= 30 \, ma^2$$

Substituting this value in equation (i), we get

$$\omega = v/5a \quad \text{Ans.}$$

(c) Total energy after collision

$$E = \frac{1}{2}I\omega^2 = \frac{1}{2}30ma^2 \times (v/5a)^2$$

or $\quad E = 3mv^2/5 \quad$ Ans.

Ex. 45 Two 2.00 kg walls are attached to the ends of a thin rod of negligible mass, 50 cm long. The rod is free to rotate in vertical plane without friction about a horizontal axis through its centre. While the rod is horizontal, a 50 g putty wad was dropped onto one of the balls with a speed of 3.0 m/s and sticks to it.
(a) What is the angular speed of the system just after the putty wad hits?
(b) What is the ratio of the kinetic energy of the entire system after the collision to that of putty wad just before?
(c) Through what angle the system rotate until momentarily stops?

Sol.
(a) Let M is the mass of each ball and m is the mass of the putty wad given:
$M = 2.00$ kg $\quad m = 0.05$ kg, Length of the rod, $L = 0.05$ m
Using the principle of conservation of angular momentum, we have

$$mv\left(\frac{L}{2}\right) + 0 = I\omega \quad \ldots \text{(i)}$$

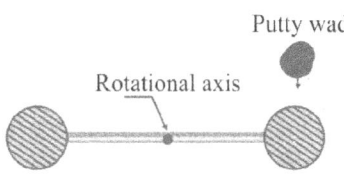

Fig. 1.105

where
$$I = M\left(\frac{L}{2}\right)^2 + M\left(\frac{L}{2}\right)^2 + m\left(\frac{L}{2}\right)^2$$

$$= (2M + m)\left(\frac{L}{2}\right)^2$$

Substituting this value in above equation, we get

$$\omega = \left(\frac{mvL}{2}\right)\Big/I = \frac{2mv}{(2M+m)L}$$

$$= 0.148 \text{ rad/s} \quad \text{Ans.}$$

(b) The initial K.E. $= \frac{1}{2}mv^2$

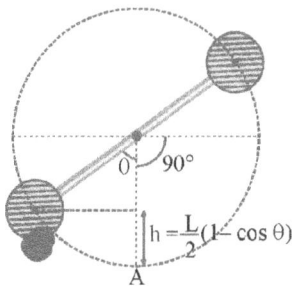

Fig. 1.106

Final K.E. $= \frac{1}{2}I\omega^2$

Their ratio $f = \dfrac{\frac{1}{2}I\omega^2}{\frac{1}{2}mv^2}$

After substituting the values of L and ω, we get

$$f = \frac{m}{(2M+m)} = 0.0123 \quad \text{Ans.}$$

(c) As the rod rotates, its mechanical energy remain constant. If one on the balls is lowered a distance d the other is raised the same distance, and the sum of the P.E. of the balls does not change. Now using principle of conservation of mechanical energy, we have mechanical energy at A = mechanical energy at B

or $mg\dfrac{L}{2} + \dfrac{1}{2}I\omega^2 = mg\dfrac{L}{2}(1-\cos\theta)$

or $mg\dfrac{L}{2} + \dfrac{1}{2}(2M+m)\left(\dfrac{L}{2}\right)^2\left[\dfrac{2mv}{2M+m}\right]^2 = mg\dfrac{L}{2}(1-\cos\theta)$

After substituting the all known values in above equation, we get

$$\theta = 92.6°$$

The total angle of the swing is $= 90° + 92.6° = \mathbf{182.6°}$ **Ans.**

Ex. 46 Four thin rods, each with mass M and length $d = 1.0$ m, are rigidly connected in the form of a plus sign; the entire assembly rotates in a horizontal plane around a vertical axle at the centre, with initial (clockwise) angular velocity $\omega_i = -2.0$ rad/s (see *Fig. 1.107*). A mud ball with mass m and initial speed $v_i = 12$ m/s is thrown at and sticks to the end of one rod. Let $M = 3m$. What is the final angular velocity ω_f of the plus sign + mud ball system if the initial path of the mud ball is each of the four paths shown in figure: path 1 (contact is made when the ball's velocity is perpendicular to the rod), path 2 (radial contact), path 3 (perpendicular contact), and path 4 (contact is made at 60° to the perpendicular)?

Sol.

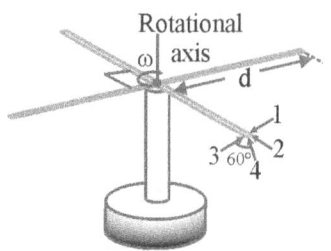

Fig. 1.107

During the collision, the total angular momentum of the system remains constant.

or $L_i = L_f$

$$I^{rod}\omega_i + L_i^{mud} = (I^{rod} + I^{mud})\omega_f \quad \ldots (i)$$

$$I_f = I^{rod} + I^{mud}$$

$$= 4\left(\frac{Md^2}{3}\right) + md^2$$

$$= \frac{4(3m)d^2}{3} + md^2 = 5md^2$$

$$\therefore \quad \omega_f = (4md^2\omega_i + L^{mud})/(5md^2) \quad \ldots (ii)$$

Angular momentum about axle taken as +ve, if it rotates counterclockwise, and -ve if rotates clockwise.

L^{mud}:

path 1 : $L_1 = -mdv$ path 2 : $L_2 = 0$
path 3 : $L_3 = mdv$ path 4 : $L_4 = (mv\cos 60°)d$

Here $v = 12$ m/s substituting these values in equation (ii) along with $v = 12$ m/s, we get ω_f

path 1 : -4.0 rad/s path 2 : -1.6 rad/s
path 3 : 0.80 rad/s path 4 : -0.40 rad/s **Ans.**

Ex. 47 A rigid body is made of three identical thin rods, each with length ℓ fastened together in the form of letter H (see *Fig. 1.159*). The body is free to rotate about a horizontal axis that runs along the length of one of the length of the H. The body is allowed to fall from rest from a position in which the plane of the H is horizontal. What is the angular speed of the body when the plane of the H is vertical ?

Sol. Using principle of conservation of mechanical energy, we have

$$\frac{mg\ell}{2} + mg\ell = \frac{1}{2}I\omega^2$$

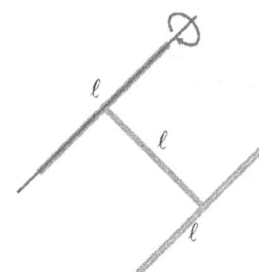

Fig. 1.108

where ω is the angular speed of the rod when it becomes vertical, and

$I = \frac{m\ell^2}{3} + m\ell^2$, assuming mass of each rod is m.

Substituting value of I in the above equation, we get

$$\omega = \sqrt{\left(\frac{9g}{4\ell}\right)} \qquad \text{Ans.}$$

Ex. 48 A uniform spherical shell of mass M and radius R rotates about a vertical axis on frictionless bearing as shown in *Fig. 1.109*. A massless cord passes around the equator of the shell, over a pulley of rotational inertia I and radius r, and is attached to a small object of mass m that is otherwise free to fall under the influence of gravity. There is no friction of pulley's axle; the cord does not slip on the pulley. What is the speed of the object after it has fallen a distance h from rest? Use work-energy considerations.

Sol. Using a conservation of energy principle, we have

Fall in P.E. of the block = Gain in K.E. of block + rotational K.E. of the pulley + rotational K.E. of the shell.

or $\qquad mgh = \frac{1}{2}mv^2 + \frac{1}{2}I\omega^2 + \frac{1}{2}\left(\frac{2MR^2}{3}\right)\omega'^2$

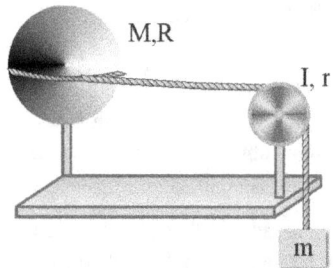

Fig. 1.109

where $\omega = v/r$ and $\omega' = v/R$.

After substituting these values in above equation, and solving, we get

$$v^2 = \frac{mgh}{\left(\frac{m}{2} + \frac{I}{2r^2} + \frac{M}{3}\right)} \qquad \text{Ans.}$$

Ex. 49 A homogeneous rod AB of length $\ell = 1.8$ m and mass M is pivoted at the centre O in such a way that it can rotate freely in the vertical plane. The rod is initially in the horizontal position. An insect S of the same mass M falls vertically with speed v on the point C, midway between the points O and B. Immediately after falling, the insect moves towards the end B such that the rod rotates with a constant angular velocity ω.

(a) Determine the angular velocity ω in terms of v and L.
(b) If the insect reaches the end B when the rod has turned through an angle of 90°, determine v.

Sol.

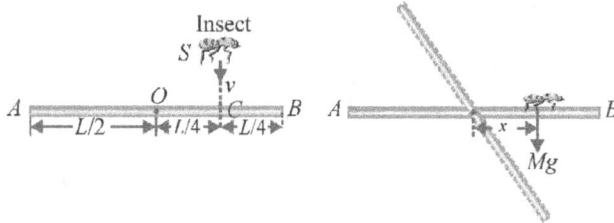

Fig. 1.110

(a) In the process the angular momentum of the system remains constant.

$$Mv \times \frac{L}{4} + 0 = I\omega \qquad \ldots (i)$$

where I is the moment of inertia of the system which is

$$\frac{ML^2}{12} + M\left(\frac{L}{4}\right)^2 = \frac{7ML^2}{48}$$

Substituting this value in above equation, we get

$$\omega = \frac{12v}{7L} \qquad \ldots (ii) \qquad \text{Ans.}$$

(b) Let the insect is at a distance x from the centre of the rod after time t, the moment of inertia of the system will be $= \frac{ML^2}{12} + Mx^2$, and

therefore angular momentum at this instant $\left(\frac{ML^2}{12} + Mx^2\right)\omega$.

Torque exerted by the weight of the insect at that moment $\tau = mgx$.

Since we have $\frac{dL}{dt} = \tau$

Therefore, $\frac{d}{dt}\left(\frac{ML^2}{12} + Mx^2\right)\omega = Mgx \qquad \ldots (iii)$

or $\qquad M\omega.2x\frac{dx}{dt} = Mgx$

or $\qquad \frac{dx}{dt} = v = \frac{g}{2\omega} \qquad \ldots (iv)$

The time taken by rod to rotate through $\frac{\pi}{2}$ rad $= \frac{(\pi/2)}{\omega}$, it is given that the rod rotates with constant angular velocity. The time taken by the insect to reach the end $B = (L/4)/v$.

It is given that both times are equal, therefore

$$\frac{(\pi/2)}{\omega} = \frac{(L/4)}{v}$$

or $\quad \dfrac{(\pi/2)}{\omega} = \dfrac{(L/4)}{(g/2\omega)}$

After solving above equation, we get

$$\omega = \sqrt{(\pi g/L)}$$

Substituting this value in equation (ii), we get

$$v = \frac{7\omega L}{12} = 7\sqrt{\frac{\pi g}{L}} \times \frac{L}{12} \quad \text{where } L = 1.8 \text{ m}$$

$$= 4.4 \text{ m/s} \qquad \text{Ans.}$$

Ex. 50 In the system shown in *Fig. 1.164*. The masses of the bodies are known to be m_1 and m_2, the coefficient of friction between the body m_1 and the horizontal plane is equal to μ, and a pulley of mass m is assumed to be a uniform disc. The thread does not slip over the pulley. At the moment $t = 0$ the body m_2 starts descending. Assuming the mass of the thread and the friction in the axle of the pulley to be negligible, find the work performed by the friction forces acting on the body m_1 over the first t second after the beginning of motion.

Sol. Let a is the acceleration of the blocks.
Equation of motion of the blocks are

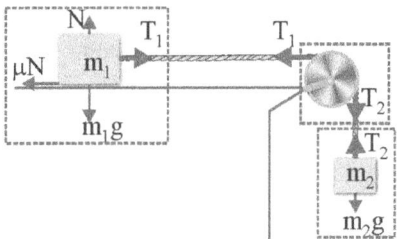

Fig. 1.111

$$T_1 - \mu N = m_1 a \qquad \ldots \text{(i)}$$
$$m_2 g - T_2 = m_2 a \qquad \ldots \text{(ii)}$$

and for the rotation of the pulley

$$T_2 R - T_1 R = I\alpha = I(a/R) \qquad \ldots \text{(iii)}$$

where $\quad I = \dfrac{mR^2}{2}$

Solving above equations, we get

$$a = \frac{(m_2 - \mu m_1)g}{(m_1 + m_2 + \frac{m}{2})}$$

The distance travelled by the block in t second

$$s = \frac{1}{2}at^2$$

Work done by the friction

$$W = f_r \times s = \mu N \times \frac{1}{2}at^2$$

$$= \frac{(\mu m_1 g) \times \frac{1}{2}(m_2 - \mu m_1)g}{(m_1 + m_2 + \frac{m}{2})} t^2$$

$$= \frac{\mu m_1 g^2 t^2 (m_2 - \mu m_1)}{(2m_1 + 2m_2 + m)} \qquad \text{Ans.}$$

Ex. 51 Two uniform thin rods A and B of length 0.6 m each and of masses 0.01 kg and 0.02 kg respectively are rigidly jointed, end to end. The combination is pivoted at the lighter end P as shown in the *Fig. 1.112*, such that it can freely rotate about the point P in a vertical plane. A small object of mass 0.05 kg, moving horizontally hits the lower end of the combination and strikes to it. What should be the velocity of the object so that the system could just be raised to the horizontal position?

Sol.
In the process of collision, the angular momentum of the system remain constant.

$$\therefore \quad mv(2L) + 0 = I\omega \qquad \ldots \text{(i)}$$

where $\quad I = \dfrac{m_A L^2}{3} + \left[\dfrac{m_B L^2}{12} + m_B\left(\dfrac{3L}{2}\right)^2 + m(2L)^2\right]$

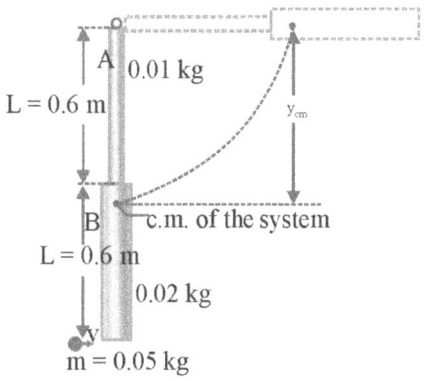

Fig. 1.112

where $\quad m_A = 0.01$ kg, $m_B = 0.02$ kg, $m = 0.05$ and $L = 0.6$ m
Substituting the values in above equation, we get

$$\omega = \frac{2v}{3}$$

Now using conservation of energy principle, we have

$$\frac{1}{2}I\omega^2 = Mgy_{cm} \qquad \ldots \text{(ii)}$$

where $M = (0.01 + 0.02 + 0.05) = 0.08$ kg and y_{cm} can be obtained as

$$y_{cm} = \frac{0.01 \times 0.3 + 0.02 \times (0.6+0.3) + 0.05 \times (0.6+0.6)}{0.01 + 0.02 + 0.05}$$

$$= 1.0125$$

Substituting the value of y_{cm} in equation (ii), we get

$$v = 6.3 \text{ m/s} \qquad \text{Ans.}$$

1.13 ROLLING MOTION

Consider a wheel moving along a straight track, the centre of the wheel moves forward in pure translation. A point on the rim of the wheel, however traces out a complex curve called cycloid. We can analyse the motion of a rolling wheel as a combination of translation and pure rotation.

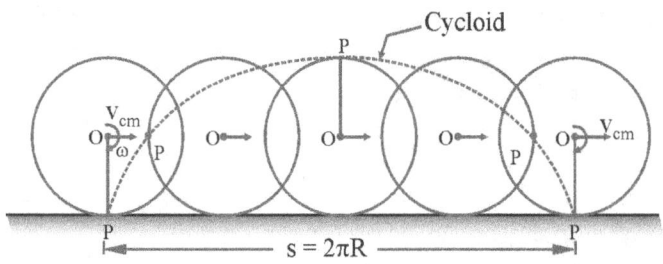

Fig. 1.13

In one complete rotation of wheel, the C.M. of the wheel moves a distance $s = 2\pi R$. In this motion there is no relative motion between point of contact of moving body and the surface. If T is the time to complete a rotation, then we have

$$\frac{s}{T} = \frac{2\pi R}{T}$$

or $\quad v_{cm} = \omega R$

Thus in pure rolling, the velocity of the point of contact is zero and the velocity of centre of mass is $v_{cm} = \omega R$. If the wheel moves through a distance greater than $2\pi R$ in one full rotation, then $v_{cm} > \omega R$ and the wheel slips forward. This type of motion occurs when you apply sudden breaks to the car. The car stops after a long distance but the wheels rotate only a little during the period.

When the wheel moves a distance shorter than $2\pi R$ in full rotation, $v_{cm} < \omega R$ and the wheel slips backward. It happens when you derive the car on muddy rod, then wheels rotate more that the forward motion of the car.

Equation of cycloid

Suppose the motion of the wheel is along the positive x-direction in xy-plane with ox along horizontal and oy along the vertical, the origin O is at the centre of the wheel. Let R be the radius of the wheel, $-\omega$, its angular velocity (being clockwise) and $-\theta$, the angle that a point P on its axis makes with the x-axis at O at $t = 0$. In time t the point is given by

$$x = R\cos(-\omega t - \theta) = R\cos(\omega t + \theta),$$
$$y = R\sin(-\omega t - \theta) = -R\sin(\omega t + \theta)$$

For an observer on the ground, the velocity of C.M. of the wheel is ωR. Hence after time t, the position of the point is given by the coordinates

$$x = v_{cm}t + R\cos(\omega t + \theta),$$
$$= \omega R t + R\cos(\omega t + \theta),$$
$$y = R - R\sin(\omega t + \theta)$$

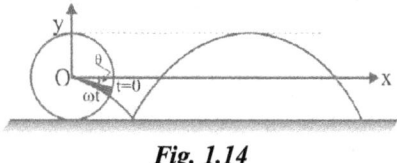

Fig. 1.14

Velocity of a point on the rolling body

Consider a point P on a rolling body, the velocity of point P is the vector sum of velocity due to translation and due to rotation. Thus

$$\vec{v}_p = \vec{v}_{translation} + \vec{v}_{rotation}$$
$$= \vec{v}_{cm} + \vec{\omega} \times \vec{r}$$

or $\quad v_p = \sqrt{v_{cm}^2 + v_{cm}^2 + 2v_{cm}v_{cm}\cos\theta}$

or $\quad v_p = 2v_{cm}\cos\dfrac{\theta}{2}$.

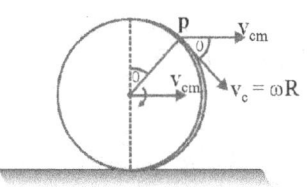

Fig. 1.15

Ex. 52 Point on the periphery of the rolling body which has velocity equal to the velocity of centre of mass of body.

Sol.

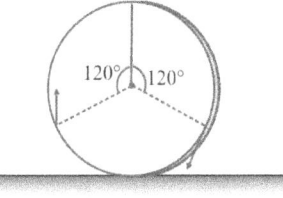

Fig. 1.116

We have $v_p = 2v_{cm} \cos\dfrac{\theta}{2}$

for $v_p = v_{cm}$;

$v_{cm} = 2v_{cm} \cos\dfrac{\theta}{2}$

or $\cos\dfrac{\theta}{2} = \dfrac{1}{2}$

or $\theta = 120°$

Geometrical method of finding velocity of any point on a rolling wheel

We know that rolling motion is the combination of translation and rotation. Figure (a) shows the purely translation motion : every point on the wheel moves with a speed v_{cm}. Figure (b) shows the purely rotational motion : every point on the wheel rotates about the centre with angular speed ω. We also have for $v_{cm} = \omega R$.

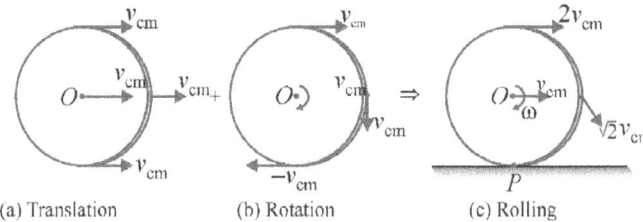

(a) Translation (b) Rotation (c) Rolling

Fig. 1.117

It is clear from the figure (c) that the point of contact of the wheel (point P) is stationary, i.e., there is no relative motion between point of contact of body and the surface. And the top most point is moving at speed $2v_{cm}$, faster than any other point on the wheel.

Note:

1. If point of contact of surface is moving with velocity u with respect to ground, then

   $v_{cm} - \omega R = u$

2. For accelerated surface (see figure 1.118 and 1.119)

   $a_{cm} - \alpha R = a$

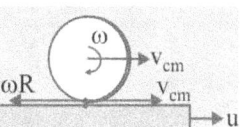

Fig. 1.118

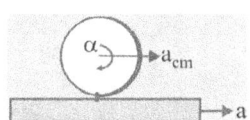

Fig. 1.119

The kinetic energy of rolling wheel

Let us calculate the kinetic energy of the rolling wheel as measured by the stationary observer.

K.E. of rolling wheel = K.E. associated with translational motion + K.E. associated with the rotation motion

or $K_{rolling} = \dfrac{1}{2}Mv_{cm}^2 + \dfrac{1}{2}I_{cm}\omega^2$

For pure rolling, $v_{cm} = \omega R$

$\therefore K_{rolling} = \dfrac{1}{2}M(\omega R)^2 + \dfrac{1}{2}I_{cm}\omega^2$

$= \dfrac{1}{2}(MR^2 + I_{cm})\omega^2$

Body	I_{cm}	Rolling K.E.
Ring	MR^2	$MR^2\omega^2$
Disc	$\dfrac{MR^2}{2}$	$\dfrac{3}{4}MR^2\omega^2$
Sphere	$\dfrac{2}{5}MR^2$	$\dfrac{7}{10}MR^2\omega^2$

As we know $(I_{cm} + MR^2)$ is the moment of inertia of the wheel about point of contact P, say it is I_p. Thus,

$K_{rolling} = \dfrac{1}{2}I_p\omega^2$

Angular momentum of rolling wheel

Angular momentum of rolling wheel about an axis passing through point of contact P and perpendicular to plane of wheel:

$$\vec{L} = \vec{L}_{\text{translation}} + \vec{L}_{\text{rotation}}$$
$$= m(\vec{R} \times \vec{v}_{cm}) + I_{cm}\vec{\omega}$$

or $\quad L = m\omega R^2 + I_{cm}\omega$

or $\quad L = (I_{cm} + mR^2)\omega = I_p\omega$

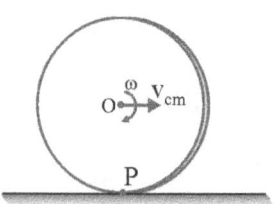

Fig. 1.120

Rolling as pure rotation

For a rolling wheel, K.E. $= \dfrac{1}{2}I_p\omega^2$. Thus rolling can be viewed as pure rotation with angular velocity ω, about an axis that always extends through point of contact P. It is clear from the figure that;

velocity of point P, $v_p = 0$

$$v_O = \omega R$$
$$v_Q = \omega(2R) = 2\omega R = 2v_{cm}$$
$$v_s = \omega(\sqrt{2}R) = \sqrt{2}\omega R = \sqrt{2}v_{cm}$$

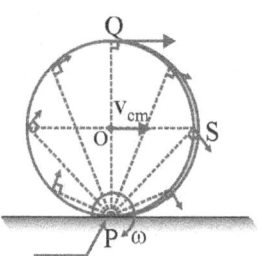

Rotational axis through P

Fig. 1.121

Acceleration of a point on a rolling wheel

Consider a rolling wheel; each point on the periphery of the wheel is rotating in a circle of radius R, due to which centripetal acceleration of each point on the wheel is $\omega^2 R$. As the wheel is moving with constant speed, so acceleration due to translation motion of each point is zero.

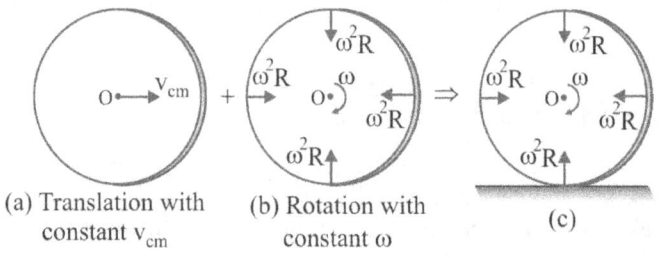

(a) Translation with constant v_{cm}
(b) Rotation with constant ω
(c)

Fig. 1.122

Ex. 53 Consider a wheel rolls without slipping and its centre moves with constant acceleration a. Find the accelerations of points O, P, Q and S when linear velocity of centre of wheel is v.

Sol.

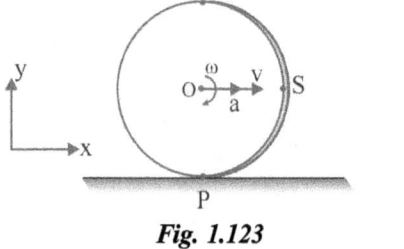

Fig. 1.123

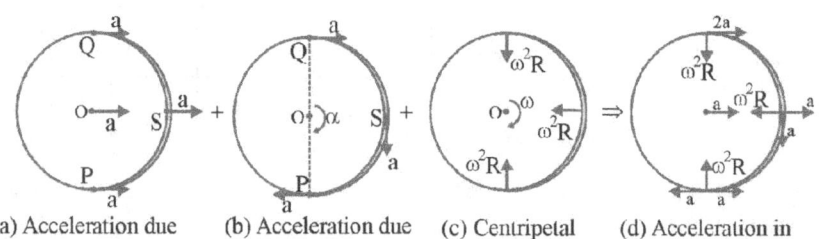

(a) Acceleration due to translation
(b) Acceleration due to rotation
(c) Centripetal acceleration
(d) Acceleration in rolling motion

Fig. 1.124

$$\alpha R = a$$
$$\omega R = v$$

From figure (d),
Resultant acceleration of point O,

$$a_O = a\hat{i}$$
$$a_P = a\hat{i} - a\hat{i} + \omega^2 R\hat{j} = \omega^2 R\hat{j}$$
$$a_Q = a\hat{i} + a\hat{i} - \omega^2 R\hat{j}$$
$$= 2a\hat{i} - \omega^2 R\hat{j}$$
$$a_S = a\hat{i} - \omega^2 R\hat{i} - a\hat{j}$$
$$= (a - \omega^2 R)\hat{i} - a\hat{j}$$

Ex. 54 Determine distance travelled by any point P on the rolling body in one revolution.

Sol.

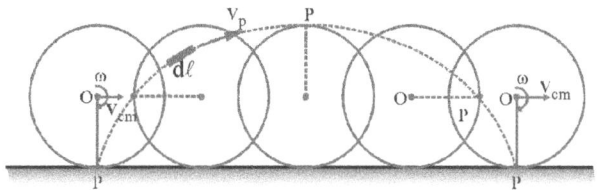

Fig. 1.125

The speed of the point P at any angular position α, as shown in *Fig. 1.126*

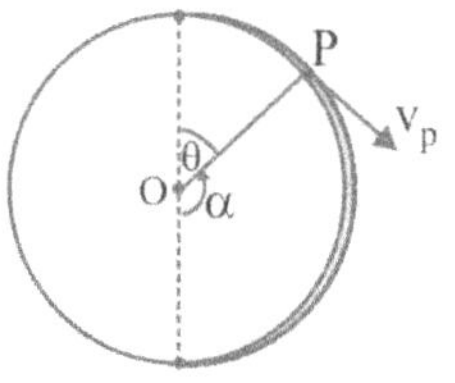

$$v_p = 2v_{cm}\cos\frac{\theta}{2}$$
$$= 2v_{cm}\cos\left(\frac{180° - \alpha}{2}\right)$$
$$= 2v_{cm}\cos(90° - \alpha/2)$$
$$= 2v_{cm}\sin\frac{\alpha}{2}$$

Fig. 1.126

The distance travelled by point P in small time dt

$$d\ell = v_p dt$$
$$= 2v_{cm}\sin\frac{\alpha}{2}(dt)$$

We have $\omega = \dfrac{d\alpha}{dt} \Rightarrow dt = \dfrac{d\alpha}{\omega}$

$$\therefore \quad d\ell = 2v_{cm}\sin\frac{\alpha}{2}\left(\frac{d\alpha}{\omega}\right)$$

The distance travelled in one complete revolution

$$\ell = \int_0^{2\pi} 2v_{cm}\sin\frac{\alpha}{2}\frac{d\alpha}{\omega}$$
$$= \frac{2v_{cm}}{\omega}\int_0^{2\pi}\sin\frac{\alpha}{2}d\alpha$$

$$= \frac{2\omega R}{\omega}\left[\frac{-\cos\alpha/2}{1/2}\right]_0^{2\pi}$$
$$= 4R[-\cos\pi - (-\cos 0)]$$
$$= 8R \qquad \textbf{Ans.}$$

Ex. 55 A rod AB of length 3m which remains in the same vertical plane has its ends A and B constrained to remain in contact with a horizontal floor and a vertical wall respectively as shown in *Fig. 127*. Determine the velocity and acceleration of the end B at the position shown in figure, if the point A has a velocity of 2 m/s and an acceleration of 1.6 m/s² rightward.

Sol.

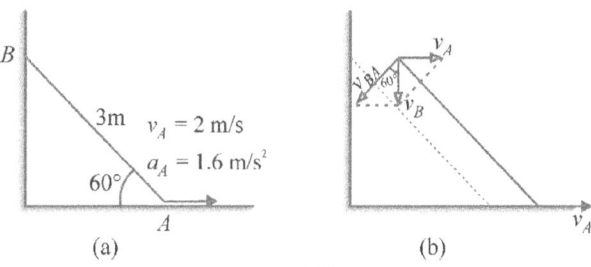

Fig. 1.127

Velocity of end A :
Method I

The motion of B can be looked as ; translation of end B with velocity v_A and rotation of B about A with tangential velocity v_{BA}. If ω be the angular velocity of B about A, then $v_{BA} = \omega \times 3 = 3\omega$. Since the velocity vector of end B moves downward, so resultant of $\vec{v}_A$ and $\vec{v}_{BA}$ must be equal to $\vec{v}_B$ (see figure).

From figure (b), $\quad \dfrac{v_A}{v_B} = \tan 60°$

$$\therefore \quad v_B = \frac{v_A}{\tan 60°} = \frac{2}{\tan 60°}$$
$$= \textbf{1.16 m/s} \qquad \textbf{Ans.}$$

Also $\quad v_{BA} = \dfrac{v_A}{\sin 60°} = \dfrac{2}{\sin 60°} = 2.3$ m/s

Method II

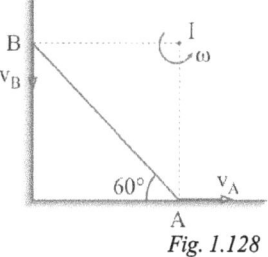

Fig. 1.128

Velocity of end A, $\vec{v}_A$ is horizontal, while velocity of the end B, $\vec{v}_B$ is vertical downward. Drop perpendiculars to the directions of $\vec{v}_A$ and $\vec{v}_B$ at points A and B respectively. The intersection point I be the instantaneous centre.

For the end A, $\quad v_A = \omega(IA)$

$$\therefore \quad \omega = \frac{v_A}{IA} = \frac{2}{3\sin 60°} = 0.77 \text{ rad/s}$$

For the end B, $\quad v_B = \omega(IB) = 0.77 \times 3\cos 60°$
$$= \textbf{1.16 m/s} \qquad \textbf{Ans.}$$

48 MECHANICS, THERMODYNAMICS & WAVES

Acceleration of end B :
The acceleration of the end B has three components.
(i)   Due to translation of end A, $a_A = 1.6$ m/s².
(ii) Due to rotation of end B about A, i.e., tangential acceleration

$$a_t = \alpha r_{AB} = \alpha \times 3 = 3\alpha \text{ m/s}^2$$

(iii) Radial acceleration (from B towards A)

$$a_n = \frac{v_{BA}^2}{r_{AB}}$$

$$= \frac{(2.3)^2}{3} = 1.76 \text{ m/s}^2$$

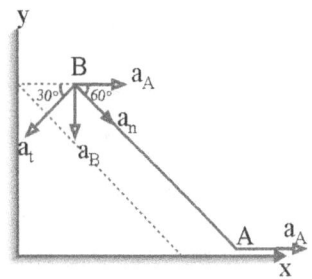

Fig. 1.129

The component of the acceleration of the end B are shown in *Fig. 1.116*. As the net acceleration of the end is vertically downward, so net horizontal component of the accelerations must be zero. i.e.,

$$a_x = 0 = 1.6 + 1.76\cos 60° - 3\alpha \cos 30°$$

or $\alpha = 0.95$ rad/s²

Considering vertical components, we get

$$a_B = a_y = 1.76\sin 60° + 3\alpha \sin 30°$$
$$= 2.98 \text{ m/s}^2 \quad \textbf{Ans.}$$

Ex. 56 A wheel of radius 1 m rolls freely with an angular velocity of 5 rad/s and with an angular acceleration of 4 rad/s², both clockwise as shown in *Fig. 1.117*. Determine the velocity and acceleration of points A and B.

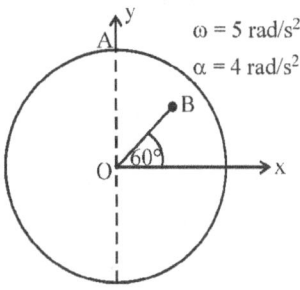

Fig. 1.130

Sol.
Velocity : Translational velocity of centre of mass O

$$v_0 = \omega r = 5 \times 1 = 5 \text{ m/s}$$

The motion of point A and B may be looked as translational of O and rotation about O.

For point A, $\vec{v}_A = \vec{v}_O + \vec{v}_{AO}$

or $v_A = v_O + \omega(OA) = 5 + 5 \times 1$
$= 10$ m/s **Ans.**

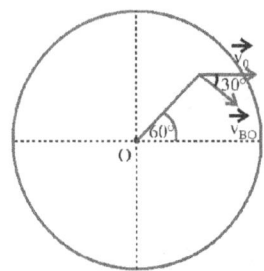

Fig. 1.131

For the point B, $\vec{v}_B = \vec{v}_O + \vec{v}_{BO}$

or $v_B = \sqrt{v_O^2 + v_{BO}^2 + 2v_O v_{BO} \cos 30°}$

Here $v_{BO} = \omega(OB)$
$= 5 \times 0.6 = 3$ m/s

∴ $v_B = \sqrt{5^2 + 3^2 + 2 \times 5 \times 3 \times \cos 30°}$
$= 7.74$ m/s **Ans.**

Acceleration : The acceleration at any point on the wheel (except centre) has three components.
(i)   Due to translation of wheel $a_0 = 4$ m/s²
(ii) Tangential acceleration $a_t = \alpha r = 4r$ m/s²
(iii) Radial acceleration, towards centre of wheel

$$a_n = \frac{v_{BO}^2}{r}$$

Acceleration of point A

$r_A = 1$ m

∴ $a_t = 4 \times 1 = 4$ m/s²

$a_n = \frac{v_{AO}^2}{r_A} = \frac{5^2}{1} = 25$ m/s²

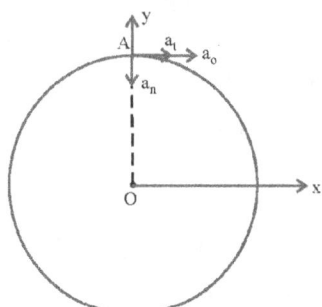

Fig. 1.132

The resultant acceleration of point A,

$$a_A = \sqrt{(a_0 + a_t)^2 + a_n^2}$$
$$= \sqrt{(4+4)^2 + 25^2} = 26.25 \text{ m/s}^2 \quad \textbf{Ans.}$$

Acceleration of point B

$r_B = 0.6$ m

∴ $a_t = 4 \times 0.6 = 2.4$ m/s²

$a_n = \frac{v_{BO}^2}{r_B} = \frac{3^2}{0.6} = 15$ m/s²

ROTATIONAL MECHANICS

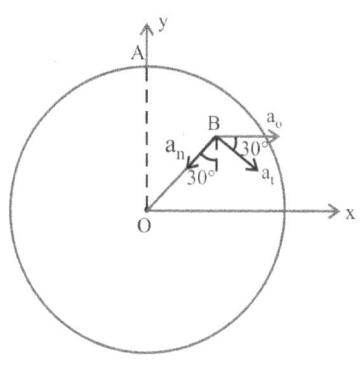

Fig. 1.133

x and y component of acceleration of point B, a_B

$$a_x = a_O + a_t \cos 30° - a_n \sin 30°$$
$$= 4 + 2.4 \cos 30° - 15 \sin 30°$$
$$= -1.4 \text{ m/s}^2$$
$$a_y = -(a_t \sin 30° + a_n \cos 30°)$$
$$= -(2.4 \sin 30° + 15 \cos 30°)$$
$$= -14.2 \text{ m/s}^2$$

The resultant acceleration of point B,

$$a_B = \sqrt{a_x^2 + a_y^2}$$
$$= \sqrt{(1.4)^2 + (14.2)^2}$$
$$= 14.27 \text{ m/s}^2 \quad \text{Ans.}$$

The role of friction in rolling

1. Take a wheel of radius R, and give it translational velcoity v_{cm} and angular velocity ω, so that $v_{cm} = \omega R$ and place the wheel on the rough horizontal surface. As $v_{cm} = \omega R$, so there is no relative motion between points of contact of the wheel and the surface. The wheel will continue its motion with constant velocity.

2. Consider a wheel acted by a force F at its centre changing the velocity of centre of the wheel or the angular speed about the centre, then there is a tendency for the wheel to slide at P, and a static frictional force acts on the wheel, at the point of contact to oppose this tendency. At subsequent motion the linear speed decreases due to force f and angular speed increases due to its torque (fR).

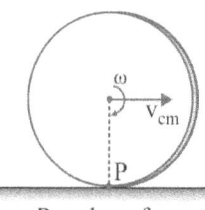

Rough surface

Fig. 1.134

For translation of wheel,
$$F - f = m a_{cm} \quad \ldots(i)$$

For rotation of wheel
$$f \times R = I\alpha \quad \ldots(ii)$$

For pure rolling of wheel, we have $\alpha = \dfrac{a_{cm}}{R}$

$$\therefore \quad f \times R = \dfrac{I a_{cm}}{R}$$

or $$f = \dfrac{I a_{cm}}{R^2} \quad \ldots(iii)$$

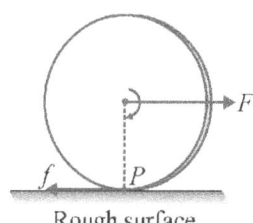

Rough surface

Fig. 1.135

Solving equations (i) and (iii), we get

$$a_{cm} = \dfrac{F}{\left(m + \dfrac{I}{R^2}\right)} \quad \ldots(iv)$$

and $$f = F\left(\dfrac{1}{1 + \dfrac{mR^2}{I}}\right) \quad \ldots(v)$$

Note:

From equation (i), we have $a_{cm} = \dfrac{F - f}{m}$ and from equation (ii), $\alpha = \dfrac{fR}{I}$

As the maximum value of frictional force f can be $f = f_{\lim} = \mu_s N$, so angular acceleration a can not be greater than a certain limit, i.e., $\alpha = \alpha_{max} = \dfrac{f_{\lim} R}{I}$. In case, if F is large, then a_{cm} becomes larger than $a_{max} R$. The wheel will have linear speed greater than angular speed and therefore wheel will not have pure rolling motion.

The minimum value of coefficient of friction required for rolling of a body on horizontal surface for given value of F

We have got $f = F\left[\dfrac{1}{1+\dfrac{mR^2}{I}}\right]$

The coefficient of friction (static)

$$\mu_{min} = \dfrac{f}{N} = \dfrac{F}{Mg}\left[\dfrac{1}{1+\dfrac{mR^2}{I}}\right]$$

Body	M.I.	μ_{min}
Ring or hoop	$I = mR^2$	$\dfrac{F}{2mg}$
Disc or cylinder	$I = \dfrac{mR^2}{2}$	$\dfrac{F}{3mg}$
Sphere	$I = \dfrac{2}{5}mR^2$	$\dfrac{2F}{7mg}$

3. Let a wheel is thrown on a rough surface with initial velocity v_0. The tendency of point of contact P is to slide forward, so frictional force acts in backward direction of motion of wheel. Due to the frictional force, the linear speed of centre of wheel decreases and angular speed increases due to the torque exerted by frictional force. A condition is reached when $v = \omega R$, and then wheel will start in pure rolling motion. Thereafter friction stops acting.
Retardation for translation motion,

$$a = \dfrac{f}{m} = \dfrac{\mu N}{m} = \dfrac{\mu mg}{m} = \mu g \qquad \ldots(i)$$

Acceleration for rotational motion,

$$\alpha = \dfrac{\tau}{I} = \dfrac{fR}{I} \qquad \ldots(ii)$$

Let the wheel starts pure rolling after time t, then

$$v = v_0 - at \qquad \ldots(iii)$$
and $$\omega = 0 + \alpha t \qquad \ldots(iv)$$

When wheel starts rolling,

$$v = \omega R \qquad \ldots(v)$$

Work done by friction $= \Delta K.E.$
$= K_f - K_i$
$$= \left(\dfrac{1}{2}mv^2 + \dfrac{1}{2}I\omega^2\right) - \dfrac{1}{2}mv_0^2 \qquad \ldots(vi)$$

We can solve above equations to get unknowns.

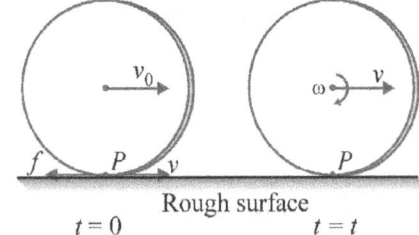

Fig. 1.136

4. Let a rotating wheel, $\omega = \omega_0$ is placed on a rough surface. The tendency of point of contact P is to slide backward, so the frictional force will act in forward direction. Because of this frictional force, the centre of wheel starts accelerating, while torque of frictional force decreases the angular speed. After some time wheel starts rolling. Thereafter friction stop acting.

ROTATIONAL MECHANICS

Acceleration for translational motion,

$$a = \frac{f_r}{m} = \frac{\mu N}{m} = \frac{\mu mg}{m} \quad \ldots(i)$$

$$= \mu g$$

Retardation for rotational motion,

$$\alpha = \frac{\tau}{I} = \frac{fR}{I} \quad \ldots(ii)$$

Let wheel starts pure rolling after time t, then we have

$$v = 0 + at \quad \ldots(iii)$$

$$\omega = \omega_0 - \alpha t \quad \ldots(iv)$$

When wheel starts rolling, we have

$$v = \omega R \quad \ldots(v)$$

Work done by friction $= \Delta K.E.$
$$= K_f - K_i$$
$$= \left(\frac{1}{2}mv^2 + \frac{1}{2}I\omega^2\right) - \frac{1}{2}I\omega_0^2 \quad \ldots(vi)$$

We can solve above equations to get unknowns.

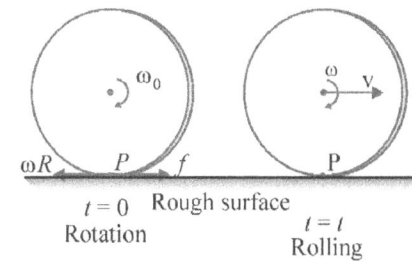

Fig. 1.137

Ex. 57 In devices shown in figure, the cylinder of mass M and radius R is connected to a small block of mass m with the help of inextensible string. The cylinder is in pure rolling motion. Find the acceleration of the block.

Sol.

(a)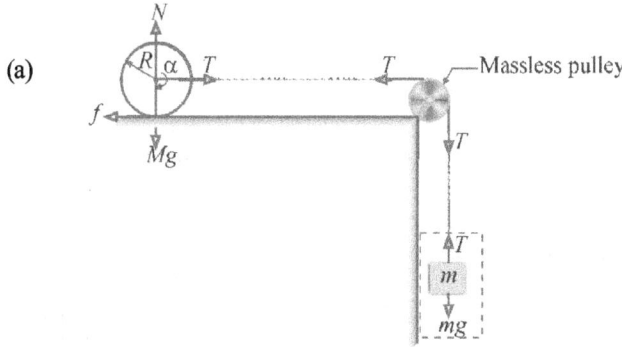

Fig. 1.138

The accelerations magnitude of the block and the centre of mass of the cylinder are equal, Let it is a.
For the motion of the cylinder :

$$T - f = Ma \quad \ldots(i)$$
and $\quad fR = I\alpha \quad \ldots(ii)$

For pure rolling, $\alpha = \dfrac{a}{R} \quad \ldots(iii)$

For the motion of the block :

$$mg - T = ma \quad \ldots(iv)$$

After solving above equations, we get

$$a = \frac{mg}{m + M + \dfrac{I}{R^2}}$$

(b)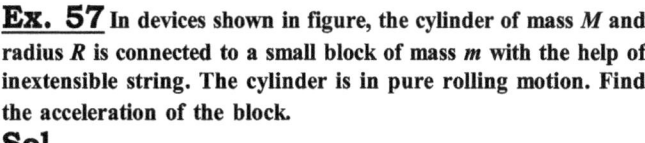

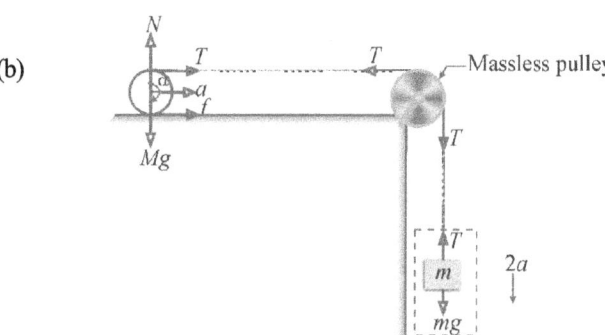

Fig. 1.139

If a be the acceleration of C.M. of the cylinder, then the acceleration of the top most point of the cylinder is $2a$, and hence acceleration of the hanging block is $2a$.

For the motion of the cylinder :

$$T + f = Ma \quad \ldots(i)$$
and $\quad TR - fR = I\alpha \quad \ldots(ii)$

For pure rolling, $\quad \alpha = \dfrac{a}{R} \quad \ldots(iii)$

For the motion of the block :

$$mg - T = m(2a) \quad \ldots(iv)$$

After solving above equations, we get

$$a = \frac{2mg}{4m + M + \dfrac{I}{R^2}}$$

1.14 Accelerated pure rolling

1. Rolling motion of spool

Take an example of a spool in which a tangential force F is acting on the axel of spool. In first case, it is applied tangentially on the top of the axel and in second case it is applied tangentially at the bottom of the axel.

Case I. In this case sliding tendency of point of contact P is backward

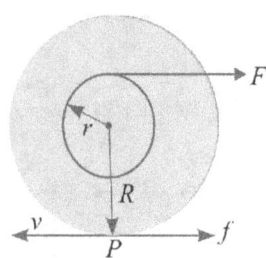

Fig. 1.140 - I

$$F + f = ma_{cm} \quad \ldots(i)$$
$$Fr - fR = I\alpha \quad \ldots(ii)$$

For pure rolling
$$\alpha = \frac{a_{cm}}{R} \quad \ldots(iii)$$

After simplifying above equation we get,

$$a_{cm} = \frac{F\left(1 + \dfrac{r}{R}\right)}{m + \dfrac{I}{R^2}}$$

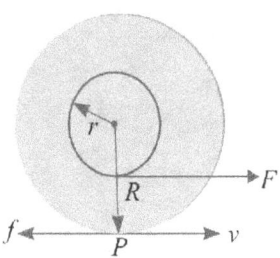

Fig. 1.141 - II

Case II. In this case sliding tendency of point of contact P is forward

$$F - f = ma_{cm} \quad \ldots(i)$$
$$fR - Fr = I\alpha \quad \ldots(ii)$$

For pure rolling motion,
$$a = \frac{a_{cm}}{R} \quad \ldots(iii)$$

After simplifying above equation we get,

$$a_{cm} = \frac{F\left(1 - \dfrac{r}{R}\right)}{m + \dfrac{I}{R^2}}$$

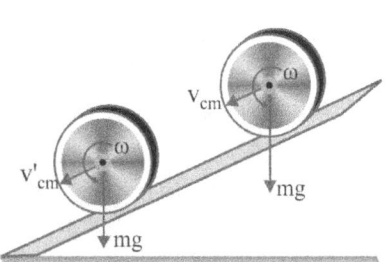

Fig. 1.142

2. Let a wheel $v_{cm} = \omega R$ lands on a smooth inclined plane. The centre of the wheel will accelerate due to a force $mg\sin\theta$, but the angular speed of wheel will remain constant as no torque is acting on the wheel about axis of rotation. So, the motion of wheel will no remain pure rolling. Thus the body can have pure rolling only on rough inclined surface.

3. Let a wheel is placed on rough inclined plane. The tendency of contact point P is to slide down the inclined due to a net force down the plane. The friction will act up the plane at the point of contact of the wheel. This frictional force constitute a torque fR. Due to which wheel starts rotating in addition to translation. Here role of friction is to transfer some part of tanslational K.E. into rotational K.E. The mechanical energy of pure rolling wheel remains constant.

Rolling on rough inclined plane :

Dynamical method

For translational motion of wheel

$$mg\sin\theta - f = ma_{cm} \quad \ldots(i)$$

For rotational motion of wheel

$$fR = I\alpha \quad \ldots(ii)$$

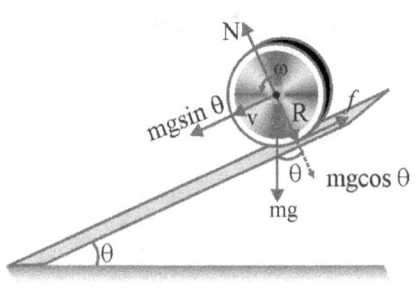

Fig. 1.143

For pure rolling motion,
$$\alpha = \frac{a_{cm}}{R}$$

$$\therefore \quad fR = \frac{Ia_{cm}}{R} \quad \ldots(iii)$$

or
$$f = \frac{Ia_{cm}}{R^2} \quad \ldots(iv)$$

Solving equations (i) and (iv), we get

$$a_{cm} = \frac{mg\sin\theta}{\left(m+\dfrac{I}{R^2}\right)} \quad \text{or} \quad a_{cm} = \left[\frac{g\sin\theta}{1+\dfrac{I}{mR^2}}\right]$$

Short-cut method: $\quad a_{cm} = \dfrac{\text{Unbalanced load}}{\{\text{Inertia of translation} + \text{inertia of rotation}\}}$

$$= \frac{mg\sin\theta}{(m+I/R^2)}$$

Velocity of C.M. after falling a height h

$$v^2 = 0 + 2a_{cm}(s)$$

$$= 2\left[\frac{g\sin\theta}{1+\dfrac{I}{mR^2}}\right] \times \frac{h}{\sin\theta}$$

or $\quad v = \sqrt{\dfrac{2gh}{1+\dfrac{I}{mR^2}}}$

The minimum frictional force and coefficient of friction required to cause pure rolling of a body can be obtained from, $f_{\min} = \dfrac{I a_{cm}}{R^2}$.

Body	Moment of inertia	Acceleration $a_{cm} = \left(\dfrac{g\sin\theta}{1+I/mR^2}\right)$	$f_{\min} = \dfrac{I a_{cm}}{R^2}$	$\mu_{\min} = \dfrac{f_{\min}}{N}$ $N = mg\cos\theta$
Ring	MR^2	$\dfrac{g}{2}\sin\theta$	$\dfrac{mg\sin\theta}{2}$	$\dfrac{\tan\theta}{2}$
Disc/Cylinder	$\dfrac{MR^2}{2}$	$\dfrac{2}{3}g\sin\theta$	$\dfrac{mg\sin\theta}{3}$	$\dfrac{\tan\theta}{3}$
Sphere	$\dfrac{2}{5}MR^2$	$\dfrac{5}{7}g\sin\theta$	$\dfrac{2}{7}mg\sin\theta$	$\dfrac{2\tan\theta}{7}$

Ex. 58 A plank of mass m_1 with uniform sphere of mass m_2 placed on it rests on a smooth horizontal plane. A constant horizontal force F is applied to the plank. With what acceleration will the plank and the centre of the sphere move provided there is no sliding between the plank and the sphere?

Sol.

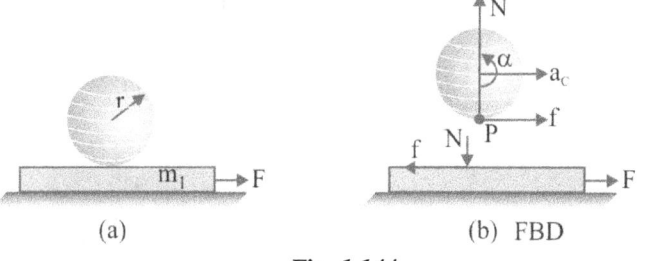

Fig. 1.144

If a_c is the acceleration of the centre of the sphere, and a_p is the acceleration of the plank (or acceleration of point of contact of the sphere), then

$$a_p = a_c + \alpha r \qquad \text{...(i)}$$

Here r is the radius of the sphere.

For the motion of sphere: If f is the frictional force, then

$$f = m_2 a_c \qquad \text{...(ii)}$$

and $\quad fr = I\alpha$

or $\quad fr = \dfrac{2}{5}m_2 r^2 \alpha \qquad \text{...(iii)}$

For the motion of the plank:

$$F - f = m_1 a_p \qquad \text{...(iv)}$$

After solving equations, we get

$$a_c = \left[\frac{2F}{2m_2 + 7m_1}\right]$$

and $\quad a_p = \left[\dfrac{7F}{2m_2 + 7m_1}\right] \qquad$ **Ans.**

Ex. 59 Two solid bodies rotate about stationary mutually perpendicular intersecting axes with constant angular velocities $\omega_1 = 3.0$ rad/s and $\omega_2 = 4.0$ rad/s. Find the angular velocity and angular acceleration of one body relative to the other.

Sol. We know that

$$\vec{\omega}_{12} = \vec{\omega}_1 - \vec{\omega}_2$$

$$\therefore \quad \omega_{12} = \sqrt{\omega_1^2 + \omega_2^2}$$

$$= \sqrt{3.0^2 + 4.0^2} = 5.0 \text{ rad/s} \quad \text{Fig. 1.145}$$

In rotating frame S' with angular velocity $\vec{\omega}$ the quantity $\vec{A}$ can be written as

$$\left|\frac{d\vec{A}}{dt}\right|_S = \left|\frac{d\vec{A}}{dt}\right|_{S'} + \vec{\omega} \times \vec{A}$$

For the body 1 relative to 2, and for $\vec{A} = \vec{\omega}_1$, we have $\vec{\omega} = \vec{\omega}_2$ and

$$\left|\frac{d\vec{A}}{dt}\right|_{S'} = \frac{d\vec{\omega}_{12}}{dt}$$

$$\therefore \quad \frac{d\vec{\omega}_1}{dt} = \frac{d\vec{\omega}_{12}}{dt} + \vec{\omega}_2 \times \vec{\omega}_1$$

According to the problem $\vec{\omega}_1$ is constant and so $\frac{d\vec{\omega}_1}{dt} = 0$.

Hence $\quad \frac{d\vec{\omega}_{12}}{dt} = -\vec{\omega}_2 \times \vec{\omega}_1$

$$= \vec{\omega}_1 \times \vec{\omega}_2$$

and $\left(\frac{d\vec{\omega}_{12}}{dt}\right) = \omega_1 \omega_2 \sin 90°$

$$= \omega_1 \omega_2$$

$$= 3.0 \times 4.0 = 12.0 \text{ rad/s}^2 \quad \text{Ans.}$$

Ex. 60 A bullet of mass m moving with velocity u just grazes the top of a solid cylinder of mass M and radius R resting on a rough horizontal surface as shown. Assuming that the cylinder rolls without slipping, find the angular velocity of the cylinder and the final velocity of bullet.

Sol. We can assume the rolling of cylinder as pure rotation about an axis passing through O.

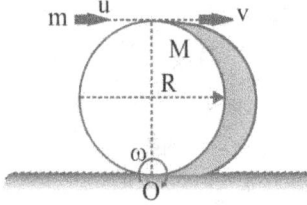

Fig. 1.146

Using conservation of angular momentum about O

$$(mu) \times 2R = (mv) \times 2R + I_o \omega$$

here $\quad v = \omega \times 2R \quad$ and $\quad I_o = \frac{MR^2}{2} + MR^2$

After substituting these values in above equation, we get

$$\omega = \frac{4mu}{(8m + 3M)R} \quad \text{and} \quad v = \left(\frac{8mu}{8m + 3M}\right) \quad \text{Ans.}$$

Ex. 61 A circular wooden hoop of mass m and radius R rests flat on a frictionless surface. A bullet, also of mass m, and moving with a velocity v strikes the hoop and gets embedded in it. The thickness of hoop is much smaller than R. Find the angular velocity with which the system rotates after the bullet strikes the hoop

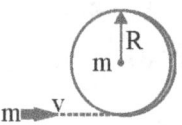

Fig. 1.147

Sol.
Let the velocity of the C.M. of the system after strike is v_c. By conservation of linear momentum

$$mv = 2m \times v_c$$

$$\Rightarrow \quad v_c = \frac{v}{2}$$

Position of C.M. $\quad y = \frac{m \times 0 + m \times R}{m + m} = \frac{R}{2} \quad$ Fig. 1.148

Using conservation of angular momentum about C.M. of the system (hoop + bullet)

$$mv \times \frac{R}{2} = I_C \omega$$

or $\quad \frac{mvR}{2} = (I_{\text{bullet}} + I_{\text{hoop}})_c \omega$

or $\quad \frac{mvR}{2} = \left[m\left(\frac{R}{2}\right)^2 + \left\{mR^2 + m\left(\frac{R}{2}\right)^2\right\}\right]\omega$

After solving, we get

$$\omega = \frac{v}{3R} \quad \text{Ans.}$$

Ex. 62 A thin spherical shell of radius R lying on a rough horizontal surface is hit sharply and horizontally by a cue. Where should it be hit so that the shell does not slip on the surface?

Sol.
Let v is the velocity attained by its centre of mass and ω be the angular velocity about centre of mass by the impact of the cue.
Suppose F is the force exerted by cue for small duration Δt, then

$$F\Delta t = m(v - 0) \quad \ldots \text{(i)}$$

and $\quad Fh\Delta t = I(\omega - 0) \quad \ldots \text{(ii)}$

From equations (i) and (ii),

$$mv \times h = I\omega$$

For pure rolling $\quad \omega = \frac{v}{R}$

$$\therefore \quad mv \times h = \frac{2}{3}mR^2 \times \frac{v}{R} \quad \text{Fig. 1.149}$$

$$\Rightarrow \quad h = \frac{2R}{3} \quad \text{Ans.}$$

Ex. 63 A solid sphere is set into motion on a rough horizontal surface with a linear velocity v in the forward direction and an angular velocity v/R in the anticlockwise direction as shown in the *Fig. 1.150*. Find the linear speed of the sphere (a) when it stops rotating and (b) when slipping finally ceases and pure rolling starts.

Sol.

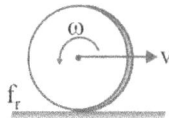

Fig. 1.150

Here friction provide retarding torque and therefore its angular velocity decreases with time. Let it becomes zero after time *t*.

(a) $\alpha = \dfrac{\tau}{I} = \dfrac{f_r R}{I} = \dfrac{\mu M g R}{\dfrac{2}{5}MR^2}$

$= \dfrac{5}{2}\dfrac{\mu g}{R}$

Now using $\omega = \omega_0 - \alpha t$

or $0 = \dfrac{v}{R} - \left(\dfrac{5\mu g}{2R}\right)t$

∴ $t = \dfrac{2v}{5\mu g}$

Let linear speed of sphere become v in this time,

$a = \dfrac{f_r}{m} = \dfrac{\mu m g}{m} = \mu g$

∴ $v' = v - at$

$= v - (\mu g) \times \dfrac{2v}{5\mu g}$

$= \dfrac{3v}{5}$ **Ans.**

(b) Let sphere has velocity v_1 and angular velocity ω_1 when it starts pure rolling

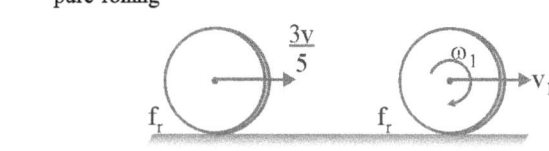

$t = 0$ $\qquad\qquad\qquad$ $t = t$

Fig. 1.151

$\omega_1 = 0 + \alpha t$

$\omega_1 = 0 + \dfrac{5\mu g}{2R}t$ ... (i)

and $v_1 = v_0 - at$

$= \dfrac{3v}{5} - (\mu g)t$ ... (ii)

After getting pure rolling

$v_1 = \omega_1 R$ ... (iii)

∴ $\dfrac{3v}{5} - \mu g t = \left(\dfrac{5\mu g t}{2R}\right)R$

or $t = \dfrac{6v}{35}$

Now from equation (i), we have

$v_1 = \dfrac{3v}{5} - \mu g \times \dfrac{6v}{35\mu g}$

$= \dfrac{3v}{7}$ **Ans.**

Ex. 64 A constant horizontal force of 10 N is applied to a wheel of mass 10 kg and radius 0.30 m as shown in *Fig. 1.152*. The wheel rolls without slipping on the horizontal surface, and the acceleration of centre of mass is 0.60 m/s².
(a) What are the magnitude and direction of the frictional force on the wheel?
(b) What is the rotational inertia of the wheel about an axis through its centre of mass and perpendicular to the plane of the wheel?

Sol.
(a) The direction of the frictional force will be in backward direction of motion of the wheel.
Equation of motion for translation of wheel
$10 - f_r = ma$

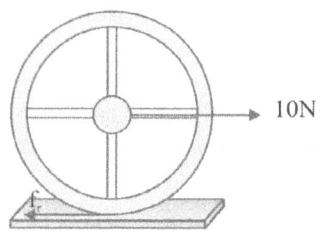

Fig. 1.152

Substituting m = 10 kg and a = 0.60 m/s² in the above equation, we get

$f_r = 4N$ **Ans.**

(b) Equation of motion for rotation of wheel

$f_r \times R = I\alpha$

which gives $I = f_r \times \dfrac{R}{\alpha} = \dfrac{4 \times 0.30}{(0.60/0.30)}$

or $I = 0.6$ kg.m² **Ans.**

Ex. 65 Two thin circular disks of mass 2 kg and radius 10 cm each are joined by a rigid massless rod of length 20 cm. The axis of the rod is along the perpendicular to the planes of the disk through their centres as shown in the *Fig.1.153*. This object is kept on a truck in such a way that the axis of the object is horizontal and perpendicular to the direction of the motion of the truck. Its friction with the floor of the truck is large enough so that the object can roll on the truck without slipping. Take x-axis as the direction of motion of the truck and z-axis as the vertically upwards direction. If the truck has an acceleration of 9 m/s², calculate :
(i) The force of friction on each disk.
(ii) The magnitude and the direction of the frictional torque acting on each disk about the centre of mass O of the object. Express the torque in the vector form in terms of unit vectors i, j and k in the x, y and z directions.

56 MECHANICS, THERMODYNAMICS & WAVES

Sol.

(i) In the reference frame of the truck, frictional force will pull the disks in the direction of motion of the truck, while pseudo force ($F = ma$), where $a = 9$ m/s^2 acts in backward direction of motion of the truck. Consider the forces on the either wheel.
For the translation of the disk

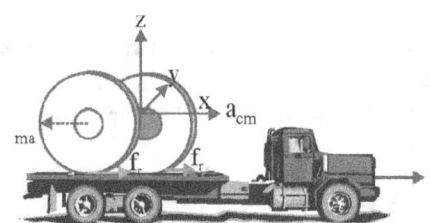

Fig. 1.153

$$F - f_r = ma_{cm} \quad \ldots (i)$$

and for rotation of the disk, we have
$$f_r \times R = I\alpha$$
or $$f_r \times R = I a_{cm}/R \quad \ldots (ii)$$

where $$I = \frac{mR^2}{2}$$

Solving above equations, and substituting $I = \frac{mR^2}{2}$, $m = 2$ kg and $R = 0.10$ m,
we get $a_{cm} = 6$ m/s^2
and $f_r = 6$ N or $\vec{f_r} = (6\hat{i})$ N

(ii) The position vectors of point of contacts are (taking c. m. of the system as the origin)

$$\vec{r_1} = (0\hat{i} - 0.1\hat{j} - 0.1\hat{k})$$
and $$\vec{r_2} = (0\hat{i} + 0.1\hat{j} - 0.1\hat{k})$$

The torque on the disks are

$$\vec{\tau_1} = \vec{r_1} \times \vec{f_r} = (0\hat{i} - 0.1\hat{j} - 0.1\hat{k}) \times (6\hat{i})$$
$$= (-0.6\hat{j} + 0.6\hat{k}) \text{N-m}$$

$$\vec{\tau_2} = \vec{r_2} \times \vec{f_r} = (0\hat{i} + 0.1\hat{j} - 0.1\hat{k}) \times (6\hat{i})$$
$$= (-0.6\hat{j} - 0.6\hat{k}) \text{N-m}$$

Ex. 66 A uniform cylinder of radius R is spinned about its axis to the angular velocity ω_0 and then placed into a corner Fig. 1.165. The coefficient of friction between the corner walls and the cylinder is equal to μ. How many turns the cylinder accomplish before it stops?

Sol.

For the vertical and horizontal equilibrium of the cylinder, we have
$$N_1 + \mu N_2 = mg \quad \ldots (i)$$

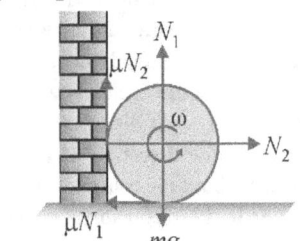

Fig. 1.154

and $$N_2 = \mu N_1 \quad \ldots (ii)$$

Solving above equations, we get

$$N_1 = \frac{mg}{(1+\mu^2)}$$

and $$N_2 = \frac{\mu mg}{(1+\mu^2)}$$

Method 1 : Dynamical method

The net retarding torque on the cylinder = $(\mu N_1 + \mu N_2) \times R$
therefore we have, $(\mu N_1 + \mu N_2) \times R = I\alpha$

Substituting the values of N_1, N_2 and $I = \frac{mR^2}{2}$, we get

$$\alpha = \frac{2\mu g(\mu+1)}{R(\mu^2+1)}$$

The time taken by the cylinder to come in rest can be obtained as
$$0 = \omega_0 - \alpha t,$$

$$\therefore \quad t = \frac{\omega_0}{\alpha} = \frac{\omega_0 R(\mu^2+1)}{2\mu g(\mu+1)}$$

Now using second equation of motion

$$\theta = \omega_0 t - \frac{1}{2}\alpha t^2$$

After substituting the values of α and t in above equation, we get

$$\theta = \frac{\omega_0^2 R(\mu^2+1)}{[4\mu g(\mu+1)]}$$

Number of turns $\quad n = \frac{\theta}{2\pi} = \frac{(1+\mu^2)\omega_0^2 R}{[8\pi g\mu(\mu+1)]} \quad$ **Ans.**

Method II : Energy method

Using work-energy theorem,
$$\Delta K = W_f$$

or $$\frac{1}{2}I\omega_0^2 = (\mu N_1 + \mu N_2) \times (2\pi R n)$$

Substituting all the known values in above equation, we get

$$n = \frac{(1+\mu^2)\omega_0^2 R}{[8\pi g\mu(\mu+1)]} \quad$$ **Ans.**

Ex. 67 A uniform solid cylinder of radius $R = 15$ cm rolls over a horizontal plane passing into an inclined plane forming an angle $\alpha = 30°$ with the horizontal shown in the Fig. 1.155. Find the maximum value of the v_0 which still permits the cylinder to roll onto the inclined plane section without a jump. The sliding is assumed to be absent.

Sol.

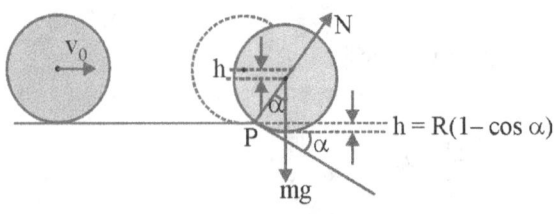

Fig. 1.155

Initial rolling kinetic energy of the cylinder

$$K_1 = \frac{1}{2}mv_0^2 + \frac{1}{2}I\omega^2$$

$$= \frac{1}{2}mv_0^2 + \frac{1}{2}\left(\frac{mR^2}{2}\right)\left(\frac{v_0}{R}\right)^2$$

$$= \frac{3}{4}mv_0^2 \qquad \ldots (i)$$

When the cylinder passes on to the inclined plane its centre of mass descends through a distance $h = R(1 - \cos\alpha)$.
If v is the velocity of its centre of mass now,

then rolling kinetic energy $= \frac{3}{4}mv^2$.

From energy conservation, we have

$$\frac{3}{4}mv_0^2 + mgR(1-\cos\alpha) = \frac{3}{4}mv^2 \qquad \ldots (ii)$$

At point P, $\quad mg\cos\alpha = N + \frac{mv^2}{R}$

Cylinder passes the point P without jump, if $N \geq 0$.
For maximum value of v_0, N should have minimum +ve value i.e., $N=0$

$$\therefore \quad mg\cos\alpha = \frac{mv^2}{R}.$$

Solving equations (i) and (ii), and substituting $\alpha = 30°$, $R = 0.15$ m and $g = 9.81$ m/s², we get

$$v_0 = \sqrt{\frac{gR}{3}(7\cos\alpha - 4)} = 1.0 \; m/s \qquad \textbf{Ans.}$$

Ex. 68 A uniform ball of radius r rolls without slipping down from the top of a sphere of radius R. Find the angular velocity of the ball at the moment it breaks off the sphere. The initial velocity of the ball is negligible.

Sol. Let v is the velocity and θ is the angle made by the radius vector with the vertical at the instant when ball break-off the sphere.

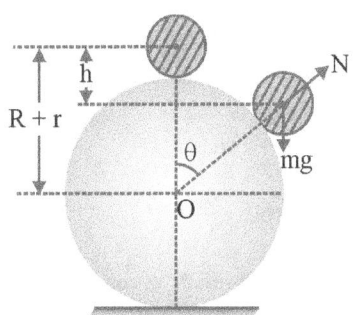

Fig. 1.156

Let it happens at a vertical height h below the top. Therefore we have,

$$mgh = \frac{1}{2}mv^2 + \frac{1}{2}I\omega^2$$

where $\quad h = (R+r)(1-\cos\theta)$

$$\therefore \quad mg(R+r)(1-\cos\theta) = \frac{1}{2}mv^2 + \frac{1}{2}I\omega^2$$

$$mg(R+r)(1-\cos\theta) = \frac{1}{2}m(\omega r)^2 + \frac{1}{2}I\omega^2 \qquad \ldots (i)$$

At the break-off

$$mg\cos\theta = N + \frac{mv^2}{(R+r)}$$

Substituting $N = 0$ and $v = \omega r$, we have

$$mg\cos\theta = \frac{m(\omega r)^2}{(R+r)} \qquad \ldots (ii)$$

Solving equations (i) and (ii), we get

$$\omega = \sqrt{\frac{10g(R+r)}{17r^2}} \qquad \textbf{Ans.}$$

Ex. 69 A uniform sphere of mass m and radius r rolls without sliding over a horizontal plane, rotating about a horizontal axle OA as shown in *Fig. 1.157*. In the process, the centre of the sphere moves with velocity v along a circle of radius R. Find the kinetic energy of the sphere.

Sol. The kinetic energy of the sphere due to its rotation about own axis and its motion along a circular path with velocity v.

$$\therefore \quad K.E. = \frac{1}{2}I_1\omega_1^2 + \frac{1}{2}I_2\omega_2^2$$

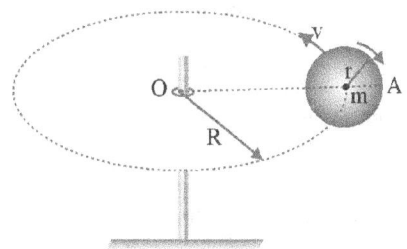

Fig. 1.157

where $\quad I_1 = \frac{2}{5}mr^2$ and $I_2 = \left(\frac{2}{5}mr^2 + mR^2\right)$

$$\omega_1 = \frac{v}{r} \text{ and } \omega_2 = \frac{v}{R}$$

Substituting these values in above equation, we get

$$K.E. = \frac{7m}{10}v^2[1 + \frac{2r^2}{7R^2}] \qquad \textbf{Ans.}$$

Ex. 70 A uniform solid cylinder of mass M and radius R rolls on a rough inclined plane with its axis perpendicular to the line of the greatest slope. As the cylinder rolls it winds up a light string which passes over a small mass m, the part of the string between pulley and the cylinder being parallel to the line of greatest slope. If θ is the inclination of the plane with the horizontal, calculate the tension in the string.

Sol.

Method 1: Dynamic method
Let the acceleration of c.m. of the cylinder is a. The acceleration of a point on its tangent will be $2a$, so the acceleration of the mass m will be $2a$.

Equation of motion for the translation of the cylinder

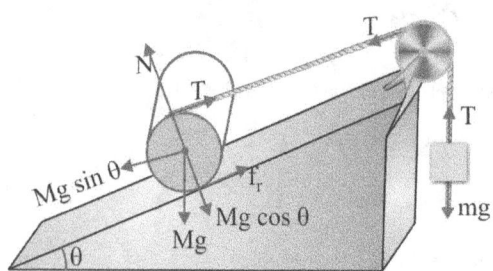

Fig. 1.158

$$Mg\sin\theta - T - f_r = Ma \qquad \text{...(i)}$$

and for its rotation about axis passing through its c.m.

$$f_r R - TR = I\alpha$$

or $$f_r R - TR = \frac{MR^2}{2}\alpha \qquad \text{...(ii)}$$

Equation of motion for mass m

$$T - mg = m(2a) \qquad \text{...(iii)}$$

Solving above equations, we get

$$a = \frac{2Mg\sin\theta - 4mg}{8m + 3M}$$

and $$T = \frac{(3 + 4\sin\theta)mMg}{8m + 3M} \qquad \text{Ans.}$$

Method II : Energy method

Let v be the velocity of the c.m. of the cylinder when it travelled a distance y along the plane. The velocity and the distance travelled by the mass m in this interval will be $2v$ and $2y$ respectively.

Decrease in P.E. of cylinder = Increase in (rolling K.E. of the cylinder
+ translational K.E. of the mass m + P.E. of the mass)

$$Mg(y\sin\theta) = \frac{1}{2}Mv^2 + \frac{1}{2}I\omega^2 + \frac{1}{2}m(2v)^2 + mg(2y)$$

where $\omega = \frac{v}{R}$ and $I = \frac{MR^2}{2}$

Substituting these values in above equation and solving for v, we get

$$v^2 = \frac{4g \times (M\sin\theta - 2m)}{8m + 3M}$$

Using third equation of motion $v^2 = u^2 + 2ay$, where $u = 0$

$$\therefore \quad a = \frac{v^2}{2y} = \frac{(2Mg\sin\theta - 4mg)}{(8m + 3M)}$$

Substituting this value in equation (iii), we can get T.

Ex. 71 A sphere of mass M and radius r shown in *Fig. 1.159* slips on a rough horizontal plane. At some instant, it has translational velocity v_0 and rotational velocity about the centre $(v_0/2r)$. Find the translational velocity after the sphere starts pure rolling.

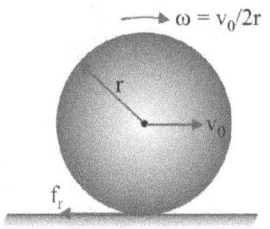

Fig. 1.159

Sol.

Given, velocity of centre = v_0

Angular velocity about the centre = $\frac{v_0}{2r}$

Here initial velocity of rotation $\omega_0 < v_0/r$, the sphere slips in forward direction. Frictional force decelerates it to decrease its translational velocity v_0 to a value v, which corresponds to pure rolling. Frictional force increases angular velocity ω_0 to a value ω, which corresponds to pure rolling and satisfies the relation $v = \omega r$.

Deceleration of the centre of mass of the sphere $a = \dfrac{f_r}{M}$

$$\therefore \quad v = v_0 - at$$

or $$v = v_0 - \left(\frac{f_r}{M}\right)t \qquad \text{...(i)}$$

and angular acceleration about centre $\alpha = \dfrac{\tau}{I}$

or $$\alpha = \frac{f_r \cdot r}{(2Mr^2/5)} = \frac{5f_r}{2Mr}$$

$$\omega = \omega_0 + \alpha t$$

or $$\omega = \omega_0 + \frac{5f_r}{(2Mr)}t$$

or $$\omega = \frac{v_0}{2r} + \frac{5f_r}{(2Mr)}t \qquad \text{...(ii)}$$

When pure rolling occurs $v = \omega r$ ...(iii)

Solving above equations, we get

$$v = \frac{6v_0}{7} \qquad \text{Ans.}$$

Ex. 72 A billiard ball, initially at rest, is given a sharp impulse by a cue. The cue is held horizontally a distance h above the centre line as shown in *Fig. 1.160*. The ball leaves the cue with a speed v_0 and because of its forward energy eventually acquires a final speed of $\left(\dfrac{9v_0}{7}\right)$, show that $h = (4/5)R$ where R is the radius of the ball.

Sol.

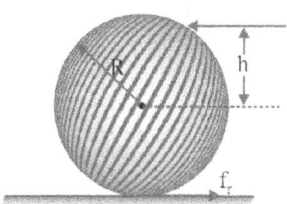

Fig. 1.160

The angular momentum acquired by the ball due to the impulse given by a cue,

$$L = mv_0 h = I\omega_0 = \frac{(2mR^2)}{5}\omega_0 \quad \ldots \text{(i)}$$

Suppose initial angular velocity $\omega_0 < \frac{v_0}{R}$, then the equations of motions are

$$v = v_0 - at \quad \ldots \text{(ii)}$$

where $\quad a = \frac{f_r}{m} = \frac{\mu mg}{m} = \mu g$

and $\quad \omega = \omega_0 + \alpha t \quad \ldots \text{(iii)}$

where $\quad \alpha = \frac{\tau}{I} = \frac{f_r R}{(2mR^2/5)} = \frac{5\mu g}{2R}$

When ball starts pure rolling $v = \omega R \quad \ldots \text{(iv)}$

From above equations, we get

$$v = \frac{5v_0 + 2\omega_0 R}{7}$$

According to the given condition, $v = \frac{9v_0}{7}$

$$\therefore \quad \frac{9v_0}{7} = \frac{5v_0 + 2\omega_0 R}{7}$$

or $\quad \omega_0 = \frac{2v_0}{R}$

Substituting this value in equation (i), we get

$$h = \frac{4R}{5} \quad \text{Ans.}$$

Review of formulae & Important Points

1. **Angular position :** To describe the rotation of a rigid body, we assume a reference line which is fixed in a the body and perpendicular to the axis of rotation. The angular position of this line is defined as

   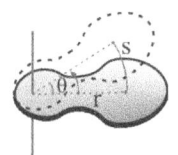

   $$\theta = \frac{s}{r}$$

   where s the arc length, and θ measured in radian.

2. **Angular displacement :** For the change in position of the body from θ_1 to θ_2, its angular displacement

   $$\Delta\theta = \theta_2 - \theta_1$$

   where $\Delta\theta$ can be taken as positive for anticlockwise and negative for clockwise rotation.

3. **Angular velocity :** If a body rotates through an angular displacement $\Delta\theta$ in a time interval Δt, its angular velocity

   $$\vec{\omega}_{av} = \frac{\Delta\vec{\theta}}{\Delta t}$$

   The instantaneous angular velocity

   $$\vec{\omega} = \frac{d\vec{\theta}}{dt}$$

   Angular velocity is a vector quantity whose direction is given by right hand rule. Its SI units is rad/s.

4. **Angular acceleration :** If the angular velocity of a body changes by $\Delta\omega$ in time interval Δt, then the average angular acceleration of the body is given by

   $$\vec{\alpha}_{av} = \frac{\Delta\vec{\omega}}{\Delta t}$$

   The instantaneous angular acceleration

   $$\vec{\alpha} = \frac{d\vec{\omega}}{dt}$$

   Angular acceleration is a vector quantity. Its SI units is rad/s^2.

5. **Equations of motion of rotating body with constant angular acceleration :**

   $$\omega = \omega_0 + \alpha t$$
   $$\theta = \omega_0 t + \frac{1}{2}\alpha t^2$$
   $$\omega^2 = \omega_0^2 + 2\alpha\theta$$
   $$\theta^n = \omega_0 + \frac{\alpha}{2}(2n-1)$$

6. **Relationship between linear and angular variables :** If a body rotates through an angle θ, the point at a radial distance r from axis of rotation moves along an arc with length s is given by

   $$s = \theta r$$
   Also, $\quad v = \omega r$
   $$a_t = \alpha r$$
   and $\quad a_n = \frac{v^2}{r} = \omega^2 r$

7. **Moment of inertia or rotational inertia :** M.I. of a particle of mass m at a distance r from axis of rotation is given by

   $$I = mr^2$$

   M.I. of a body can be defined as $\quad I = \Sigma m_i r_i^2$

   For a system of discrete particles $\quad I = \int r^2 dm$

8. **Parallel-axes theorem :** The parallel-axes theorem relates the moment of inertia of a body about any axis to that about a parallel axis passing through centre of mass of the body :

$$I = I_{cm} + Md^2$$

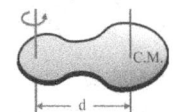

9. **Perpendicular-axes theorem :** If I_x and I_y are the moment of inertia of the planer body about the x and y-axis respectively, then moment of inertia about z axis is given by

$$I_z = I_x + I_y$$

10. **Radius of gyration :** Radius of gyration of system of particles about an axis is given by

$$K = \sqrt{\frac{I}{M}}$$

where $I = \Sigma m_i r_i^2$ and $M = \Sigma m_i$

Radius of gyration of a body of mass M and moment of inertia about an axis is given by $K = \sqrt{\dfrac{I}{M}}$

11. **Some moment of inertias :**

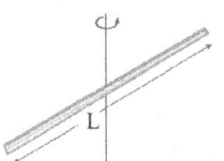

$$I = \frac{ML^2}{12}$$

Thin rod about axis through centre perpendicular to length

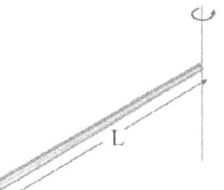

$$I = \frac{ML^2}{3}$$

Thin rod about axis through one end perpendicular to length

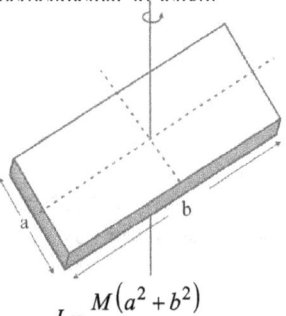

$$I = \frac{M(a^2 + b^2)}{12}$$

Thin rectangular lamina about perpendicular axis about centre

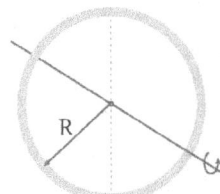

$$I = MR^2$$

Ring or hoop about central axis

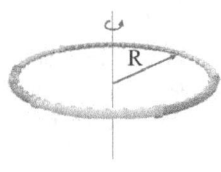

$$I = \frac{MR^2}{2}$$

Hoop about any diameter

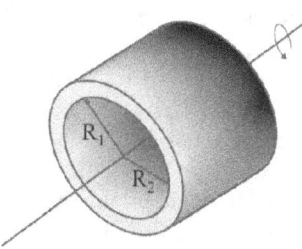

$$I = \frac{M}{2}\left(R_1^2 + R_2^2\right)$$

Annular ring or cylinder

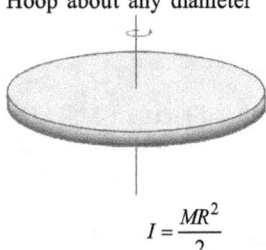

$$I = \frac{MR^2}{2}$$

Circular disc

Circular disc about diameter

$$I = \frac{MR^2}{4}$$

ROTATIONAL MECHANICS

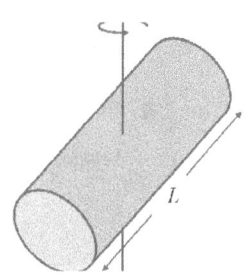

$I = \dfrac{MR^2}{2}$
Solid cylinder or disc

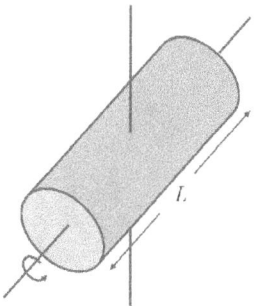

$I = \dfrac{ML^2}{12} + \dfrac{MR^2}{4}$
Solid cylinder about equatorial axis

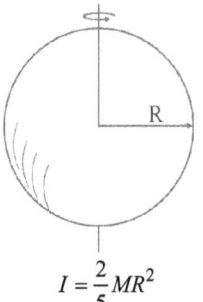

$I = \dfrac{2}{5}MR^2$
Sphere about any diameter

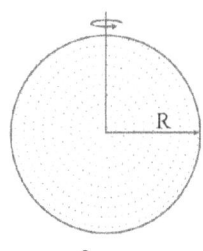

$I = \dfrac{2}{3}MR^2$
Thin spherical shell about any diameter

12. **Moment of force or torque :** Torque is a turning effect of a force. If $\vec{F}$ is exerted at a point given by the position vector $\vec{r}$ relative to the axis, then the magnitude of the torque is given by

$$\tau = rF_\perp = r_\perp F = Fr \sin\theta$$

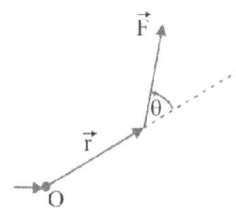

where $\vec{F_\perp}$ is the perpendicular component of the force. In vector notation $\vec{\tau} = \vec{r} \times \vec{F}$.

13. **Angular momentum of a particle :**

The angular momentum $\vec{L}$ of a particle of momentum $\vec{P}$ relative to an axis passing through O is defined as

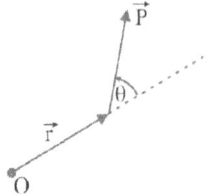

$$L = rP_\perp = r_\perp P = Pr \sin\theta$$
$$= mvr \sin\theta$$

where $P_\perp$ is the perpendicular component of the momentum. In vector notation, it can be written as :

$$\vec{L} = \vec{r} \times \vec{P} = m(\vec{r} \times \vec{v})$$

The direction of $\vec{\tau}$ and $\vec{L}$ can be obtained by right hand screw rule.

14. **Angular momentum of system of particles :**

$$\vec{L} = \vec{L_1} + \vec{L_2} + ... + \vec{L_n}$$

$$= \sum_{i=1}^{n} \vec{L_i}$$

15. **Angular momentum of a rigid body :**
For a rigid body rotating about a fixed axis, its angular momentum is given by

$$\vec{L} = I\vec{\omega}$$

16. **Newton's second law in angular form :**

$$\vec{\tau}_{net} = \dfrac{d\vec{L}}{dt} = I\vec{\alpha}$$

where $\vec{\tau}_{net}$ is the net torque acting on a particle or rigid body, I is the moment of inertia of the particle or body about the axis of rotation, and α is the resulting angular acceleration about that axis.

17. Work and rotational kinetic energy : Work done by torque τ in rotating body from θ_i to θ_f is:

$$W = \int_{\theta_1}^{\theta_2} \tau \, d\theta$$

and $$P = \frac{dW}{dt} = \tau \omega$$

For constant $\tau, W = \tau(\theta_f - \theta_i)$

18. Work-energy theorem for rotating body :

$$W = \Delta K = \frac{1}{2} I \omega_f^2 - \frac{1}{2} I \omega_i^2$$

19. Rolling motion :
(i) For a wheel of radius R rolling with constant velocity
$$v_{cm} = \omega R$$
(ii) For rolling with constant acceleration
$$a_{cm} = \alpha R$$

20. Velocity of different points of a rolling wheel :

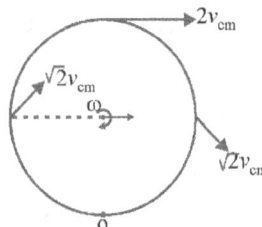

21. Angular momentum of a rolling wheel :

$$\vec{L} = \vec{L}_{Translation} + \vec{L}_{Rotation}$$

or $$\vec{L} = m(\vec{R} \times \vec{v}_{cm}) + I_{cm}\vec{\omega}$$

22. Kinetic energy of a rolling wheel :

$$K = K_{Translation} + K_{Rotation}$$
$$= \frac{1}{2} m v_{cm}^2 + \frac{1}{2} I_{cm} \omega^2$$

23. Rolling on rough inclined plane : Acceleration of C.M.

$$a_{cm} = \left(\frac{g \sin\theta}{1 + \frac{I}{mR^2}} \right)$$

Velocity of C.M. after falling height h

$$v_{cm} = \sqrt{\frac{2gh}{1 + \frac{I}{mR^2}}}$$

Minimum friction required to cause pure rolling

$$f_{min} = \frac{I a_{cm}}{1 + \frac{I}{mR^2}}$$

24. Rolling of cylinder on inclined plane :

$$a_{cm} = \frac{2g}{3} \sin\theta$$

$$f_{min} = \frac{mg}{3} \sin\theta$$

and $$\mu_{min} = \frac{\tan\theta}{3}$$

ROTATIONAL MECHANICS

MECHANICS — MCQ Type 1 — *Exercise 1.1*

LEVEL - 1

Only one option correct

1. Fly wheel is an important part of an engine :
   (a) it gives strength to engine
   (b) it accelerates the speed of the wheel
   (c) it reduces the moment of inertia
   (d) it helps the engine in keeping the speed uniform

2. A body is in pure rotation. The linear speed v of a particle, the distance r of the particle from the axis and the angular velocity ω of the body are related as $\omega = v/r$. Then :
   (a) $\omega \propto 1/r$ (b) $\omega \propto r$
   (c) ω is independent of r (d) all

3. A uniform rod is kept vertically on a horizontal smooth surface at O. If it is rotated slightly and released, it falls down on the horizontal surface. The lower end will remain :
   (a) at O
   (b) at a distance less than $\dfrac{l}{2}$ from O
   (c) at a distance $\dfrac{l}{2}$ from O
   (d) at a distance larger than $\dfrac{l}{2}$ from O

4. Consider the following two equations
   (A) $\vec{L} = I\vec{\omega}$ (B) $\vec{\tau} = \dfrac{d\vec{L}}{dt}$,
   in non inertial frame :
   (a) both A and B are true   (b) A is true but B is false
   (c) B is true but A is false   (d) both A and B are false

5. Which of the following equations can be used for uniformly accelerated rotating body :
   (a) $\omega = 5$ (b) $\omega = t - 3$
   (c) $\omega = 5t^2 - 3$ (d) $\omega = 4t^2 + t + 3$

6. Figure is a graph of the angular position of the rotating disk. The angular velocity of the disk at $t = 3$ s :

   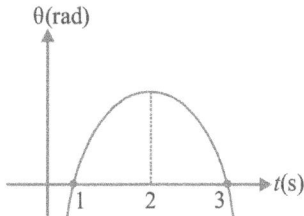

   (a) Zero   (b) Positive
   (c) Negative   (d) None

7. Figure shows a graph of the angular velocity versus time for the rotating disk. For a point on the rim of the disk, the only radial acceleration is represented by :

   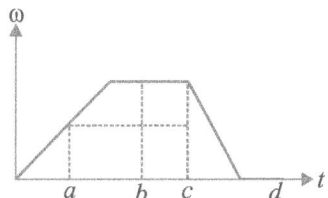

   (a) ab (b) ac
   (c) bc (d) cd

8. Figure shows the overhead view of a disk rotating counter clockwise. The angular speed of the disk is decreasing. Which of the vector correctly represents total acceleration of a point on the rim of the disk :

   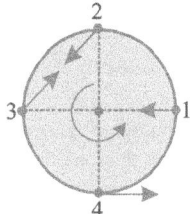

   (a) 1   (b) 2
   (c) 3   (d) 4

9. Figure shows an assembly of three small spheres of the same mass that are attached to a massless rod with the indicated spacings. Consider the moment of inertia I of the assembly about each sphere, in turn. The sphere(s) about which moment of inertia is greatest is :

   (a) 1   (b) 2
   (c) 3   (d) 1 and 3

10. A body is rotating uniformly about a vertical axis fixed in an inertial frame. The resultant force on a particle of the body not on the axis is :
    (a) vertical
    (b) horizontal and skew with the axis
    (c) horizontal and intersecting the axis
    (d) none of these

Answer Key Solution from page 95	1	(d)	3	(c)	5	(b)	7	(c)	9	(c)
	2	(c)	4	(b)	6	(c)	8	(c)	10	(c)

MECHANICS, THERMODYNAMICS & WAVES

11. Figure shows an overhead view of a horizontal bar that can pivot about the point indicated. Two horizontal forces act on the bar, but the bar is stationary. If the angle between the bar and force F_2 is now decreased from the initial 90^0 and the bar is still not turn, then :

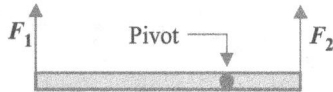

(a) F_2 be made smaller
(b) F_2 be made larger
(c) F_2 be remain as such
(d) none of the above

12. Four forces of the same magnitude act on a square as shown in figure. The square can rotate about point O; mid point of one of the edges. The force which can produce greatest torque is

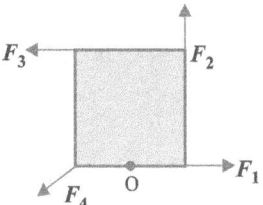

(a) F_1
(b) F_2
(c) F_3
(d) F_4

13. A body is rotating nonuniformly about a vertical axis fixed in an inertial frame. The resultant force on a particle of the body not on the axis is
(a) vertical
(b) horizontal and skew with the axis
(c) horizontal and intersecting the axis
(d) none of these

14. A solid sphere, a hollow sphere and a disc, all having same mass and radius, are placed at the top of a smooth incline and released. The friction coefficients between the objects and the incline are same and not sufficient to allow pure rolling. Least time will be taken in reaching the bottom by :
(a) the solid sphere
(b) the hollow sphere
(c) the disc
(d) all will take same time

15. The density of a rod gradually decreases from one end to the other. It is pivoted at an end so that it can move about a vertical axis through the pivot. A horizontal force F is applied on the free end in a direction perpedicular to the rod. The quantities, that do not depend on which end of the rod is pivoted, are :
(a) angular acceleration
(b) angular velocity when the rod completes one rotation
(c) angular momentum, when the rod completes one rotation
(d) torque of the applied force

16. A hollow sphere and a solid sphere having same mass and same radii are rolled down a rough inclined plane :
(a) The hollow sphere reaches the bottom first
(b) The soild sphere reaches the bottom with greater speed
(c) The soild sphere reaches the bottom with greater kinetic energy
(d) The two spheres will reach the bottom with same linear momentum

17. A bola, which consists of three heavy balls connected to a common point by identical lengths of sturdy string, is readied for launch by holding one of the balls overhead and rotating the wrist, causing the other two balls to rotate in a horizontal circle about the hand. The bola is then released, and its configuration rapidly changes from that of figure (a) to the figure (b). Thus, the rotation is initially around axis1 through the ball that was held, then it is around axis 2 through the centre of mass. If ω_1 and ω_2 are the angular speeds in two cases of figure (a) and (b) respectively, then

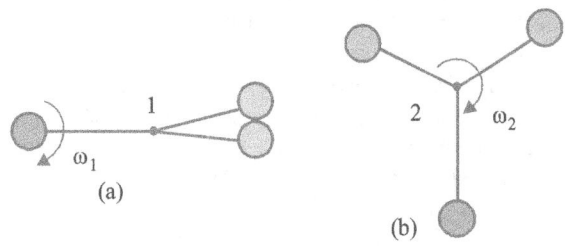

(a) $\omega_1 = \omega_2$
(b) $\omega_1 < \omega_2$
(c) $\omega_1 > \omega_2$
(d) none of the above

18. Figure shows a particle moving at constant velocity v and four points with their xy coordinates. If L_1, L_2, L_3 and L_4 are the angular momentum about the points a, b, c and d respectively, then :

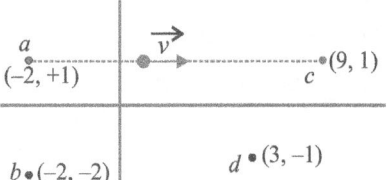

(a) $L_1 < L_3$
(b) $L_1 > L_4$
(c) $L_1 = L_3 = L_4$
(d) $(L_1 = L_3) < L_4 < L_2$

19. Figure shows three particles of the same mass and the same constant speed moving as indicated by the velocity vectors. Points a, b, c and d form a square with point e at the centre. The points about which angular momentum is greatest :

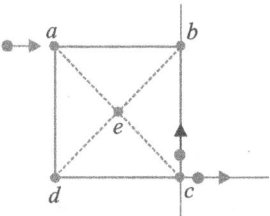

(a) a
(b) a, b
(c) c, d
(d) e

Answer Key
Solution from page 95

11	(b)	13	(b)	15	(d)	17	(b)	19	(a)
12	(c)	14	(d)	16	(b)	18	(d)		

ROTATIONAL MECHANICS

20. Figure shows a smooth inclined plane fixed in a car accelerating on a horizontal road. The angle of incline θ is related to the acceleration a of the car as $a = g \tan θ$. If the sphere is set in pure rolling on the inclined :

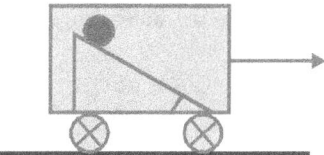

(a) it will continue pure rolling
(b) it will slip down the plane
(c) its linear velocity will increase
(d) its linear velocity will decrease

21. A mass is moving with constant velocity parallel to x - axis. Its angular momentum with respect to origin :
(a) remains constant
(b) goes on increasing
(c) goes on decreasing
(d) zero

22. Four spheres each of diameter 2r and the mass M are placed with their centres on the four corners of a square of side l then the moment of inertia of the system about an axis along one of the sides of the square is :
(a) $M[\frac{4}{5} r^2 + 2 l^2]$
(b) $M[\frac{8}{5} r^2 + 2 l^2]$
(c) $\frac{8}{5} Mr^2$
(d) $M[\frac{4}{5} r^2 + 4 l^2]$

23. Three point masses, each of mass m are placed at corners of an equilateral triangle of side l then the moment of inertia of this system about an axis along one side of the triangle is :
(a) ml^2
(b) $3 ml^2$
(c) $\frac{3}{4} ml^2$
(d) $\frac{2}{3} ml^2$

24. A body slides down on an incline and reaches the bottom with a velocity v. If the same body were in the form of a ring, its velocity at the bottom would have been :
(a) v
(b) $v\sqrt{2}$
(c) $\frac{v}{\sqrt{2}}$
(d) $v\sqrt{\frac{2}{5}}$

25. A ring rolls on a plane surface. The fraction of its total energy associated with its rotation is:
(a) $\frac{1}{2}$
(b) 1
(c) $\frac{1}{3}$
(d) 2

26. A soild cylinder of mass M and radius R rolls down an inclined plane with height h without slipping. The speed of its centre of mass when it reaches the bottom is :
(a) $\sqrt{2gh}$
(b) $\sqrt{\frac{4}{3} gh}$
(c) $\sqrt{\frac{3}{4} gh}$
(d) $\sqrt{4gh}$

27. A force $(3i + 4j)$ N is applied to a point whose radius vector relative to origin O is equal to $(2i + j)$ m. The moment arm of the force relative to point O is :
(a) $5 m$
(b) $3 m$
(c) $\sqrt{5} m$
(d) $1 m$

28. The moment of the force about the origin, from the data as shown in the figure is:

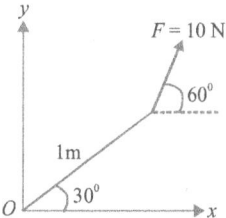

(a) $10k$ N-m
(b) $5\sqrt{3} j$ N-m
(c) $5k$ N-m
(d) $5j$ N-m

29. Two point masses m_1 and m_2 joined by a masssless string of length r. The moment of inertia of the system about an axis passing through the centre of mass and perpendicular to the string is :
(a) $(m_1 + m_2)r^2$
(b) $\frac{m_1 m_2 r^2}{m_1 + m_2}$
(c) $\frac{m_1 r^2}{m_2(m_1 + m_2)}$
(d) $\frac{m_2 r^2}{m_1(m_1 + m_2)}$

30. A uniform cylinder has a length l and radius R. If moment of interia of this cylinder about its own geometrical axis is equal to moment of inertia of the same cylinder about an axis passing through centre and perpendicular to its length is :
(a) $l = R$
(b) $l = \sqrt{3} R$
(c) $l = \frac{1}{\sqrt{3}} R$
(d) $l = 3 R$

31. A rod of mass m and length l is bent in to shape of L. Its moment of inertia about the axis shown in figure :

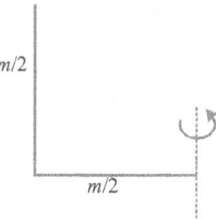

(a) $\frac{ml^2}{6}$
(b) $\frac{ml^2}{3}$
(c) $\frac{ml^2}{2}$
(d) None

Answer Key Solution from page 95	20	(a)	22	(b)	24	(c)	26	(b)	28	(c)	30	(b)
	21	(a)	23	(c)	25	(d)	27	(d)	29	(b)	31	(a)

32. A sphere of mass M and radius R moves on a horizontal surface with a velocity v and then climbs up an inclined plane up to a height h where it stops. The height up to which it rises will be:

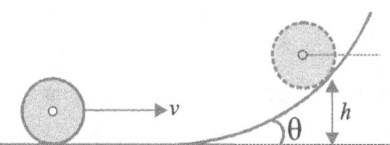

(a) directly proportional to the square of the velocity and inversely proportional to the angle of the inclination
(b) directly proportional to the velocity and inversely proportional to its mass.
(c) directly proportional to the square of the velocity and independent of mass and the angle of the inclination
(d) directly proportional to its velocity and inversely proportional to the angle of the inclination

33. Two particles, each of mass m and moving with speed v in opposite directions along parallel lines, are separated by a distance d. The vector angular momentum of this system of paricles will be :
(a) Maximum when the origin is taken beyond the two parallel lines on either side
(b) Minimum when the origin is taken beyond the two parallel lines on either side
(c) Maximum when the origin lies anywhere on the middle line between the two.
(d) Same no matter which point is taken as the origin

34. A particle P with a mass 2.0 kg has position vector $r = 3.0$ m and velocity $v = 4.0$ m/s as shown. It is accelerated by the force = 2.0 N. All these vectors lie in a common plane. The angular momentum vector is :

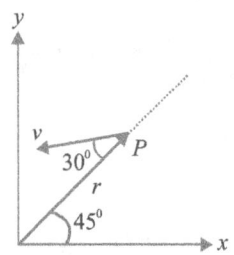

(a) 12 kg m²/s out of he plane of the figure
(b) 12 kg m²/s in to the plane of the figure
(c) Zero
(d) 24 kg m²/s in to the plane of the figure

35. A strip of length 1 m rotates about the z-axis passing through the point O in the xy-plane with an angular velocity of 10 rad/s in the counterclockwise direction, and O is at rest. The velocity of point A is :

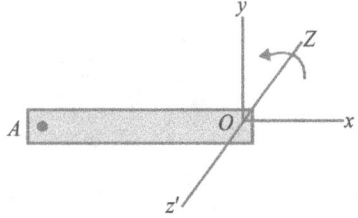

(a) $10\,\mathbf{k}$ m/s
(b) $-10\,\mathbf{j}$ m/s
(c) $+10\,\mathbf{j}$ m/s
(d) $100\,\mathbf{k}$ m/s

36. A thin circular ring of mass M and radius R is rotating about its axis with a constant angular velocity ω. Two objects each of the mass m are attached gently to the opposite ends of a diameter of the ring. The wheel now rotates with an angular velocity :

(a) $\dfrac{\omega M}{M+m}$
(b) $\dfrac{\omega(M-2m)}{M+2m}$
(c) $\dfrac{\omega M}{M+2m}$
(d) $\dfrac{\omega(M-2m)}{M}$

37. ABC is a rectangular plate of uniform thickness. The side AB, BC and AC are in the ratio 4,3,5 as shown in figure. $I_{AB}, I_{BC},$ and I_{CA} are the moments of interia of the plate about AB, BC and CA respectively. Which one of the following statements is correct :

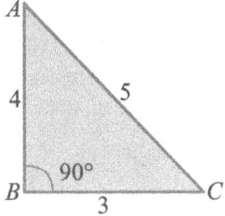

(a) I_{CA} is maximum
(b) $I_{AB} > I_{BC}$
(c) $I_{BC} > I_{AB}$
(d) $I_{AB} + I_{BC} = I_{CA}$

38. If I is the moment of inertia of a solid sphere about an axis parallel to a diameter and at a distance x from it. Which of the following graphs represents the variation of I with x :

(a)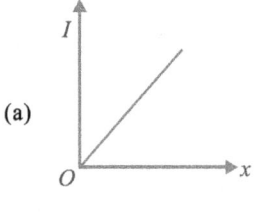
(b)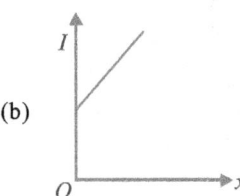
(c)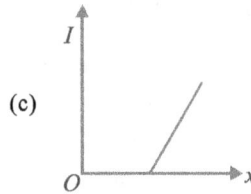
(d)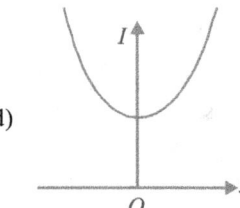

39. A disc is rolling (without slipping) on a horizontal surface C is the centre, P and Q are two points equidistant from C. Let v_P, v_Q and v_C be the magnitudes of velocities of points P, Q and C respectively, then :
(a) $v_Q > v_C > v_P$
(b) $v_Q < v_C < v_P$
(c) $v_Q = v_P, v_C = \dfrac{1}{2} v_P$
(d) $v_Q < v_C > v_P$

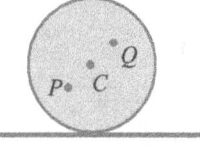

Answer Key
Solution from page 95

| 32 | (c) | 34 | (a) | 36 | (c) | 38 | (d) |
| 33 | (d) | 35 | (b) | 37 | (c) | 39 | (a) |

ROTATIONAL MECHANICS

40. A child is standing with folded hands at the centre of platform rotating about its central axis. The kinetic energy of the system is K. The child is now stretches his arms so that the moment of inertia of the system doubles. The kinetic energy of the system now is :

(a) $2K$ (b) $\dfrac{K}{2}$

(c) $\dfrac{K}{4}$ (d) $4K$

41. One quarter section is cut from a uniform circular disc of radius R. This section has a mass M. It is made to rotate about a line perpendicular to its plane and passing through the centre of original disc. Its moment of inertia about the axis of rotation is :

(a) $\dfrac{1}{2}MR^2$

(b) $\dfrac{1}{4}MR$

(c) $\dfrac{1}{8}MR^2$

(d) $\sqrt{2}MR^2$

42. A cylinder rolls up an inclined plane, reaches some height and then rolls down (without slipping throughout these motions). The directions of the frictional force acting on the cylinder are :
(a) up the incline while ascending and down the incline while descending
(b) up the incline while ascending as well as descending
(c) down the incline while ascending and up the incline while descending
(d) down the incline while ascending as well as descending

43. An equilateral triangle ABC formed from a uniform wire has two small identical beads initially located at A. A triangle is set rotating about the vertical axis AO. Then the beads are released from rest simultaneously and allowed to slide down. One along AB the other along AC as shown. Neglecting frictional effects, the quantities that are conserved as beads slide down are :

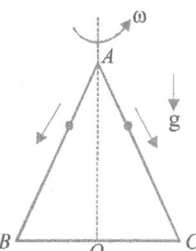

(a) Angular velocity and total energy (kinetic and potential)
(b) Total angular momentum and total energy
(c) Angular velocity and moment of inertia about the axis of rotation
(d) Total angular momentum and moment of inertia about the axis of rotation

44. Two identical rods each of mass M and length L are joined to form a symmetrical X. The smaller angle between the rods is θ. The moment of inertia of the system about an axis passing through the point of intersection of the rods and perpendicular to this plane is:

(a) $\dfrac{ML^2}{12}$ (b) $\dfrac{ML^2}{6}$

(c) $\dfrac{ML^2}{6}\sin^2\theta$ (d) $\dfrac{ML^2}{6}\cos^2\theta$

45. A disc of mass M and radius R is rolling with angular velocity ω on a horizontal plane as shown in figure. The magnitude of angular momentum of disc about the origin O is :

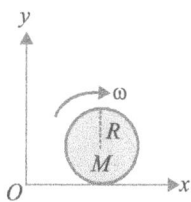

(a) $\dfrac{1}{2}MR^2\omega$ (b) $MR^2\omega$

(c) $\dfrac{3}{2}MR^2\omega$ (d) $2MR^2\omega$

46. The moment of inertia of a uniform semicircular disc of mass M and radius R about a line perpendicular to the plane of disc through the centre is :

(a) $\dfrac{2}{5}MR^2$ (b) $\dfrac{1}{4}MR^2$

(c) $\dfrac{1}{2}MR^2$ (d) MR^2

47. A uniform solid sphere of radius R having moment of inertia I about its diameter is melted to form a uniform disc of thickness t and radius r. The moment of inertia of the disc about an axis passing through its edge and perpendicular to its plane is I, then the radius of the disc is :

(a) $\dfrac{2}{\sqrt{15}}R$ (b) $\dfrac{2}{\sqrt{5}}R$

(c) $\sqrt{\dfrac{2}{5}}R$ (d) $\sqrt{\dfrac{2}{15}}R$

48. Four point masses each of value m are placed at the corners of a square $ABCD$ of side ℓ. The moment of inertia of this system about an axis passing through A and parallel to BD is :

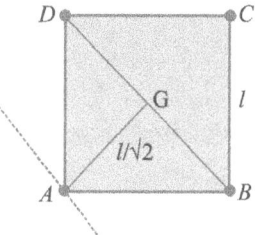

(a) $2m\ell^2$ (b) $\sqrt{3}\,m\ell^2$

(c) $3m\ell^2$ (d) $m\ell^2$

Answer Key	40	(b)	42	(b)	44	(b)	46	(c)	48	(c)
Solution from page 95	41	(a)	43	(b)	45	(c)	47	(a)		

MECHANICS, THERMODYNAMICS & WAVES

49. A horizontal platform is rotating with uniform angular velocity arround the vertical axis passing through its centre. At some instant of time a viscous fluid of mass m is dropped at the centre and is allowed to spread out and finally fall. The angular velocity during this period :
    (a) Decreases continuously
    (b) Decreases initially and increases again
    (c) Remains unaltered
    (d) Increases continuously

50. A solid sphere is rolling on a frictionless surface, shown in figure with a translational velocity v m/s. If sphere climbs upto height h then value of v should be :

    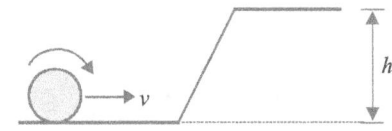

    (a) $\sqrt{\dfrac{10}{7}gh}$ (b) $\sqrt{2gh}$

    (c) $2gh$ (d) $\sqrt{\dfrac{10}{7}}gh$

51. A uniform cylinder oscillates without slipping on rough inclined plane. The cylinder is connected to a spring at the centre, whose other end is fixed. The force of friction on the cylinder

    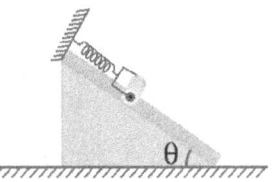

    (a) is always upwards
    (b) is always downwards
    (c) is initially upwards and then downwards periodically
    (d) none of these.

52. A disc is performing pure rolling on a smooth stationary surface with constant velocity v. For the point of contact of the disc
    (a) velocity is v, acceleration is zero
    (b) velocity is zero, acceleration is zero
    (c) velocity is v, acceleration is v^2/R
    (d) velocity is zero, acceleration is v^2/R

    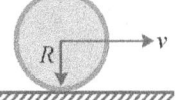

53. A disc of radius R rolls on a horizontal surface with linear velocity v and angular velocity ω. This is a point P on the circumference of the disc at an angle θ which has a vertical velocity. Here θ is equal to

    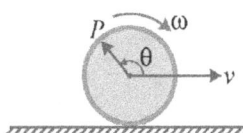

    (a) $\pi + \sin^{-1}\left(\dfrac{v}{\omega R}\right)$ (b) $\dfrac{\pi}{2} - \sin^{-1}\left(\dfrac{v}{\omega R}\right)$

    (c) $\pi - \cos^{-1}\left(\dfrac{v}{\omega R}\right)$ (d) $\pi + \cos^{-1}\left(\dfrac{v}{\omega R}\right)$

54. A ball of mass m moving with velocity v, collide with the wall elastically as shown in the figure. After impact the change in angular momentum about P is
    (a) $2mvd \sin\theta$
    (b) $2mvd \cos\theta$
    (c) $2mvd$
    (d) zero

    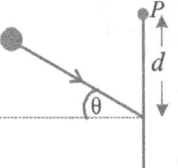

55. A cylinder is in pure rolling up an inclined plane. It stops momentarily and then rolls back. Therefore friction
    (a) on the cylinder is zero throughout the journey
    (b) is directed opposite to the velocity of the centre of mass throughout the journey
    (c) is directed up the plane throughout the journey
    (d) is directed down the plane throughout the journey

56. A solid cylinder is wrapped with a string and placed on an inclined plane as shown in the figure. Then the frictional force acting between cylinder and plane is
    (a) zero
    (b) $5\,mg$
    (c) $\dfrac{7mg}{2}$
    (d) $\dfrac{mg}{5}$

    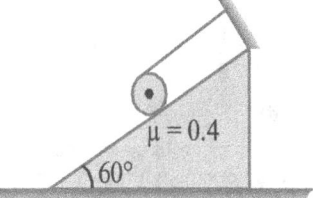

57. A spool is pulled horizontally by two equal and opposite forces on rough surface. The correct statement is :

    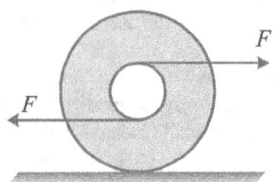

    (a) centre of mass of spool moves towards right
    (b) centre of mass of spool moves towards left
    (c) centre of mass remains at rest
    (d) none of these

58. A horizontal force F is applied at the top of an equilateral triangular block having mass m and side a as shown in figure. The minimum value of the coefficient of friction required to topple the block before translation will be

    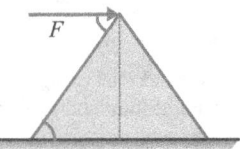

    (a) $\dfrac{2}{\sqrt{3}}$ (b) $\dfrac{1}{2}$

    (c) $\dfrac{1}{\sqrt{3}}$ (d) $\dfrac{1}{3}$

Answer Key	49	(b)	51	(c)	53	(c, d)	55	(c)	57	(a)
Solution from page 95	50	(b)	52	(d)	54	(b)	56	(d)	58	(c)

ROTATIONAL MECHANICS

59. Linear acceleration of cylinder of mass m_2 is a_2. Then angular acceleration α_2 is (given that there is no slipping).

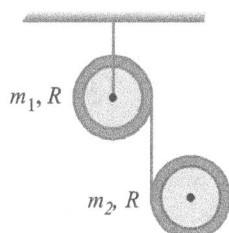

(a) $\dfrac{a_2}{R}$ (b) $\dfrac{(a_2+g)}{R}$

(c) $\dfrac{2(a_2+g)}{R}$ (d) None of these

60. A particle of mass m is attached to a rod of length L and it rotates in a circle with a constant angular velocity ω. An observer P is rigidly fixed on the rod at a distance $L/2$ from the centre. The acceleration of m and the pseudo force on m from the frame of reference of P must be respectively.

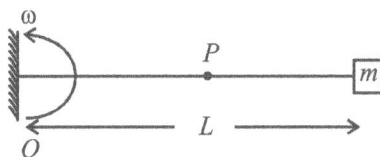

(a) zero, zero   (b) zero, $m\omega^2 \dfrac{L}{2}$

(c) $\omega^2 \dfrac{L}{2}, m\omega^2 \dfrac{L}{2}$ (d) zero, $m\omega^2 L$

61. Consider the two bobs are shown in the figure. The bobs are pivoted to the hinges through massless rods. If t_A be the time taken by the bob A to reach the lowest position and t_B be the time taken by the bob B to reach the lowest position. (Both bobs are released from rest from a horizontal position) then ratio t_A / t_B is

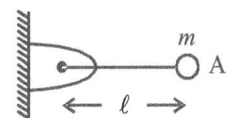 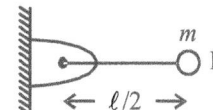

(a) $\sqrt{3}$ (b) $\sqrt{5}$

(c) $\sqrt{2}$ (d) $\dfrac{1}{\sqrt{2}}$

62. A hemispherical shell of mass m and radius R is hinged at point O and placed on a horizontal surface. A ball of mass m moving with a velocity u inclined at an angle $\theta = \tan^{-1}(1/2)$ strikes the shell at point A (as shown in the figure) and stops. What is the minimum speed u if the given shell is to reach the horizontal surface OP ?

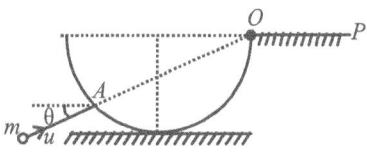

(a) Zero

(b) $\sqrt{\dfrac{2gR}{3}}$

(c) $\dfrac{gR}{\sqrt{5}}$

(d) it cannot come on the surface for any value of u.

63. A hoop of radius 0.10m and mass 0.50 kg rolls across a table parallel to one edge with a speed of 0.50 m/s. Refer its motion to a rectangular coordinate system with the origin at the left rear corner of the table. At a certain time t, a line drawn from the origin to the point of contact of the hoop with the table has length 1m and makes an angle of 30° with the X-axis (figure). What is the spin angular momentum of the hoop with respect to the origin at this time t ?

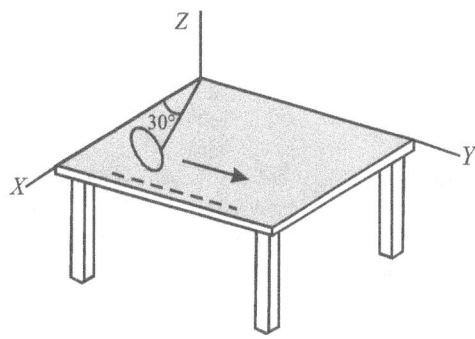

(a) $-0.25\,\hat{i}\ \text{kg m}^2/\text{s}$ (b) $-0.005\,\hat{i}\ \text{kg m}^2/\text{s}$

(c) $-0.025\,\hat{i}\ \text{kg m}^2/\text{s}$ (d) $-0.5\,\hat{i}\ \text{kg m}^2/\text{s}$

Answer Key	59	(c)	61	(c)	63	(c)
Solution from page 95	60	(d)	62	(d)		

Level -2

Only one option correct

1. Figure shows four rotating disks that are sliding across a frictionless floor. Three forces F, $2F$ or $3F$ act on each disk, either at the rim, at the centre, or halfway between rim and centre. Which disks are in equilibrium :

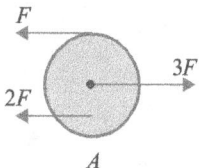
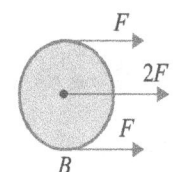
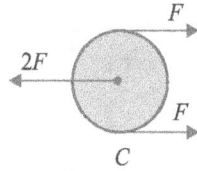
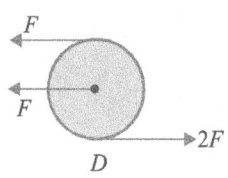

   (a) A, D   (b) A, B
   (c) C, D   (d) A, C

2. Figure shows overhead views of three structures on which three forces act. The direction of the forces are as indicated. If the magnitude of the forces are adjusted properly, which structure can be in stable equilibrium :

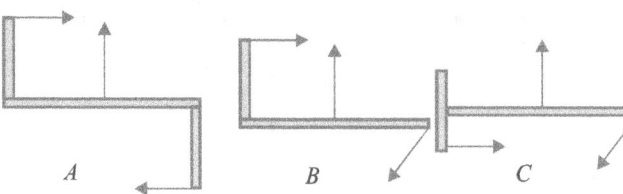

   (a) A   (b) B
   (c) C   (d) None

3. In figure, a block slides down a frictionless inclined plane and a sphere rolls without sliding down a ramp of the same angle θ. The block and sphere have the same mass, start from rest at point A, and descend to point B. If work done by gravitational force on the block is W_1 and that on sphere is W_2, then :

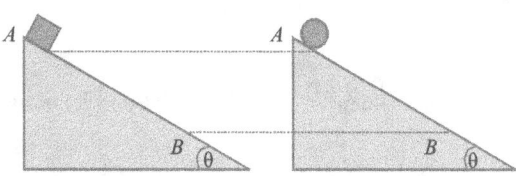

   (a) $W_1 = W_2$ (b) $W_1 < W_2$
   (c) $W_1 > W_2$ (d) None of the above

4. In the previous problem, if v_1 is the speed of block at B and v_2 is the speed of sphere at the same position, then :
   (a) $v_1 = v_2$ (b) $v_1 < v_2$
   (c) $v_1 > v_2$ (d) none of the above

5. If E_1 is the kinetic energy of the block and E_2 is the kinetic energy of sphere at the position B, then :
   (a) $E_1 = E_2$ (b) $E_1 < E_2$
   (c) $E_1 > E_2$ (d) none of the above

6. If K_1 is the translational kinetic energy of block and K_2 is the translational kinetic energy of the sphere at B, then:
   (a) $K_1 = K_2$ (b) $K_1 < K_2$
   (c) $K_1 > K_2$ (d) none of the above

7. Two spheres of radii R and $2R$ roll on an inclined plane without slipping. If v_1, v_2 and ω_1, ω_2 are their velocities of centre of mass and angular velocities of rotation after moving a distance l, then :
   (a) $v_1 = v_2, \omega_1 = \omega_2$ (b) $v_1 < v_2, \omega_1 < \omega_2$
   (c) $v_1 < v_2, \omega_1 = \omega_2$ (d) $v_1 = v_2, \omega_1 > \omega_2$

8. Figure shows the motions of three identical spheres on three different ramps of same inclination.

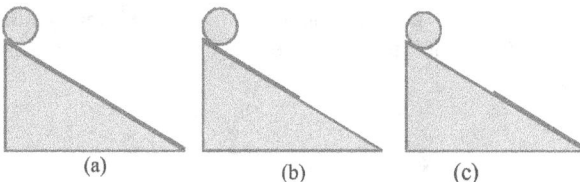

   The rough part of the ramps are shown by bold line. If K_A, K_B and K_C are their kinetic energy at the bottom of the ramp, then :
   (a) $K_A < K_B$ (b) $(K_A = K_B) < K_C$
   (c) $K_A < (K_B = K_C)$ (d) $(K_A = K_B) > K_C$

9. End of the bar AB in figure rests on a horizontal surface, while end B is hinged. A horizontal force P of 60 N is exerted on end A. Neglect the weight of the bar. The vertical component of the force exerted by the bar on the hinge at B is :

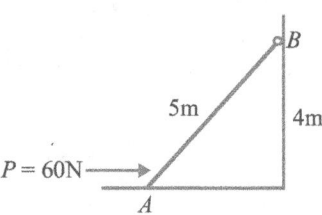

   (a) 60 N   (b) 80 N
   (c) 100 N   (d) 120 N

10. Minimum coefficient of friction required to cause pure rolling of a cylinder down on an inclined plane of inclination θ is :
    (a) $\sin\theta$ (b) $\dfrac{\sin\theta}{3}$
    (c) $\dfrac{\tan\theta}{3}$ (d) $\dfrac{\tan\theta}{2}$

Answer Key

| 1 | (d) | 3 | (a) | 5 | (a) | 7 | (d) | 9 | (b) |
| 2 | (c) | 4 | (c) | 6 | (c) | 8 | (d) | 10 | (c) |

11. A rod of mass m and length is hinged to its one end and held vertical. A point mass m is attached to the other end, is allowed to rotate about the hinge. The velocity of the rod when it becomes horizontal is :

    (a) $3gl$ (b) $\frac{3}{2}\sqrt{gl}$

    (c) $\frac{3}{4}\sqrt{gl}$ (d) None

12. A hoop of radius r rolls on a horizontal plane with constant velocity v without slipping. The velocity of any point, t second after it passes the top position is :

    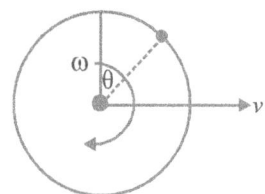

    (a) $2v$ (b) $2vt$

    (c) $2v\cos\left(\frac{vt}{2r}\right)$ (d) $2v\sin\left(\frac{vt}{2r}\right)$

13. A block of mass M rests on a turntable that is rotating at constant angular velocity ω. A smooth cord runs from the block through a hole in the centre of the table down to hanging block of mass m. The coefficient of friction between the first block and the turnable is μ (see figure). The smallest value of the radius r for which the first block will remain at rest relative to the turntable:

    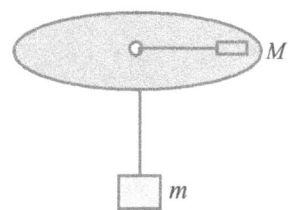

    (a) $r=\frac{mg-\mu Mg}{M\omega^2}$ (b) $r=\frac{mg+\mu Mg}{M\omega^2}$

    (c) $r=\frac{\mu g}{M\omega^2}$ (d) None of the above

14. Moment of inertia of a uniform circular disc about a diameter is I. Its moment of inertia about an axis perpendicular to its plane and passing through a point its rim will be :
    (a) $5I$ (b) $3I$
    (c) $6I$ (d) $4I$

15. A uniform spherical shell of mass M and radius R rotates about a vertical axis on frictionless bearing as shown in figure. A massless cord passes around the equator of the shell over a pulley of rotational inertia I and radius r and is attached to a small object of mass m that is otherwise free to fall under the influence of gravity. There is no friction of pulley axle. The cord does not slip on the pulley. The speed of the object after it has fallen a distance h from rest is

    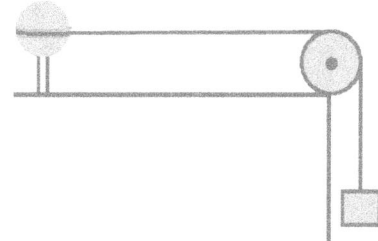

    (a) $v^2 = 2gh$ (b) $v^2 = \dfrac{mgh}{\dfrac{m}{2}+\dfrac{I}{2r^2}+M}$

    (c) $v^2 = \dfrac{mgh}{\dfrac{m}{2}+\dfrac{I}{2r^2}+\dfrac{M}{3}}$ (d) $v^2 = \dfrac{mgh}{\dfrac{m}{2}+\dfrac{I}{r^2}+M}$

16. The angular momentum of a particle relative to a point O varies with time as $\vec{J}=\vec{a}+\vec{b}t^2$, where $\vec{a}$ and $\vec{b}$ are constant vectors, with $\vec{a}$ perpendicular $\vec{b}$. The moment of force (τ) relative to the point O acting on the particle when the angle between the vectors $\vec{\tau}$ and $\vec{J}$ equal 45° :

    (a) $\sqrt{\dfrac{a}{b}}$ (b) $2\sqrt{\dfrac{a}{b}}$

    (c) $2b\sqrt{\dfrac{a}{b}}$ (d) $2a\sqrt{\dfrac{b}{a}}$

17. A rod AB of length L slides in the xy- plane. If the rod makes an angle θ with the vertical, the angular velocity of the rod will be :

    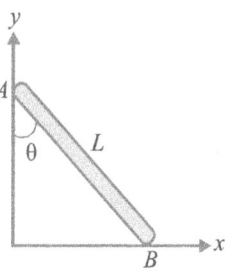

    (a) Directly proportional to the length of the rod and the linear velocity of the end A at that instant.
    (b) Independent of the length of the rod but will depend on the angle θ.
    (c) Independent of θ but will depend on the length of the rod and linear velocity of the end A at that instant.
    (d) Dependent upon the length of the rod, the angle θ and also on the linear velocity of the end A of the rod at that instant.

Answer Key	11	(c)	13	(a)	15	(c)	17	(d)
Solution from page 97	12	(c)	14	(c)	16	(c)		

72 MECHANICS, THERMODYNAMICS & WAVES

18. A hole of radius $R/2$ is cut from a thin circular plate of radius R. The mass of the remaining plate is M. The moment of inertia of the plate about an axis through O perpendicular to the xy- plane (i.e. about the z- axis) is : (The mass of remaining disc is M)

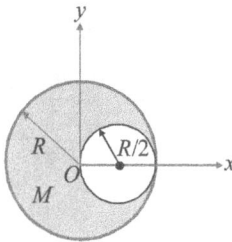

(a) $\dfrac{5}{7} MR^2$ (b) $\dfrac{7}{12} MR^2$

(c) $\dfrac{11}{24} MR^2$ (d) $\dfrac{13}{24} MR^2$

19. A uniform disc of mass M and radius R is mounted on an axle supported on fixed frictionless bearings. A light cord wrapped around the rim is pulled with a force 5 N. On the same system of pulley and string, instead of pulling it down, a body of weight 5 N is suspended. If the first process is termed A and the second B, the tangential acceleration will be:

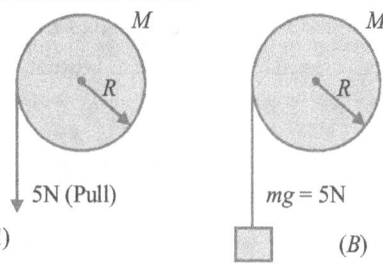

(a) equal in the processes A and B
(b) greater in process A than in B
(c) greater in process B than in A
(d) independent of the two processes

20. A uniform cylindrical disc of radius R and mass M is pulled over a horizontal frictionless surface by a constant force. The force is applied by means of a string wound around the disc as shown in the figure. If it starts from rest at $t = 0$, the linear and angular displacements respectively at time t are :

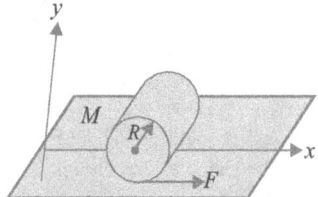

(a) $\left(\dfrac{F}{M}\right)t^2, \left(\dfrac{F}{M}\right)t^2$ (b) $\left(\dfrac{F}{2M}\right)t, \left(\dfrac{F}{2MR}\right)t^2$

(c) $\left(\dfrac{F}{2M}\right)t^2, \left(\dfrac{F}{MR}\right)t^2$ (d) $\left(\dfrac{2F}{M}\right)t^2, \left(\dfrac{2F}{MR}\right)t^2$

21. A straight bar, of mass 15 kg and length 2 m, at rest on a frictionless horizontal surface, receives an instantaneous impulse of 7.5 Ns perpendicular to the bar. If the impulse is applied at the centre of mass of the bar, the energy transferred is :
(a) 3.2 J
(b) 1.9 J
(c) 3.8 J
(d) 2.5 J

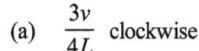

22. A bar of mass M and length L is in pure translatory motion with its centre of mass velocity v. it collides with and sticks to a second identical bar which is initially at rest. (Assume that it becomes one composite bar of length $2L$). The angular velocity of the composite bar will be :

(a) $\dfrac{3v}{4L}$ clockwise

(b) $\dfrac{4v}{3L}$ clockwise

(c) $\dfrac{3v}{4L}$ counterclockwise

(d) $\dfrac{v}{L}$ counterclockwise

23. A circular wooden hoop of mass m and radius R rests flat on a horizontal frictionless surface. A bullet, also of mass m, and moving with a velocity v, strikes the hoop and gets embedded in it. The thickness of the hoop is much smaller than R. The angular velocity with which the system rotates after the bullet strikes the hoop is:

(a) $\dfrac{v}{4R}$
(b) $\dfrac{v}{3R}$
(c) $\dfrac{2v}{3R}$
(d) $\dfrac{3v}{4R}$

24. A uniform rod AB of length L is hinged at one end A. The rod is kept in the horizontal position by a massless string tied to point B as shown in figure. If the string is cut, the initial angular acceleration of the rod will be:

(a) $\dfrac{g}{L}$
(b) $\dfrac{2g}{L}$
(c) $\dfrac{2g}{3L}$
(d) $\dfrac{3g}{2L}$

Answer Key (Solution from page 97)

18	(d)	20	(c)	22	(c)	24	(d)
19	(b)	21	(b)	23	(b)		

25. Consider a body consisting two identical balls, each of mass M, connected by a light rigid rod. If an impulse $J = Mv$ is imparted to the body at one of its ends, what should be its angular velocity :

(a) $\dfrac{v}{L}$ (b) $\dfrac{2v}{L}$

(c) $\dfrac{v}{3L}$ (d) $\dfrac{v}{4L}$

26. A circular platform is free to rotate in a horizontal plane about a vertical axis passing through its centre. A tortoise is sitting at the edge of the platform. Now the platform given an angular velocity ω_0. When the tortoise moves along a chord of platform with a constant velocity (with respect to the platform) the angular velocity of the platform $\omega(t)$ will vary with time t as :

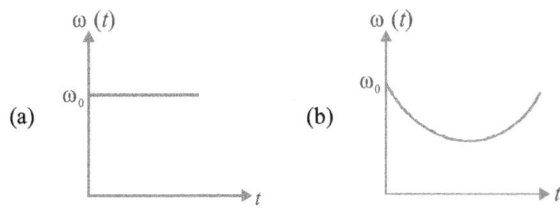

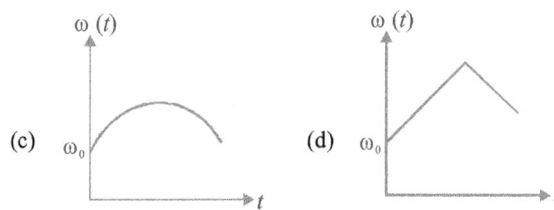

27. A symmetrical lamina of mass M consists of a square shape with a semi-circular section over each edge of the square as shown in figure. The side of the square is $2a$. The moment of inertia of the lamina about an axis through its centre of mass and perpendicular to the plane is $1.6Ma^2$. The moment of inertia of the lamina about the tangent AB in the plane of the lamina is :

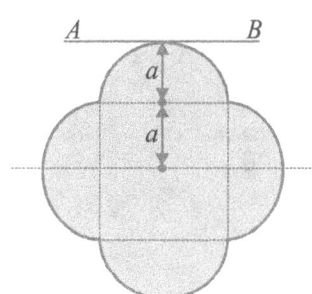

(a) $0.8\,Ma^2$ (b) $2.6\,Ma^2$
(c) $3.6\,Ma^2$ (d) $4.8\,Ma^2$

28. A disc of radius R has mass $9m$. A hole of radius $\dfrac{R}{3}$ is cut from it as shown is figure. The moment of inertia of the remaining part about an axis passing through centre O of the disc and perpendicular of the plane of disc is :

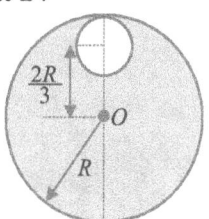

(a) $8\,mR^2$ (b) $4\,mR^2$
(c) $\dfrac{40}{9}\,mR^2$ (d) $\dfrac{37}{9}\,mR^2$

29. A circular disc X of radius R is made from an iron plate of thickness t and another plate Y of radius $4R$ is made from an iron plate of thickness $\dfrac{t}{4}$. The ratio between moments of inertia $\dfrac{I_y}{I_x}$ is :

(a) 1   (b) 16
(c) 32   (d) 64

30. A thin wire of length L and uniform linear mass density ρ is bent into a circular loop with centre at O as shown. The moment of inertia of the loop about the axis xx' is :

(a) $\dfrac{\rho L^3}{8\pi^2}$ (b) $\dfrac{\rho L^3}{16\pi^2}$

(c) $\dfrac{5\rho L^3}{16\pi^2}$ (d) $\dfrac{3\rho L^3}{8\pi^2}$

31. In the device shown in figure, the cylinder in the pure rolling motion. At certain instant the angular speed of the cylinder is ω. The velocity of the block at that instant is

(a) ωR
(b) $2\omega R$
(c) $3\omega R$
(d) $4\omega R$

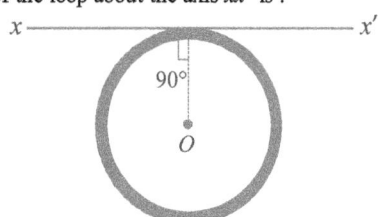

Answer Key	25	(a)	27	(d)	29	(d)	31	(c)
Solution from page 97	26	(c)	28	(b)	30	(d)		

74 MECHANICS, THERMODYNAMICS & WAVES

32. A cubical block of side L rests on a rough horizontal surface with coefficient of friction μ. A horizontal force F is applied on the block as shown. If the coefficient of friction is sufficiently high so that the block does not slide before toppling, the minimum force required to topple the block is :

(a) infinitesimal (b) $\dfrac{Mg}{4}$

(c) $\dfrac{Mg}{2}$ (d) $Mg(1-\mu)$

33. A rectangular piece of dimension $l \times b$ is cut out of central portion of a uniform circular disc of mass m and radius r. The moment of inertia of the remaining piece about an axis perpendicular to the plane of the disc and passing through its centre is :

(a) $m\left[r^2 - \dfrac{lb}{6\pi r^2}(l^2+b^2)\right]$ (b) $\dfrac{m}{2}\left[r^2 - \dfrac{lb}{6\pi r^2}(l^2+b^2)\right]$

(c) $\dfrac{m}{2}\left[r^2 - \dfrac{(l^2+b^2)}{6}\right]$

(d) not determinable as mass of the rectangular piece is not given

34. A small particle of mass m is given an initial high velocity in the horizontal plane and winds its cord around the fixed vertical shaft of radius a. All motion occurs essentially in horizontal plane. If the angular velocity of the cord is ω_0 when the distance from the particle to the tangency point is r_0, then the angular velocity of the cord ω after it has turned through an angle θ is : :

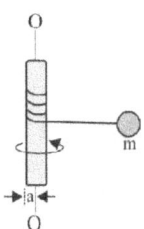

(a) $\omega = \omega_0$ (b) $\omega = \dfrac{a}{r_0}\omega_0$

(c) $\omega = \left(\dfrac{\omega_0}{1-\dfrac{a}{r_0}\theta}\right)$ (d) $\omega = \omega_0\theta$

35. Moment of inertia of a uniform–disc of mass m about an axis $x = a$ is mk^2, where k is the radius of gyration. What is its moment of inertia about an axis $x = a + b$:

(a) $mk^2 + m(a+b)^2 - ma^2$ (b) $mk^2 + m\dfrac{(a+b)^2}{2}$

(c) $mk^2 + m\dfrac{b^2}{2}$ (d) $mk^2 + mb^2$

36. A plank P is placed on a hollow cylinder C, which rolls on a horizontal surface as shown. No slippage is there at any of the surfaces in contact. Both have equal mass say M (each) and if v is the velocity of centre of mass of the cylinder C, then the ratio of the kinetic energy of plank P to the cylinder C is :

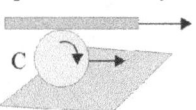

(a) 1 : 1   (b) 2 : 1
(c) 3 : 8   (d) 8 : 11

37. A sphere is given some angular velocity about a horizontal axis through the centre, and gently placed on a plank with coefficient of friction μ. The plank rests on a smooth horizontal surface. The initial acceleration of the sphere relative to the plank is : (mass of sphere = mass of plank)

(a) μg

(b) $\dfrac{7}{5}\mu g$

(c) $2\mu g$

(d) zero

38. A force F is applied at the top of a ring placed on a rough horizontal surface as shown in figure. Friction is sufficient to cause pure rolling. The frictional force acting on the ring is :

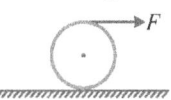

(a) $\dfrac{F}{2}$ towards left   (b) $\dfrac{F}{2}$ towards right

(c) $\dfrac{F}{3}$ towards left   (d) zero

39. A cylinder rolls without slipping on a plank is device shown in figure. The acceleration of the plank to keep the cylinder in a fixed position during the motion is

(a) $\dfrac{g}{2}\sin\theta$

(b) $g\sin\theta$

(c) $\sqrt{2}\,g\sin\theta$

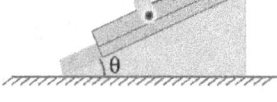

(d) $2g\sin\theta$

40. A time varying force $F = 2t$ is applied on a spool as shown in figure. The angular momentum of the spool at time t about bottommost point is

(a) $\dfrac{r^2t^2}{2}$

(b) $\dfrac{(R+r)^2}{r}t^2$

(c) $(R+r)t^2$

(d) none of these

Answer Key	32	(c)	34	(c)	36	(b)	38	(d)	40	(c)
Solution from page 97	33	(b)	35	(a)	37	(c)	39	(d)		

ROTATIONAL MECHANICS

41. A cubical block of side a moving with velocity v on a horizontal smooth plane as shown in figure. It hits a ridge at point O. The angular speed of the block after it hits O is :

(a) $\dfrac{3v}{4a}$

(b) $\dfrac{3v}{2a}$

(c) $\sqrt{\dfrac{3}{2}}\dfrac{v}{a}$

(d) zero

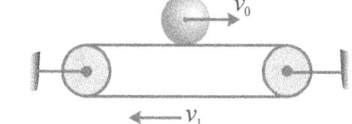

42. A sphere of radius r and mass m has a velocity v_0 directed to the left and no angular velocity as it is placed on a belt moving to the right with a constant velocity v_1. If after sliding on the belt the sphere is to have no linear velocity relative to the ground as it starts rolling on the belt without sliding. In terms of v_1, the velocity v_0 is

(a) $v_0 = \dfrac{2}{5}v_1$

(b) $v_0 = \dfrac{3}{5}v_1$

(c) $v_0 = \dfrac{1}{5}v_1$

(d) $v_0 = 3v_1$

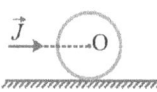

43. An impulse J is applied on a ring of mass m along a line passing through its centre O. The ring is placed on a rough horizontal surface. The linear velocity of centre of ring once it starts rolling without slipping is

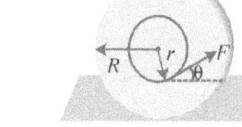

(a) J/m

(b) $J/2m$

(c) $J/3m$

(d) $J/4m$

44. A particle of mass 1 kg located at the position $(\hat{i}+\hat{j})$m has a velocity $2(\hat{i}-\hat{j}+\hat{k})$m/s. Its angular momentum about z-axis is

(a) zero kg-m²/s

(b) +4 kg-m²/s

(c) –4 kg-m²/s

(d) +8 kg-m²/s

45. The spool shown in figure is placed on a rough horizontal surface has inner radius r and outer radius R. The angle θ between the applied force and the horizontal can be varied. The critical angle (θ) for which the spool does not roll and remains stationary is given by

(a) $\sin\theta = \dfrac{r}{R}$

(b) $\cos\theta = \dfrac{r}{R}$

(c) $\cos\theta = \sqrt{\dfrac{r}{R}}$

(d) $\cos\theta = \dfrac{2r}{R}$

46. A hollow sphere of mass 2 kg is kept on a rough horizontal surface. A force on 10 N is applied at the centre of the sphere as shown in the figure. The minimum value of μ so that the sphere starts pure rolling is (g = 10 m/s²)

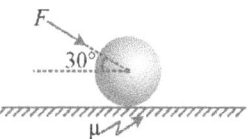

(a) $\sqrt{3}\times 0.16$

(b) $\sqrt{3}\times 0.08$

(c) $\sqrt{3}\times 0.1$

(d) none of these

47. A rigid body can be hinged about any point on the x-axis. When it is hinged such that the hinge is at a distance x, the moment of inertia is given by

$$I = 2x^2 - 12x + 15$$

The x-coordinate of centre of mass is

(a) $x = 0$

(b) $x = 1$

(c) $x = 2$

(d) $x = 3$

48. A thin uniform straight rod of mass 2 kg and length, 1 m is free to rotate about its upper end, when at rest, it recieves an impulse of 10 N-s at its lower end, normal to its length. The kinetic energy of rod after impact is

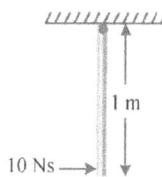

(a) 75 J

(b) 100 J

(c) 200 J

(d) 225 J

49. A uniform rod of mass M is hinged at its upper end. A particle of mass m moving horizontally strikes the rod at its mid point elastically. If the particle comes to rest after collision, then M/m is

(a) $\dfrac{2}{3}$

(b) $\dfrac{3}{4}$

(c) $\dfrac{4}{3}$

(d) none

50. A uniform sphere of radius R is placed on a rough horizontal surface and given a linear velocity v_0 and angular velocity ω_0 as shown. The sphere comes to rest after moving some distance to the right. It follows that :

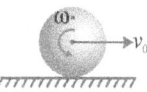

(a) $v_0 = \omega_0 R$

(b) $2v_0 = 5\omega_0 R$

(c) $5v_0 = 2\omega_0 R$

(d) $2v_0 = \omega_0 R$

Answer Key	41	(a)	43	(b)	45	(b)	47	(d)	49	(b)
Solution from page 97	42	(a)	44	(c)	46	(b)	48	(a)	50	(c)

51. A spool is pulled vertically by a constant force F ($<Mg$) as shown in figure. The frictional force is best represented in

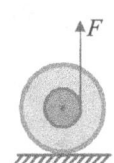

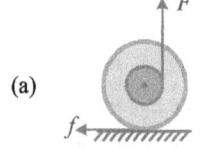
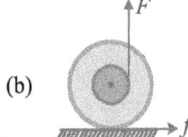

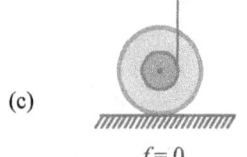

52. A uniform rod AB of length l and mass m is laying on a smooth table. A small particle of mass m strike the rod with a velocity is at C a distance x from the centre O. The particle comes to rest after collision. The value of x, so that point A of the rod remains stationary just after collision is

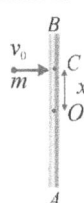

(a) $\ell/3$ (b) $\ell/6$
(c) $\ell/4$ (d) $\ell/12$

53. Two thin rods; each of mass m and length l are joined to form L shape as shown. The moment of inertia of rods about an axis passing through free end (O) of a rod end and perpendicular to both the ends is

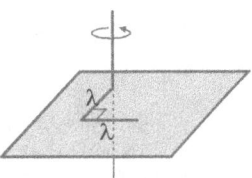

(a) $\dfrac{2}{7}ml^2$ (b) $\dfrac{ml^2}{6}$
(c) $\dfrac{5}{3}ml^2$ (d) ml^2

54. A block of mass $\dfrac{\sqrt{3}}{10}$ kg is placed on a rough horizontal surface as shown in the figure. A force of 1 N is applied at one end of the block and the block remains stationary. The normal force exerted by the surface on the block acts ($g = 10$ m/s^2)

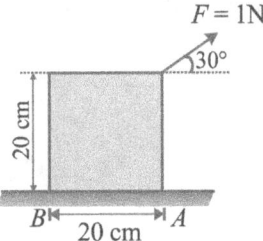

(a) through the centre of mass of the block
(b) through point A
(c) through point B
(d) through the point at a distance 5 cm. from A

55. Two particles A and B of mass m each and moving with velocity v, hit the ends of a rigid bar of the same mass m and length l simultaneously and stick to the bar as shown in the figure. The bar is kept on a smooth horizontal plane. The linear and angular speed of the system (bar + particle) after the collision are

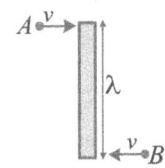

(a) $v_{cm} = 0, \omega = \dfrac{12}{7}\dfrac{v}{l}$ (b) $v_{cm} = 0, \omega = \dfrac{4v}{l}$
(c) $v_{cm} = 0, \omega = \dfrac{5v}{l}$ (d) $v_{cm} = 0, \omega = \dfrac{v}{5l}$

56. A straight uniform metal rod of length $3l$ is bent through angle as shown. The bent rod is then placed on a rough horizontal table. A light string is attached to the vertex of the right angle. The string is then pulled horizontally so that the rod translates at constant velocity. Then the angle α which the side $2l$ makes with string is

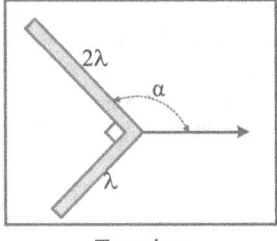

Top view

(a) $\pi - \tan^{-1}\dfrac{1}{2}$ (b) $\pi - \tan^{-1}\dfrac{1}{4}$
(c) $r - \sin^{-1}\dfrac{1}{2}$ (d) $\pi - \sin^{-1}\dfrac{1}{4}$

Answer Key	51	(a)	53	(c)	55	(a)
Solution from page 97	52	(b)	54	(b)	56	(d)

57. A ring of mass m and radius R has four particles each of mass m attached to the ring as shown in figure. The centre of ring has a speed v_0. The kinetic energy of the system is

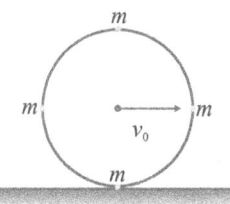

(a) mv_0^2 (b) $3mv_0^2$
(c) $5mv_0^2$ (d) $6mv_0^2$

58. A particle of mass m is attached to a disc of equal mass m by means of a slack string as shown. The disc is hinged about its centre c. on a horizontal smooth table. The particle is projected with initial velocity v_0. Its velocity when the string becomes taut is

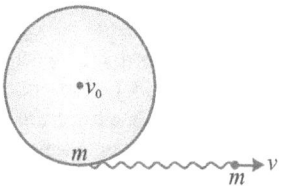

(a) v (b) $v/3$
(c) $2v/3$ (d) $\dfrac{3v}{4}$

59. Three identical rods are hinged at point A as shown. The angle made by rod AB with vertical is

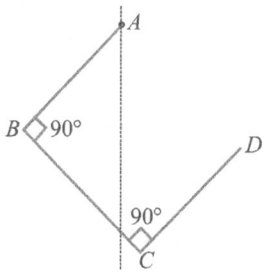

(a) $\tan^{-1}\left(\dfrac{1}{\sqrt{3}}\right)$ (b) $\tan^{-1}\left(\dfrac{3}{4}\right)$
(c) $\tan^{-1}(1)$ (d) $\tan^{-1}\left(\dfrac{4}{3}\right)$

60. A weight W rests on the bar AB as shown in figure. The cable connecting W and B passes over frictionless pulleys. If bar AB has negligible weight, the vertical component of reaction at A is

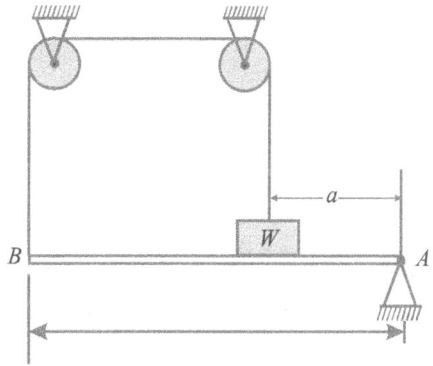

(a) $W\dfrac{L-a}{L+a}$ (b) $W\dfrac{L+a}{L-a}$
(c) $W\dfrac{L-2a}{L+a}$ (d) $W\dfrac{L-a}{L+2a}$

Answer Key
Solution from page 97

| 57 | (c) | 58 | (c) | 59 | (b) | 60 | (a) |

MECHANICS — MCQ Type 2 — Exercise 1.2

Multiple correct options

1. A body can have :
   (a) Three moment of inertia
   (b) Infinite number of moment of inertia
   (c) Infinite moment of inertia
   (d) None of the above

2. The moment of inertia of a body depends on :
   (a) mass of body
   (b) distribution of mass
   (c) location of axis of rotation
   (d) angular velocity of the body

3. In which of the following cases the angular momentum is constant:
   (a) a particle moving on a circular path with constant speed
   (b) a satellite revolving in elliptical orbit
   (c) earth revolving around the sun
   (d) during opening of a door by applying force on the handle

4. A man stands at the centre of a turn table and the turn table is rotating about its centre. If man walk away from the axis of rotation, then :
   (a) moment of inertia of system increases
   (b) angular momentum of system increases
   (c) angular velocity of system decreases
   (d) kinetic energy of system increases

5. Let F be a force acting on a particle having vector $\vec{r}$. Let τ be the torque of this force about the origin, then :
   (a) $\vec{r} \cdot \vec{\tau} = 0$
   (b) $\vec{F} \cdot \vec{\tau} = 0$
   (c) $\vec{r} \times \vec{\tau} = 0$
   (d) $\vec{r} \times \vec{\tau} \neq 0$

6. A ring of mass M and radius R can have moment of inertia :
   (a) MR^2
   (b) $2MR^2$
   (c) $3MR^2$
   (d) $4MR^2$

7. In the figure shown the lines of action and moment arms of two forces about the origin O. Imagining these forces to be acting on a rigid body pivoted at O, all vectors shown being the plane of the figure, the magnitude and direction of the resultant torque will be:

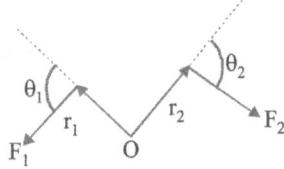

   (a) $(F_2 r_2 \sin \theta_2 - F_1 r_1 \sin \theta_1)$ out of the plane of the page.
   (b) $(F_1 r_1 \sin \theta_1 - F_2 r_2 \sin \theta_2)$ out of the plane of the page.
   (c) $(F_2 r_2 \sin \theta_2 - F_1 r_1 \sin \theta_1)$ in to the plane of the page.
   (d) Zero

8. Let I_A and I_B be moments of inertia of a body about cm and B respectively. Then
   (a) $I_A < I_B$
   (b) If the axes are parallel, $I_A < I_B$
   (c) If the axes are not parallel, $I_A \leq I_B$
   (d) none of the above

9. When a sphere of radius R is thrown on a rough horizontal surface with velocity v_0, then
   (a) Its linear velocity decreases and becomes zero
   (b) Its angular velocity increases to $\dfrac{v_0}{R}$
   (c) Its angular velocity increases but can not be equal to $\dfrac{v_0}{R}$
   (d) the frictional force acts in backward direction of v_0.

10. In front-wheel drive cars, the engine rotates the front wheels and the rear wheels rotate only because the car moves. If such a car accelerates on a horizontal road, the frictional force
    (a) on the front wheels is in the forward direction
    (b) on the rear wheels is in the beckward direction
    (c) on the fornt wheels has larger magnitude than the rear wheels
    (d) on the car in backward direction

11. A sphre is rolled on a rough horizontal surface. It gradually shows down and stops. The force of friction tries to
    (a) decrease the linear velocity
    (b) increases the angular velocity
    (c) increase the angular momentum
    (d) decrease the linear momentum.

12. A particle is moving along an expanding spiral in such a manner that magnitude of normal acceleration of particle remains constant. Choose the correct options
    (a) Linear speed of particle is increasing
    (b) Linear speed of particle is decreasing
    (c) Angular speed of paricle is increasing
    (d) Angular speed of particle is decreasing

13. A wheel is rolling on a horizontal plane without slipping. At a certain instant, it has velocity 'v' and acceleration 'a' of c.m. as shown in the figure. Acceleration of

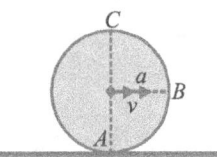

    (a) A is vertically upwards
    (b) B may be vertically downwards
    (c) C cannot be horizontal
    (d) Some point on the rim may be horizontal leftwards.

Answer Key (Sol. from page 103)

1	(b, c)	5	(a, b, d)	9	(c, d)	13	(a, b, c, d)
2	(a, b, c)	6	(a, b, c, d)	10	(a, b, c)		
3	(a, b, c)	7	(b, c)	11	(a, b, d)		
4	(a, c)	8	(b, c)	12	(a, d)		

14. A disc is given an initial angular velocity ω_0 and placed on rough horizontal surface as shown. The quantities which will not depend on the coefficient of friction is/are

    (a) The time until rolling begins.
    (b) The displacement of the disc until rolling begins.
    (c) The velocity when rolling begins.
    (d) The work done by the force of friction.

15. The angular acceleration of the toppling pole shown in figure is given by $\alpha = k \sin \theta$, where θ is the angle between the axis of the pole and the vertical, and k is a constant. The pole starts from rest at $\theta = 0$. Choose the correct options

    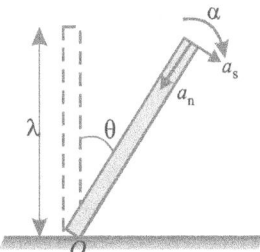

    (a) The tangential acceleration of the upper end of the pole is $\ell k \sin \theta$
    (b) The centripetal acceleration of the upper end of the pole is $2k\ell (1 - \cos \theta)$
    (c) The tangential acceleration of the upper end of the pole is $2k\ell (1 - \cos \theta)$
    (d) The centripetal acceleration of the upper end of the pole is $\ell k \sin \theta$

16. A particle of mass m is projected with a velocity v, making an angle 45° with the horizontal. The magnitude of the angular momentum of the particle about the point of projection when the particle is at its maximum height h is

    (a) zero
    (b) $\dfrac{mv^3}{4\sqrt{2}g}$
    (c) $\dfrac{mv^3}{\sqrt{2}g}$
    (d) $m\sqrt{2gh^3}$

17. A sphere is rolling without slipping on a fixed horizontal plane surface. In figure, A is the point of contact, B is the centre of the sphere and C is its topmost point. Then

    (a) $\vec{v}_C - \vec{v}_A = 2(\vec{v}_B - \vec{v}_C)$
    (b) $\vec{v}_C - \vec{v}_B = \vec{v}_B - \vec{v}_A$
    (c) $|\vec{v}_C - \vec{v}_A| = 2|\vec{v}_B - \vec{v}_C|$
    (d) $|\vec{v}_C - \vec{v}_A| = 4|\vec{v}_B|$

18. In the figure shown, the plank is being pulled to the right with a constant velocity v. If the cylinder does not slip, then

    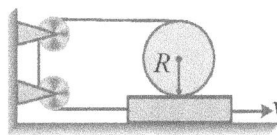

    (a) the speed of the centre of mass of the cylinder is $2v$.
    (b) the speed of the centre of mass of the cylinder is zero
    (c) the angular velocity of the cylinder is v/R
    (d) the angular velocity of the cylinder is zero

19. If a cylinder is rolling down the incline with sliding
    (a) after sometime it may start pure rolling
    (b) after some time it will start pure rolling
    (c) it may be possible that it will never start pure rolling
    (d) none of these

20. The moment of inertia of a thin square plate ABCD of uniform thickness about an axis passing through the centre O and perpendicular to the plane of the plate is

    (a) $I_1 + I_3$
    (b) $I_1 + 2I_2$
    (c) $I_1 + I_2$
    (d) $\dfrac{I_1 + I_2 + I_3 + I_4}{2}$

    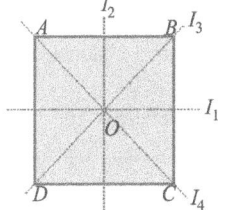

21. A small ball is connected to a block by a light string of length ℓ. Both are initially on the ground. There is sufficeint friction on the ground to prevent the block from slipping. The ball is projected vertically up with a velocity u, where $2g\ell < u^2 < 3g\ell$. The centre of mass of the block + ball system is C.

    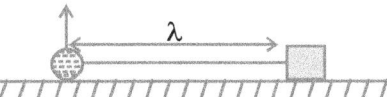

    (a) C will move along a circle.
    (b) C will move along a parabola.
    (c) C will move along a straight line.
    (d) The horizontal component of the velocity of the ball will be maximum when the string makes an angle $\theta = \sin^{-1}(u^2/3g\ell)$ with the horizontal

22. The torque τ on a body about a given point is found to be equal to $A \times L$ where A is a constant vector, and L is the angular momentum of the body about that point. From this it follows that

    (a) $\dfrac{d\mathbf{L}}{dt}$ is perpendicular to $\mathbf{L}$ at all instants of time.
    (b) the component of $\mathbf{L}$ in the direction of $\mathbf{A}$ does not change with time.
    (c) the magnitude of $\mathbf{L}$ does not change with time.
    (d) $\mathbf{L}$ does not change with time

Answer Key Sol. from page 103	14	(c, d)	17	(b, c)	20	(a, c, d)
	15	(a, b)	18	(b, c)	21	(a, d)
	16	(b, d)	19	(a, c)	22	(a, b, c)

MECHANICS — Statement Questions — Exercise 1.3

Read the two statements carefully to mark the correct option out of the options given below:
(a) If both the statements are true and the *statement - 2* is the correct explanation of *statement - 1*.
(b) If both the statements are true but *statement - 2* is not the correct explanation of the *statement - 1*.
(c) If *statement - 1* true but *statement - 2* is false.
(d) If *statement - 1* is false but *statement - 2* is true.

1. **Statement - 1**
   It is harder to open and shut the door if we apply force close to the hinge.
   Statement - 2
   Torque is minimum about the hinge.

2. **Statement - 1**
   Torque is equal to rate of change of angular momentum.
   Statement - 2
   Angular momentum depends on moment of inertia and angular velocity.

3. **Statement - 1**
   The radius of gyration of a circular ring is equal to the radius of the ring.
   Statement - 2
   $I = mk^2$, where k is the radius of gyration.

4. **Statement - 1**
   A person standing on a rotating table when suddenly folds his arms, the platform moves fast.
   Statement - 2
   The angular momentum in the process remain constant.

5. **Statement - 1**
   Moment of inertia of a particle is same, whatever be the axis of rotation.
   Statement - 2
   Moment of inertia depends on mass and distance of the particle from the axis.

6. **Statement - 1**
   In a rotating body, $a = \alpha r$ and $v = \omega r$, so $\dfrac{a}{\alpha} = \dfrac{v}{\omega}$.
   Statement - 2
   It is possible to equate $\dfrac{a+\alpha}{a-\alpha} = \dfrac{v+\omega}{v-\omega}$.

7. **Statement - 1**
   The torque of the weight of any body about any vertical line is always zero.
   Statement - 2
   Moment arm about vertical line is zero.

8. **Statement - 1**
   The sum of all the forces acting on a particle is zero.
   Statement - 2
   The body must be in equilibrium.

9. **Statement - 1**
   A rod placed on two rigid support be in equilibrium..
   Statement - 2
   The net torque about any point must be zero.

10. **Statement - 1**
    When tall buildings are constructed on earth, the duration of day-night slightly increases.
    Statement - 2
    Moment of inertia of earth about the axis of rotation increases.

11. **Statement - 1**
    If the ice at poles melts, the moment of inertia of earth increases.
    Statement - 2
    The angular momentum of the earth about axis of rotation increases.

12. **Statement - 1**
    The total kinetic energy of a rolling ring is the twice of its translational kinetic energy.
    Statement - 2
    For any body rolling kinetic energy is twice of its translational kinetic energy

13. **Statement - 1**
    The total kinetic energy of a rolling ring is the twice of its translational kinetic energy.
    Statement - 2
    Rolling kinetic energy is the sum of translational kinetic energy and rotational kinetic energy.

14. **Statement - 1**
    On smooth inclined plane rolling motion is not possible.
    Statement - 2
    Friction does no work on a rolling body on inclined plane.

Answer Key (Sol. from page 104)

1	(a)	3	(a)	5	(d)	7	(a)	9	(b)	11	(c)	13	(a)
2	(b)	4	(a)	6	(c)	8	(c)	10	(a)	12	(c)	14	(b)

ROTATIONAL MECHANICS

MECHANICS — Passage & Matrix — Exercise 1.4

PASSAGES

Passage for (Q. 1 - 3):
Two disc A and B are mounted coaxially on a vertical axle. The discs have moment of inertia I and $2I$ respectively about the common axis. Disc A is imparted an initial angular velocity 2ω using the entire potential energy of a spring compressed by a distance x_1. Disc B is imparted an angular velocity ω by a spring having the same spring constant and compressed by a distance x_2. Both the discs rotate in the clockwise direction.

1. The ratio x_1/x_2 is
   (a) $\dfrac{1}{2}$
   (b) $\dfrac{1}{\sqrt{2}}$
   (c) $\sqrt{2}$
   (d) 2

2. When disc B is brought in contact with disc A they acquire a common angular velocity in time t. The average frictional torque on one disc by the other during this peirod is
   (a) $\dfrac{2I\omega}{3t}$
   (b) $\dfrac{9I\omega}{2t}$
   (c) $\dfrac{9I\omega}{4t}$
   (d) $\dfrac{3I\omega}{2t}$

3. The loss of kinetic energy in the above process is
   (a) $\dfrac{1}{2}I\omega^2$
   (b) $\dfrac{1}{3}I\omega^2$
   (c) $\dfrac{1}{4}I\omega^2$
   (d) $\dfrac{1}{5}I\omega^2$

Passage for (Q. 4 - 6):
A non uniform cylinder of mass $2M$ and radius $2R$ is released from the position shown. The moment of inertia of the cylinder about longitudinal axis passing through A is $4MR^2$. Point B (distance R from the axis) is the centre of mass of the cylinder. Friction between the cylinder and the horizontal surface is sufficient to prevent slipping.

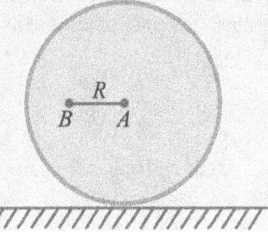

4. Initial angular acceleration of the cylinder is
   (a) g/R
   (b) $\dfrac{g}{3R}$
   (c) $\dfrac{g}{5R}$
   (d) $\dfrac{g}{6R}$

5. Frictional force acting on the cylinder just after its release is
   (a) Mg
   (b) $\dfrac{Mg}{3}$
   (c) $\dfrac{2Mg}{3}$
   (d) $\dfrac{4Mg}{7}$

6. Angular speed of the cylinder as the line AB becomes vertical is
   (a) $\sqrt{\dfrac{g}{R}}$
   (b) $\sqrt{\dfrac{g}{3R}}$
   (c) $\sqrt{\dfrac{g}{5R}}$
   (d) $\sqrt{\dfrac{g}{6R}}$

Passage for (Q. 7 - 9):
Consider a cylinder of mass $M = 1$ kg and radius $R = 1$ m lying on a rough horizontal plane. It has a plank lying on its top as shown in the figure.

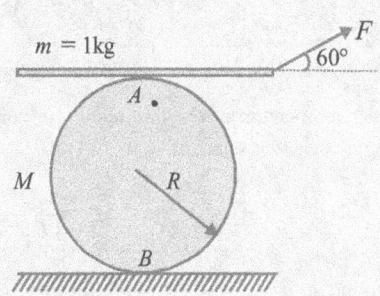

A force $F = 55$ N is applied on the plank such that the plank moves and causes the cylinder to roll. The plank always remains horizontal. There is no slipping at any point of contact.

7. Calculate the acceleration of cylinder.
   (a) 20 m/s^2
   (b) 10 m/s^2
   (c) 5 m/s^2
   (d) None of these

8. Find the value of frictional force at A
   (a) 7.5 N
   (b) 5.0 N
   (c) 2.5 N
   (d) None of these

9. Find the value of frictional force at B
   (a) 7.5 N
   (b) 5.0 N
   (c) 2.5 N
   (d) None of these

Answer Key (Sol. from page 104)

1	(c)	3	(b)	5	(c)	7	(b)	9	(c)
2	(a)	4	(d)	6	(a)	8	(a)		

Passage for (Q. 10 - 12) :
A disc of radius R is spun to an angular speed ω_0 about its axis and then imparted a horizontal velocity $v_0 = \dfrac{\omega_0 R}{4}$ (at $t = 0$) with its plane remaining vertical. The coefficient of friction between the disc and plane is μ. The direction of v_0 and ω_0 are shown in the figure.

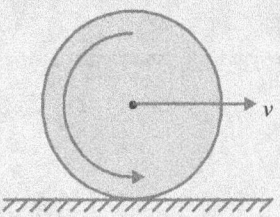

10. The disc will return to starting point at time
    (a) $\left(\dfrac{25}{48}\right)\dfrac{R\omega_0}{\mu g}$ (b) $\dfrac{5}{12}\dfrac{R\omega_0}{\mu g}$
    (c) $\dfrac{5}{48}\dfrac{R\omega_0}{\mu g}$ (d) $\dfrac{R\omega_0}{6\mu g}$

11. The disc will start rolling without slipping at time
    (a) $\dfrac{R\omega_0}{6\mu g}$ (b) $\dfrac{5R\omega_0}{12\mu g}$
    (c) $\dfrac{R\omega_0}{\mu g}$ (d) $\dfrac{R\omega_0}{4\mu g}$

12. The angular momentum of the disc about the point of contact, when slipping ceases is equal to
    (a) $MR^2 \dfrac{\omega_0}{2}$ (b) $MR^2 \dfrac{\omega_0}{12}$
    (c) $MR^2 \dfrac{\omega_0}{4}$ (d) $MR^2 \dfrac{\omega_0}{3}$

Passage for (Q. 13 - 15) :
A uniform rod AB of length 2ℓ falls without rotation on a smooth horizontal surface at an angle θ to the horizontal. The speed of rod just before collision is v_0 and the collision is elastic. The magnitude of the angular velocity and magnitude of the velocity of centre of mass after collision are ω and v' respectively.

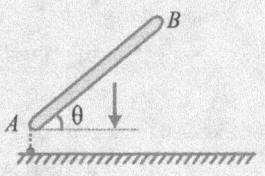

13. The direction of force of impact on the rod is
    (a) along the surface   (b) vertically upward
    (c) along the rod   (d) any direction is possible

14. The relation between v_0, ω and v' is
    (a) $v_0 = v'$ (b) $v_0 = v' + \ell\omega$
    (c) $v_0 = v' - \ell\omega$ (d) $v_0 = v' + \ell\omega \cos\theta$.

15. The angular momentum before collision about the point on the ground at which the rod strikes has the magnitude (m : mass of rod)
    (a) $\dfrac{mv_0\ell}{2}$ (b) $mv_0\ell \cos\theta$
    (c) $\dfrac{mv_0\ell}{2\cos\theta}$ (d) $\left(\dfrac{m\ell}{3}\right)\dfrac{v_0}{\ell}$.

Passage for (Q. 16 - 18) :
A rectangular rigid fixed block has a long horizontal edge. A solid homogeneous cylinder of radius R is placed horizontally at rest with its length parallel to edge such that the axis of the cylinder and the edge O of the block are in the same vertical plane as shown in the figure. There is sufficient friction present at the edge so that a very small displacement causes the cylinder to roll of the edge without slipping.

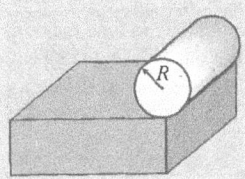

16. Determine the angle θ through which the cylinder rotates before it leave contact with the edge.
    (a) $\cos^{-1}(3/4)$ (b) $\cos^{-1}(4/7)$
    (c) $\cos^{-1}(5/7)$ (d) $\sin^{-1}(4/5)$

17. Determine the speed of the centre of mass of the cylinder before leaving contact with edge.
    (a) $\sqrt{3gR/7}$ (b) $\sqrt{2gR}$
    (c) $\sqrt{(4gR/7)}$ (d) $\sqrt{7/4gR}$

18. Determine the ratio of the translational to rotational kinetic energies of the cylinder when its centre of mass is in horizontal line with its edge.
    (a) 3   (b) 6
    (c) 4   (d) 2

Passage for (Q. 19 - 21) :
A uniform flat disc of mass M and radius R rotates about a horizontal axis through its centre with angular speed ω_0

| Answer Key | 10 | (a) | 12 | (c) | 14 | (d) | 16 | (b) | 18 | (b) |
| Sol. from page 104 | 11 | (b) | 13 | (b) | 15 | (b) | 17 | (c) | | |

19. What is its angular momentum?

    (a) $\frac{1}{2}MR^2\omega_0$ (b) $MR^2\omega_0$

    (c) $2MR^2\omega_0$ (d) $\frac{2}{3}MR^2\omega_0$

20. A chip of mass m breaks off the edge of the disc at an instant such that the chip rises vertically about the point at which it broke off. How high above the point does it rise before starting to fall?

    (a) $h = \frac{R^2\omega_0^2}{g}$ (b) $h = \frac{2R^2\omega_0^2}{g}$

    (c) $h = \frac{R^2\omega_0^2}{2g}$ (d) $h = \frac{R^2\omega_0^2}{3g}$

21. What is the final angular momentum and energy of the disc?

    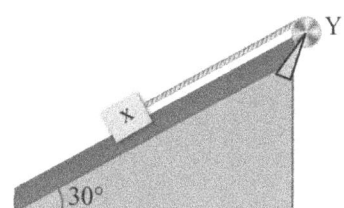

    (a) $MR^2\omega_0, \frac{1}{2}MR^2\omega^2$ (b) $mR^2\omega_0, \frac{1}{2}mR^2\omega_0$

    (c) $\left(\frac{M}{2}-m\right)R^2\omega_0, \left(\frac{M}{2}-m\right)R^2\omega_0^2$

    (d) $\left(\frac{M}{2}-m\right)R^2\omega_0, \frac{1}{2}\left[\left(\frac{M}{2}-m\right)R^2\omega_0^2\right]$

Passage for (Q. 22 - 24) :
A rod AB of mass M and length L is lying on a horizontal frictionless surface. A particle of mass m travelling along the surface hits the end A of the rod with a velocity v_0 in a direction perpendicular to AB. The collision is completely elastic. After the collision the particle comes to rest.

22. Find the ratio m/M.
    (a) 1/4 (b) 1/3
    (c) 1/2 (d) 3/4

23. A point P on the rod is at rest immediately after the collision. Find the distance AP.
    (a) 3L/4 (b) (2/3) L
    (c) L/2 (d) 3L/8

24. Find the linear speed of the point P at a time $\pi/3v_0$ after the collision.

    (a) $v_0/2$ (b) $\sqrt{3}v_0/2$
    (c) $v_0/4)\sqrt{2}$ (d) $v_0/2\sqrt{2}$

Passage for (Q. 25 - 27) :
A ring of mass m and radius R is rolling on a rough horizontal surface (coefficient friction µ) with constant velocity. The velocity of the point P is v.

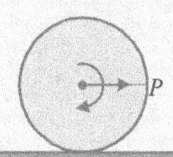

25. The angular velocity of the ring is

    (a) $\frac{v}{R}$ (b) $\frac{v}{2R}$

    (c) $\frac{v}{\sqrt{2}R}$ (d) $\frac{\sqrt{2}v}{R}$

26. The kinetic energy of ring is

    (a) $\frac{1}{2}mv^2$ (b) mv^2

    (c) $\frac{3}{2}mv^2$ (d) $2mv^2$

27. The work done by friction on the ring in a displacement πR is :
    (a) µmg × R (b) µmg × 2πR
    (c) zero (d) none of these

Passage for (Q. 28 - 30) :
A cylinder of mass 6 kg is suspended through two ideal strings wrapped around it symmetrically as shown in the figure. The strings are taut and the cylinder is initially at rest. Take g = 10 m/s².

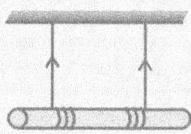

28. The acceleration of the C.M. of the cylinder is

    (a) $\frac{20}{3}$ m/s² (b) 10 m/s²

    (b) $\frac{10}{3}$ m/s² (d) 12 m/s²

29. The tension in one of the strings is
    (a) 60 N (b) 40 N
    (c) 10 N (d) 24 N

30. The velocity of the center of the cylinder after at falls through a height 7.5 m is
    (a) $10\sqrt{3}$ m/s (b) 10 m/s
    (c) $6\sqrt{5}$ m/s (d) $5\sqrt{3}$ m/s

Answer Key	19	(a)	21	(d)	23	(b)	25	(c)	27	(c)	29	(c)
Sol. from page 104	20	(c)	22	(a)	24	(c)	26	(a)	28	(a)	30	(b)

MECHANICS, THERMODYNAMICS & WAVES

Passage for (Q. 31 - 33):
A disc rolls over a horizontal surface with velocity and acceleration as shown in the fig. P_1 and P_2 are two points on the disc ($OP_1 = OP_2 = R/2$)

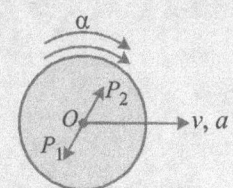

31. The speed of point P_1 with respect to P_2 is
    (a) $\frac{R}{2}\omega + v$
    (b) $\frac{3}{2}R\omega$
    (c) $\frac{R}{2}\omega$
    (d) $\frac{R}{3}\omega$

32. If the disc has mass m and radius R then the torque acting on the disc about centre of mass at the given instant is
    (a) $\frac{3}{2}mR^2\alpha$
    (b) $\frac{mR^2}{2}\alpha$
    (c) $\frac{mR^2}{3}\alpha$
    (d) data insufficient

33. The magnitude of acceleration of the point of disc, which is in contact with ground is
    (a) zero
    (b) $a = R\alpha$
    (c) $2a$
    (d) none of these

MATRIX MATCHING

34. Match **Column I** with **Column II** and select the correct answer:

Column-I (Quantity)		Column-II (Expression)
A. Angular momentum	(p)	$\vec{r} \times (m\vec{v})$
B. Impulse	(q)	$\frac{1}{2}I\omega^2$
C. Torque	(r)	$\vec{r} \times \vec{F}$
D. Energy	(s)	$m\Delta\vec{v}$

35. Match the following columns.

Column-I (Object)		Column-II (Moment of inertia about any axis)
A. ring	(p)	$\frac{mR^2}{4}$
B. sphere	(q)	$\frac{mR^2}{2}$
C. disc	(r)	$\frac{3}{2}mR^2$
D. cylinder	(s)	$2mR^2$

36. Match **Column I** (Body rolling on a surface without slipping) with **Column II** (Ratio of Translational energy to Rotational energy) and select the correct answer using the codes given below:

Column I		Column II
A. Circular ring	(p)	1/2
B. Circular disc	(q)	1
C. Solid sphere	(r)	3/2
D. Spherical shell	(s)	2
	(t)	5/2

Answer Key (Sol. from page 104)

| 31 | (c) | 32 | (b) | 33 | (d) | 34 | A→(p); B→(s); C→(r); D→(q) |
| 35 | A→(q,r,s); B→(q,r,s); C→(p,q,r,s); D→(p,q,r,s) | | | | | 36 | A→q; B→s; C→t; D→r |

37. Match the following columns.
    Column-I
    (*Devices*)
    A. A planet around sun in circular orbit
    B. A planet around sun in elliptical orbit

    Column-II
    (p) Angular momentum constant
    (q) Angular momentum changes

    (r) Kinetic energy constant

    C.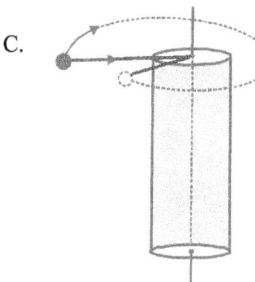
    A small particle is rotating in horizontal plane with decreasing radius in the device shown

    D.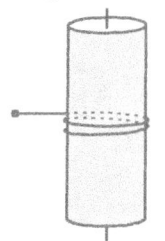
    (s) Kinetic energy changes

    A small particle is rotating in horizontal plane with decreasing radius in the device shown

38. For the following statements, except gravity and contact force between the contact surfaces, no other force is acting on the body.
    Column-I
    A. When a sphere is in pure-rolling on a fixed horizontal surface
    B. When a cylinder is in pure rolling on a fixed inclined plane in upward direction then friction force acts in
    C. When a cylinder is in pure rolling down a fixed incline plane, friction force acts is
    D. When a sphere of radius R is rolling with slipping on a fixed horizontal surface, the relation between v_{cm} and ω is

    Column-II
    (p) Upward direction
    (q) $v_{cm} > R\omega$
    (r) $v_{cm} < R\omega$
    (s) No frictional force acts

39. In each, there is sufficient friction for regular rigid uniform body to undergo pure rolling on a rigid on a horizontal surface. Now match the column I and II.
    Column-I

    A.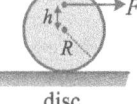

    Column-II
    (p) The direction of static friction may be backward or static friction may be forward or friction may be zero

    B.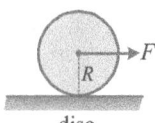
    (q) The direction of static friction is towards backward

    C.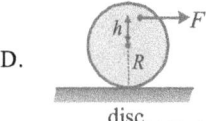
    (r) The angular acceleration will be clockwise

    D.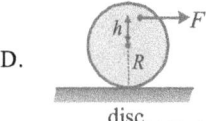
    (s) Acceleration of the centre mass will be along the direction of F

Answer Key	37	A → (p, r); B → (p, s); C → (p, s); D → (q, r)	38	A → (s); B → (p); C → (p); D → (q, r)
Sol. from page 104	39	A → (p, s, r); B → (q, r, s); C → (q, r, s); D → (p, r, s)		

MECHANICS, THERMODYNAMICS & WAVES

40. Match **Column I** with **Column II** and select the correct answer :

Column I

A. Moment of Inertia of a solid uniform sphere about the diameter

B. Moment of inertia of a thin uniform spherical shell about the tangent

C. Moment of inertia of a uniform disc through centre of a mass and perpendicular to plane of the disc

D. Moment of inertia of disc about tangent in the plane of disc.

Column II

(p) MR^2

(q) $\dfrac{1}{2} MR^2$

(r) $\dfrac{5}{3} MR^2$

(s) $\dfrac{2}{5} MR^2$

(t) $\dfrac{5}{4} MR^2$

41. The following figures shows different bodies which are either free to rotate or translate on smooth horizontal surface. An impulse J is given to the bodies in the direction shown in figure. Match the columns:

Column I

A.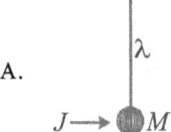
Dumbell with a massless rod placed on smooth table

B.

C.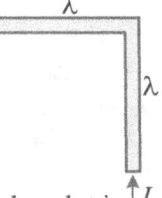
L-shaped strip not fixed anywhere

D.
L-shaped strip with hinge

Column II

(p) Translation

(q) Rotation occurs

(r) Angular momentum about CM increases

(s) Linear momentum increses.

Answer Key — Sol. from page 104

| 40 | A → s, ; B → r ; C → q ; D → t |
| 41 | A → p, q, r, s ; B → p, s ; C → p, q, r, s ; D → q, r, s |

42. A rigid body of mass *M* and radius *R* rolls without slipping on an inclined plane of inclination θ, under gravity. Match the type of body with magnitude of the force of friction.

	Column I		Column II
A.	For ring	(p)	$\dfrac{Mg \sin\theta}{2.5}$
B.	For solid sphere	(q)	$\dfrac{Mg \sin\theta}{3}$
C.	For solid cylinder	(r)	$\dfrac{Mg \sin\theta}{3.5}$
D.	For hollow spherical shell	(s)	$\dfrac{Mg \sin\theta}{2}$

43. A uniform solid cylinder of mass m and radius *R* is placed on a rough horizontal surface where friction is sufficient to provide pure rolling. A horizontal force of magnitude *F* is applied on cylinder at different positions with respect to its centre *O* in each of four situations of column-I, due to which magnitude of acceleration of centre of mass of cylinder is '*a*'. Match the appropriate results in column-II for conditions of column-I.

Column I

A.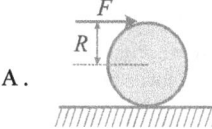

B.

C.

D.

Column II

(p) Friction force on cylinder will not be zero

(q) $a = \dfrac{F}{m}$

(r) $a \neq \dfrac{F}{m}$

(s) the direction of friction force acting on cylinder is towards left

Answer Key (Sol. from page 104)

42. A→ s; B→ r; C→ q; D → p

43. A→ p, r; B →q, r; C→ p, r, s; D→ p, r, s

MECHANICS — Subjective Integer Type — Exercise 1.5

Solution from page 108

1. A hoop of radius 2 m weighs 100 kg. It rolls along a horizontal floor so that its centre of mass has a speed of 20 cm/s. How much work has to be done to stop it?

   Ans. 4 J.

2. A cord of negligible mass is wound round the rim of a fly wheel of mass 20 kg and radius 20 cm. A steady pull of 25 N is applied on the cord as shown in figure. The flywheel is mounted on a horizontal axle with frictionless bearings.
   (a) Compute the angular acceleration of the wheel.
   (b) Find the work done by the pull, when 2 m of the cord is unwound.
   (c) Find also the kinetic energy of the wheel at this point. Assume that the wheel starts from rest.
   (d) Compare answers to parts (b) and (c).

   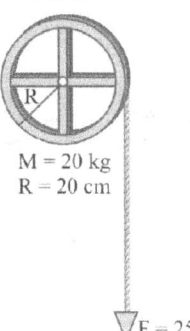

   Ans. (a) 12.5 rad/s^2 (b) 50 J (c) 50 J (d) there is no loss of energy due to friction.

3. Wheels A and B in figure are connected by a belt that does not slip. The radius of wheel B is three times the radius of wheel A. What would be the ratio of rotational inertias $\dfrac{I_A}{I_B}$ if (a) both wheels had the same momenta (b) both wheels had the same rotational kinetic energy?

   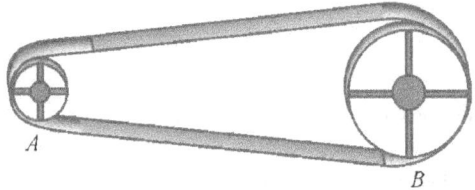

   Ans. (a) 1/3 (b) 1/9

4. The rigid body shown in figure consists of three particles connected by massless rods. It is to be rotated about an axis perpendicular to its plane through point P. If $M = 0.40$ kg, $a = 30$ cm, and $b = 50$ cm, how much work is required to take the body from rest to an angular speed of 5.0 rad/s?

   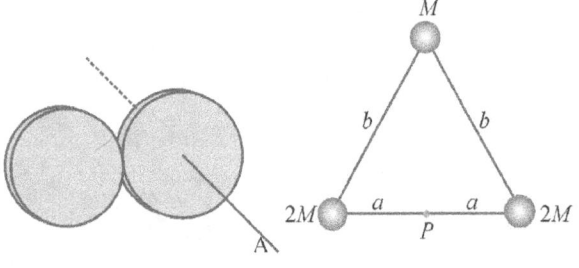

   Ans. $W = \dfrac{1}{2} M (3a^2 + b^2) \omega^2 = 2.6$ J

5. Two flywheels, A and B, are mounted on shaft that can be connected or disconnected by a friction clutch C. The moment of inertia of wheel A is 8 kg.m^2. With the clutch disengaged wheel A is brought upto an angular velocity of 600 rev/min. Wheel B is initially at rest. The clutch is now engaged, accelerating B and decelerating A, until both wheels have the same angular velocity. The final angular velocity of the system is 400 rev/min.
   (a) What was the moment of inertia of wheel B?
   (b) How much mechanical energy was lost in the process? (Neglect all bearing friction)

   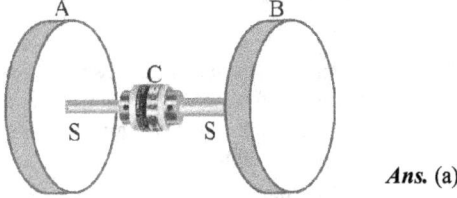

   Ans. (a) 4 kg-m^2, (b) 5200 J

6. A thin uniform rod AB of mass $m = 1.0$ kg moves translationally with acceleration $a = 2.0$ m/s^2 due to two antiparallel forces F_1 and F_2 as shown in figure. The distance between the points at which these forces are applied is equal to $y = 20$ cm. Besides, it is known that $F_2 = 5.0$ N. Find the length of the rod.

   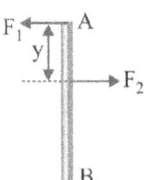

   Ans. $\ell = \dfrac{2yF_2}{ma} = 1.0$ m.

7. A flywheel with the initial angular velocity 90 rad/sec decelerates due to the forces whose moment relative to the axis is proportional to the square root of its angular velocity. Find the mean angular velocity of the flywheel averaged over the total deceleration time.

   Ans. 30

8. A uniform cylinder of mass $m = 8.0$ kg and radius $R = 1.3$ cm as shown in the figure starts descending at a moment $t = 0$ due to gravity. Neglecting the mass of the thread, find;
   (a) the tension of each thread and the angular acceleration of the cylinder,
   (b) the time dependence of the instantaneous power developed by the gravitational force.

   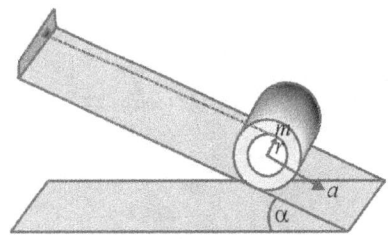

   Ans. $T = \dfrac{1}{6} mg = 13$ N, $\alpha = \dfrac{2}{3}\dfrac{g}{R} = 5.10^2$ rad/s^2 (b) $P = \dfrac{2}{3} m g^2 t$

ROTATIONAL MECHANICS

9. A uniform rod of mass m = 5.0 kg length L = 90 cm rests on a smooth horizontal surface. One of the ends of the rod is struck with the impulse J = 3.0 N. s in a horizontal direction perpendicular to the rod. As a result the rod obtains the momentum p = 3.0 N.s. Find the force with which one half of the rod will act on the other in the process of motion.

   Ans. $F = \dfrac{9J^2}{2mL} = 9N$

10. A roller of diameter 6 cm rides between two horizontal bars moving in opposite direction as shown in figure. Find the distance of defining the position of the path of the instantaneous centre of rotation of the roller. (Assume no slip at points of contact P and Q)

    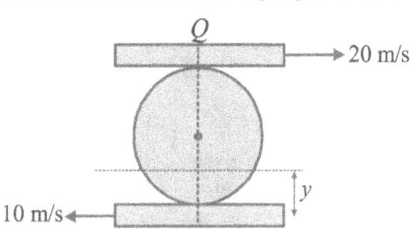

    Ans. 2 cm

MECHANICS — Subjective

Exercise 1.6
Solution from page 110

1. A solid cylinder rolls up an inclined plane of angle of inclination 30^0. At the bottom of the inclined plane the centre of mass of the cylinder has a speed of 5 m/s.
   (a) How far will the cylinder go up the plane ?
   (b) How long will it take to return to the bottom ?

   Ans. (a) 3.8 m (b) 3.0 s.

2. A flywheel of mass 25 kg has a radius of 0.2 m. It is making 240 rpm. What is the torque necessary to bring it to rest in 20 s ? If the torque is due to a force applied tangentially on the rim of the flywheel, what is the magnitude of the force ?

   Ans. $-(\pi/5)$ Nm, π N.

3. A solid disc and a ring, both of radius 10 cm are placed on a horizontal table simultaneously, with initial angular speed equal to 10π rad/s. Which of the two will start to roll earlier ? The coefficient of kinetic friction is $\mu_k = 0.2$.

   Ans. $t_{disc} = 0.53$ s, $t_{ring} = 0.80$ s; Disc begins to roll earlier than the ring.

4. A man stands on a rotating platform, with his arms stretched horizontally holding a 5 kg weight in each hand. The angular speed of the platform is 30 revolutions per minute. The man then brings his arms close to his body with the distance of each weight from the axis changing from 90 cm to 20 cm. The moment of inertia of the man together with the platform may be taken to be constant and equal to 7.6 kg m^2.
   (a) What is his new angular speed ?
   (b) Is kinetic energy conserved in the process ? If not, from where does the change come about ?

   Ans. (a) 59 rpm (b) 1.97.

5. A rigid body rotates about a fixed axis with variable angular velocity equal to $\omega = a - bt$, where a and b are constant. Find the angle through which it rotates before it comes to rest.

   Ans. $a^2/2b$

6. The four bodies shown in figure have equal masses m. Body A is a solid cylinder of radius R. Body B is a hollow thin cylinder of radius R. Body C is a solid square with length of side = 2R. Body D as the same size as C, but hollow i.e., made up of four thin sticks. The bodies have axis of rotation perpendicular to page and through the centre of gravity of each body.
   (a) Which body has the smallest moment of inertia ?
   (b) Which body has the largest moment of inertia ?

   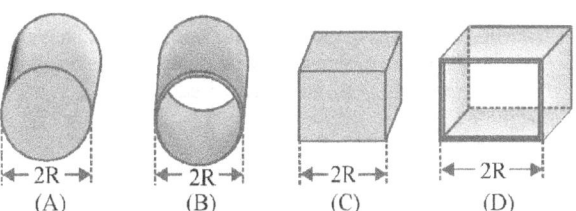

   Ans. (a) A (b) D

7. Two thin disks, each of mass 4.0 kg and radius 0.40 m, are attached as shown in figure to form a rigid body. What is the rotational inertia of this body about an axis A that is perpendicular to the plane of the disks and passes through the centre of one of the disks?

   Ans. $5mR^2 = 3.20$ kg m^2

8. A 60 kg grind stone is 1 m in diameter and has a moment of inertia of 3.75 kg. m^2. A tool is pressed down on the rim with a normal force of 50 N. The coefficient of sliding friction between the tool and stone is 0.60 and there is a constant frictional torque of 5 N-m between the axle of the stone and its bearings.
   (a) How much force must be applied normally at the end of a crank handle 0.5 m long to bring the stone from rest to 120 rev/min in 9s?
   (b) After attaining a speed of 120 rev/min, what must the normal force at the end of the handle becomes to maintain a constant speed of 120 rev/min?
   (c) How long will it take the grind stone to come from 120 rev/min to rest if it is acted on the axle friction alone ?

   Ans. (a) 49 N (b) 40 N (c) 9.44 s

9. A bucket of water of mass 20 kg is suspended by a rope wrapped around a windlass in the form of a solid cylinder 0.2 m in diameter, also of mass 20 kg. The bucket is released from rest at the top of a well and falls 20 m to the water.
   (a) What is the tension in the rope while bucket is falling?
   (b) With what velocity does the bucket strikes the water?
   (c) What was the time of fall? Neglect the weight of the rope.

   Ans. (a) 65.3 N (b) 16.2 m/s (c) 2.47 s

90 MECHANICS, THERMODYNAMICS & WAVES

10. A man of mass 60 kg runs around the edge of a horizontal turntable mounted on a vertical frictionless axis through its centre. The velocity of the man, relative to the earth, is 1 m/s. The turntable is rotating in the opposite direction with an angular velocity of 0.2 rad/s. The radius of the turntable is 2m and its moment of inertia about the axis of rotation is 400 kg. m². Find the final angular velocity of the system if the man comes to rest, relative to the turntable.

    Ans. 0.0625 rad/s

11. The particle of mass m as shown in figure slides down the frictionless surface and collides with the uniform vertical rod, sticking to it. The rod pivots about O, through the angle θ before momentarily coming to rest. Find θ in terms of the other parameters given in the figure.

    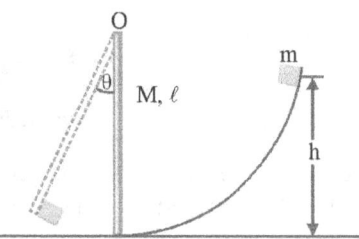

12. A small solid marble of mass m and radius r rolls without slipping along the loop, the-loop track shown in figure, having been released from rest somewhere on the straight section of track.

    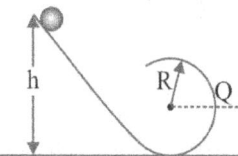

    (a) From what minimum height h above the bottom of the track must the marble be released in order that it is not leave the track at the top of the loop? (The radius of the loop-the-loop is R; assume $R >> r$)
    (b) If the marble is released from the height $6R$ above the bottom of the track, what is the horizontal component of the force acting on it at point Q?

    Ans. (a) 2.7 R, (b) 50 mg/ 7

13. Figure shows two blocks, each of mass m, suspended from the ends of a rigid weightless rod of length $\ell_1 + \ell_2$, with $\ell_1 = 20$ cm and $\ell_2 = 80$ cm. The rod is held in horizontal position shown in figure and then released. Calculate the accelerations of the two blocks as they starts to move.

    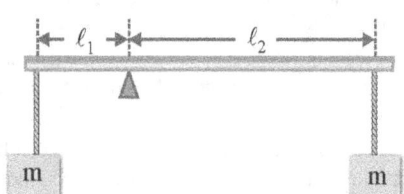

    Ans. $a_1 = 1.73$ m/s², $a_2 = 6.92$ m/s²

14. A 2.0 kg object moves in a plane with velocity components $v_x = 30$ m/s and $v_y = 60$ m/s as it passes through the point $(x, y) = (3.0, -4.0)$m.
    (a) What is its angular momentum relative to the origin at this moment?
    (b) What is its angular momentum relative to the point $(-2.0, -2.0)$m at the same moment.

    Ans. (a) 600 kg. m²/s (b) 720 kg.m²/s both about z-axis

15. A rigid sculpture, consisting of thin hoop (of mass m and radius $R = 0.15$ m) and two thin rods (each of mass m and length $L = 2.0R$), is arranged as shown in figure. The sculpture can be pivot around a horizontal axis in the plane of the hoop, passing through its centre.
    (a) In terms of m and R, what is the sculpture's rotational inertia I about the rotational axis?
    (b) Starting from rest, the sculpture rotates around the rotation axis from the initial upright orientation of figure. What is its angular speed ω about the axis when it is inverted?

    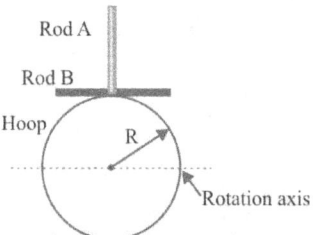

    Ans. (a) 5.83 mR^2, (b) 12 rad/s

16. A carpet of mass M made of inextensible material is rolled along its length in the form of a cylinder of radius R and is kept on a rough floor. The carpet starts unrolling without sliding on the floor when a negligibly small push is given to it. Calculate the horizontal velocity of the axis of the cylindrical part of the carpet when it radius reduces to $R/2$.

    Ans. $\sqrt{(14gR/3)}$

17. A force $F = A\hat{i} + B\hat{j}$ is applied to a point whose radius vector relative to the origin of co-ordinates O is equal to $r = a\hat{i} + b\hat{j}$, where a, b, A, B are constants, and $\hat{i}, \hat{j}$ are the unit vectors of the x and y-axes. Find the moment N and the arm ℓ of the force F relative to the point O.

    Ans. $N = (aB - bA)\hat{k}$, where $\hat{k}$ is the unit vector of the z-axis; $\ell = \dfrac{aB - bA}{\sqrt{A^2 + B^2}}$

18. A force $F_1 = A\hat{j}$ is applied to a point whose radius vector $r_1 = a\hat{i}$, while a force $F_2 = B\hat{i}$ is applied to the point whose radius vector $r_2 = b\hat{j}$. Both radius vectors are determined relative to the origin of co-ordinates O, $\hat{i}$ and $\hat{j}$ are the unit vectors of the x and y-axes, a, b, A, B are constants. Find the arm ℓ of the resultant force relative to the point O.

    Ans. $\ell = \dfrac{[aA - bB]}{(A^2 + B^2)}$

19. Three forces are applied to a square plane as shown in the figure. Find the modulus, direction and the point of application of the resultant force, if this point is taken on the side AB.

    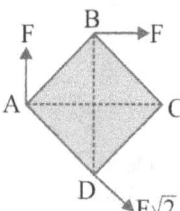

    Ans. $F_{res} = 2F$. This force is parallel to the diagonal AC and is applied at the midpoint of the side BC.

20. Find the moment of inertia
    (a) of a thin uniform rod relative to the axis which is perpendicular to the rod and passes through its end, if the mass of the rod is m and its length ℓ;
    (b) of a thin uniform rectangular plate relative to the axis passing perpendicular to the plane of the plate through one of its vertices, if the sides of the plate are equal to a and b, and its mass is m.

    Ans. (a) $L = \frac{1}{3}m\ell^2$ (b) $I = \frac{1}{3}m(a^2+b^2)$

21. Calculate the moment of inertia
    (a) of a copper uniform disc relative to the symmetry axis perpendicular to the plane of the disc. If its thickness is equal to $b = 2.0$ mm and its radius $R = 100$ mm;
    (b) of a uniform solid cone relative to its symmetry axis, if the mass of the cone is equal to m and the radius of its base to R.

    Ans. (a) $I = \frac{1}{2}\pi\rho b R^2 = 2.8 g.m^2$; (b) $I = \frac{3}{10}mR^2$

22. A thin horizontal uniform rod AB of mass m and length ℓ can rotate freely about a vertical axis passing through its end A. At a certain moment the end B starts experiencing a constant force F which is always perpendicular to the original position of the stationary rod and directed in a horizontal plane. Find the angular velocity of the rod as a function of its rotation angle ϕ counted relative to the initial position. **Ans.** $\omega = \sqrt{6F\sin\phi/m\ell}$

23. In the arrangement shown in figure. The mass of the uniform solid cylinder of radius R is equal to m and the masses of two bodies are equal to m_1 and m_2. The thread slipping and the friction is the axle of the cylinder are supposed to be absent. Find the angular acceleration of the cylinder and the ratio of tensions T_1/T_2 of the vertical sections of the thread in the process of motion.

    Ans. $\alpha = \frac{(m_2 - m_1)g}{(m_1 + m_2 + m/2)R}$, $\frac{T_1}{T_2} = \frac{m_1(m + 4m_2)}{m_2(m + 4m_1)}$

24. A uniform disc of radius R is spinned to the angular velocity ω and then carefully placed on a horizontal surface. How long will the disc be rotating on the surface if the friction coefficient is equal to μ? The pressure exerted by the disc on the surface can be regarded as uniform.

    Ans. $t = 3\omega R/4\mu g$

25. A uniform cylinder of radius R and mass M can rotate freely about a stationary horizontal axis O figure. A thin cord of length ℓ and mass m is wound on the cylinder in a single layer. Find the angular acceleration of the cylinder as function of the length x of the hanging part of the cord. The wound part of the cord is supposed to have its centre on gravity of the cylinder axis.

    Ans. $\alpha = 2mgx/R\ell(M+2m)$

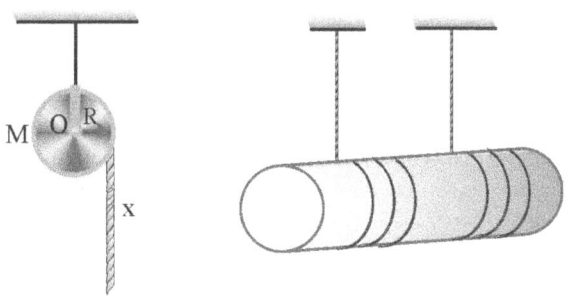

26. A spool with a thread would on it is placed on an inclined smooth plane set at an angle $\alpha = 30°$ to the horizontal. The free end of the thread is attached to the wall as shown in figure. The mass of the spool is $m = 300g$, its moment of inertia relative to its own axis $I = 0.45$ g- m^2, the radius of the would thread layer $r = 3.0$ cm . Find the acceleration of the spool axis.

    Ans. $a = g\sin\alpha/(1 + I/mr^2) = 1.6$ m/s^2

27. A uniform solid cylinder of mass m rests on two horizontal planks. A thread is wound on the cylinder. The hanging end of the thread is pulled vertically down with a constant force shown in the figure. Find the maximum magnitude of the force F which still does not bring about any sliding of the cylinder, if the coefficient of friction between the cylinder and the planks is equal to μ. What is the acceleration a_{max} of the axis of the cylinder rolling down the inclined plane?

    Ans. $F_{max} = 3\mu mg/(2-3\mu)$; $a_{max} = \frac{2\mu g}{(2-3\mu)}$

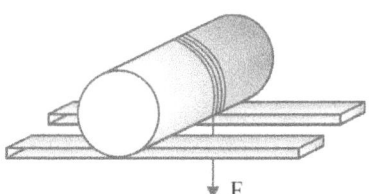

28. A spool with thread wound on it, of mass m, rests on a rough horizontal surface. Its moment of inertia relative to its own axis is equal to $I = \gamma mR^2$, where γ is a numerical factor and R is the outside radius of the spool. The radius of the wound thread layer is equal to r. The spool is pulled without sliding by the thread with a constant force F directed at an angle α to the horizontal as shown in the figure. Find

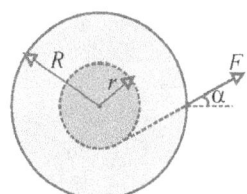

    (a) the projection of the acceleration vector of the spool axis on the x-axis.
    (b) the work performed by the force F during the first t seconds after the beginning of motion

    Ans. (a) $a_x = F(\cos\alpha - r/R)/m(1+\gamma)$;
    (b) $W = F^2 t^2 (\cos\alpha - r/R)^2/2m(1+\gamma)$

29. A uniform solid cylinder of mass m and radius R is set in rotation about its axis with an angular velocity ω_0, then lowered with its lateral surface onto a horizontal plane and released. The coefficient of friction between the cylinder and the plane is equal to μ. Find
    (a) how long the cylinder will move with sliding
    (b) the total work performed by the sliding friction force acting on the cylinder.

    Ans. (a) $t = \frac{\omega_0 R}{3\mu g}$; (b) $W = \frac{-m\omega_0^2 R^2}{6}$

30. A block of mass M is moving with a velocity v_1 on a frictionless surface as shown in figure. It passes over to a cylinder of radius R and moment of inertia I which has a fixed axis and initially at rest. When it first make contact with the cylinder, it slips on the cylinder, but the friction is large enough so that slipping ceases before it losses contact with the cylinder. Final it goes to the dotted position with velocity v_2. Compute v_2 in terms of v_1, M, I and R.

Ans. $v_2 = \dfrac{v_1}{\left[1 + \dfrac{I}{MR^2}\right]}$

31. A conical pendulum, a thin uniform rod of length L and mass M, rotates uniformly about a vertical axis with angular velocity ω (the upper end of the rod is hinged). Find the angle θ between the rod and the vertical.   **Ans.** $\cos\theta = \dfrac{3g}{2\omega^2 \ell}$

32. A smooth uniform rod AB of mass M and length L rotates freely with an angular velocity ω_0 in a horizontal plane about a stationary vertical axis passing through its end A. A small sleeve of mass m starts sliding along the rod from the point A. Find the velocity v of the sleeve relative to the rod at the moment it reaches its other end B.

Ans. $v' = \dfrac{\omega_0 L}{\sqrt{1 + \dfrac{3m}{M}}}$

33. A horizontally oriented uniform disc of mass M and radius R rotates freely about a stationary vertical axis passing through its centre. The disc has a radial guide along which can slide without friction a small body of mass m. A light thread running down through the hollow axle of the disc is tied to the body. Initially the body was located at the edge of the disc and the whole system rotated with an angular velocity ω_0. Then by means of a force F applied to the lower end of the thread the body was slowly pulled to the rotation axis. Find
(a) the angular velocity of the system in its final state;
(b) the work performed by the force F.

Ans. (a) $\omega = \left(1 + \dfrac{2m}{M}\right)\omega_0$ (b) $\dfrac{1}{2} m\omega_0^2 R^2 \left(1 + \dfrac{2m}{M}\right)$

34. Two horizontal discs rotate freely about a vertical axis passing through their centres. The moment of inertia of the discs relative to this axis are equal to I_1 and I_2 and the angular velocities to ω_1 and ω_2. When the upper disc falls on the lower one, both discs began rotating, after some time, as a single whole (due to friction). Find:
(a) the steady-state angular rotation velocity of this discs;
(b) the work performed by the friction forces in this process.

Ans. (a) $\omega = \dfrac{I_1\omega_1 + I_2\omega_2}{(I_1 + I_2)}$ (b) $\dfrac{I_1 I_2 (\omega_1 - \omega_2)^2}{2(I_1 + I_2)}$

35. A hollow sphere of radius 4.9 m is rotating about a horizontal axis at 10 rad/s. It is gently lowered on the ground ($\mu = 0.34$). How far does the sphere move before it starts pure rolling?

Ans. 0.58 m.

36. A long uniform rod of length L and mass M is pivoted about a horizontal, frictionless pin through one end. The rod is released from rest in a vertical position as shown in the figure. At the instant the rod is horizontal, find (a) the angular velocity of the rod (b) its angular acceleration (c) the x and y component of the acceleration of its c.m. (d) the component of reaction force at the pivot.

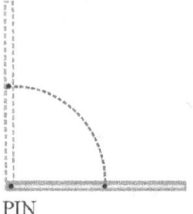

Ans. (a) $\omega = \sqrt{\dfrac{3g}{L}}$ (b) $\alpha = \dfrac{3g}{2L}$ (c) $a_x = \dfrac{3}{2}g$, $a_y = \dfrac{3}{4}g$

(d) $R_x = \dfrac{3}{2}Mg$, $R_y = \dfrac{Mg}{4}$

37. Two small flat discs, one with a mass of 3 kg and other with a mass of 2 kg, are connected by a massless stiff rod 1.5 m long and are rest on a frictionless horizontal surface. A third disc of mass 4 kg slides at a constant velocity of 3 m/s in a direction perpendicular to the rod, strikes the 2 kg mass, and sticks to it. (a) Determine the position and the velocity of c.m. of the entire system following the impact. (b) What is the angular frequency of rotation of the rod after impact? (c) Is energy conserved in this impact, if not how much kinetic energy is lost?

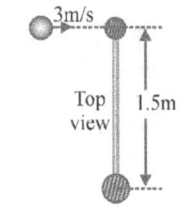

Ans. (a) $x = 0.5$ m from the top of the rod, $v = 4/3$ m/s

(b) $\omega = \dfrac{4}{3}$ rad/s (c) 7 J

38. A block X of mass 0.5 kg is held by a long massless string on a frictionless inclined plane of inclination 30° to the horizontal. The string is wound on a uniform solid cylindrical drum Y of mass 2 kg and of radius 0.2 m as shown in the figure. The drum is given an initial angular velocity, such that the block starts moving up the plane.
(i) Find the tension in the string during motion
(ii) At a certain instant of time, the magnitude of angular velocity of Y is 10 rad/s. Calculate the distance travelled by X from that instant of time until it comes to rest.

Ans. 1.63 N, 1.224 m

39. Two discs of moments of inertia I_1 and I_2 about their respective axes (normal to the disc and passing through the centre), and rotating with angular speed ω_1 and ω_2 are brought into contact face to face with their axes of rotation coincident. (i) What is the angular speed of the two-disc system? (ii) Show that the kinetic energy of the combined system is less than the sum of the initial kinetic energies of the two discs. How do you account for this loss in energy? Take $\omega_1 \neq \omega_2$ **Ans.** (i) $\omega = \dfrac{I_1\omega_1 + I_2\omega_2}{I_1 + I_2}$ (ii) $\dfrac{I_1 I_2}{2(I_1 + I_2)}(\omega_1 - \omega_2)^2$

40. A uniform disc of mass and radius R is projected horizontally with velocity v_0 on a rough horizontal floor so that it starts off with a purely sliding motion at $t = 0$. After t_0 second, it acquires purely rolling motion as shown in figure.

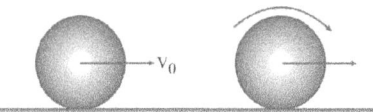

(a) Calculate the velocity of the centre of mass of the disc at t_0.
(b) Assuming that the coefficient of friction to be μ, calculate t_0. Also calculate the work done by the frictional force as a function of time and the total work done by it over a time t much longer than t_0 **Ans** : $2v_0/3, v_0/3\mu g, , -\dfrac{1}{6}mv_0^2$.

41. Two heavy metallic plates are joined together at 90^0 to each other. A linear sheet of mass 30 kg is hinged at the line AB joining the two heavy metallic plates. The hinges are frictionless. The moment of inertia of the laminar sheet about an axis parallel to AB and passing through its centre of mass is 1.2 kg-m². Two rubber obstacles P and Q are fixed one on each metallic plate at a distance 0.5 m from the line AB. This distance is chosen so that the reaction due to the hinges on the laminar sheet is zero during the impact. Initially the laminar sheet hits one of the obstacles with an angular velocity 1 rad/s and turns back. If the impulse on the sheet due to each obstacle is 6 N-s.

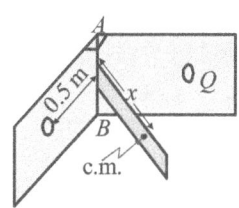

(a) Find the location of the centre of mass of the laminar sheet from AB.
(b) At what angular velocity does the laminar sheet come back after the first impact ?
(c) After how many impacts does the laminar sheet come to rest?

Ans : (a) 0.1 m (b) 1 rad/s (c) infinite.

42. A man pushes a cylinder of mass m_1 with the help of a plank of mass m_2 as shown. There is no slipping at any contact. The horizontal component of the force applied by the man is F. Find

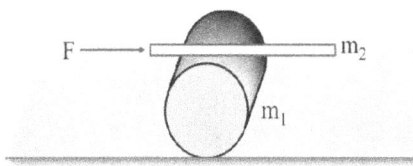

(a) the acceleration of the plank and the centre of mass of the cylinder, and
(b) the magnitude and direction of frictional force at contact points.

Ans : (a) $a_1 = \dfrac{4F}{8m_2+3m_1}, a_2 = \dfrac{8F}{8m_2+3m_1}$

(b) $f_1 = \dfrac{m_1 F}{3m_1+8m_2}, f_2 = \dfrac{3m_1 F}{8m_2+3m_1}$

43. Figure shows two cylinders of radii r_1 and r_2 having moments of inertia I_1 and I_2 about their respective axes. Initially, the cylinders rotate about their axes with angular speed ω_1 and ω_2 as shown in the figure. The cylinders are moved closer to touch each other keeping the axes parallel. The cylinders first slip over each other at the contact but the slipping finally ceases due to the friction between them. Find the angular speeds of the cylinders after the slipping ceases.

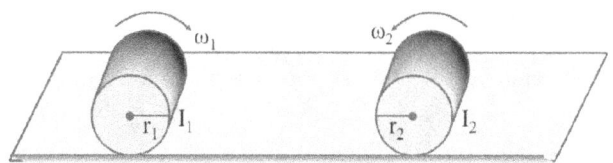

Ans. $\omega'_1 = \dfrac{I_1\omega_1 r_2 + I_2\omega_2 r_1}{I_2 r_1^2 + I_1 r_2^2} r_2$ and $\omega'_2 = \dfrac{I_1\omega_1 r_2 + I_2\omega_2 r_1}{I_2 r_1^2 + I_1 r_2^2} r_1$

44. A light rod with the balls A and B is clamped at the centre in such a way that it can rotate freely about a horizontal axis through the clamp. The system is kept at rest in the horizontal position. A particle P of the same mass m is dropped from a height h on the ball B. The particle collide with B and sticks to it.

B ———————————— A

(a) Find the angular momentum and the angular speed of the system just after the collision.
(b) What should be the minimum value of h so that the system makes a full rotation after the collision.

Ans. (a) $\dfrac{mL\sqrt{gh}}{\sqrt{2}}, \dfrac{\sqrt{8gh}}{3L}$ (b) $\dfrac{3}{2}L$.

45. A hollow sphere is released from the top of an inclined plane of inclination θ.
(a) What should be the minimum coefficient of friction between the sphere and the plane to prevent sliding ?
(b) Find the kinetic energy of the sphere as it moves down a length l on the incline if the friction coefficient is half the value calculated in part (a).

Ans. (a) $\dfrac{2}{5}\tan\theta$ (b) $\dfrac{7}{8}mgl\sin\theta$.

46. A uniform plate of length $a = 0.6$ m and width $b = 0.4$ m having mass $M = 3$ kg is free to rotate about an edge. Initially the plate is kept horizontally and small particles each of mass $M = 0.01$ kg collide elastically and perpendicular to the plate on the second half of the plate at the rate $n = 100$ particles per unit time per unit area as shown. What will be the velocity of striking particles so that plate does not rotate ?

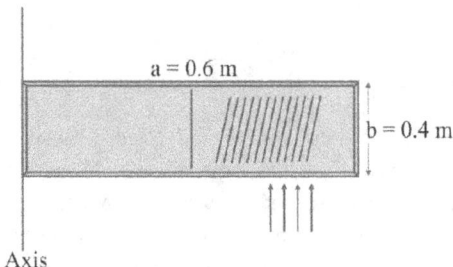

Ans. 83.3 m/s.

47. Three particles A, B and C each of mass m are connected to each other by three massless rigid rods to form a rigid equilateral triangular body of side l. This body is placed on a horizontal frictionless table (x-y plane) and is hinged to it at point A so that it can move without friction about a vertical axis through A. The body is set into rotational motion on the table about A with a constant angular velocity ω.

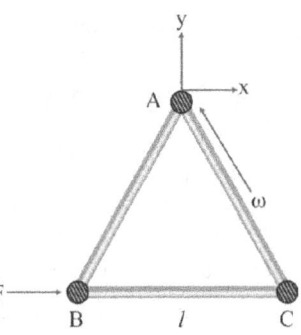

(a) Find the magnitude of the horizontal force exerted by the hinge on the body.
(b) At time T, when the side BC is parallel to x-axis, a force F is applied on B along BC (as shown). Obtain the x-component and the y-component of the force exerted by the hinge on the body, immediately after time T.

Ans. (a) $\sqrt{3}\; ml\omega^2$

(b) $F_x = -(F/4)$ F_y = centripetal force = $\sqrt{3}\; ml\omega^2$.

ROTATIONAL MECHANICS

Hints & Solutions

Solutions Exercise 1.1 Level-1

1. (d) Flywheel is the wheel of large moment of inertia. So $\alpha = \dfrac{\tau}{I}$ becomes smaller.

2. (c) $\omega = \dfrac{v}{r}$ or $v = \omega r$ in which ω is constant and $v \propto r$.

3. (c) The only force acts on the rod is gravitational force, so its C.G. falls vertically at O.

4. (b) In non inertial frame, there is a torque of pseudo force, so (B) should be changed accordingly.

5. (b) $\alpha = \dfrac{d(t-3)}{dt} = 1$ (const)

6. (c) At $t = 3s$ the slope $\dfrac{d\theta}{dt}$ is negative.

7. (c) For only radial acceleration, ω must be constant.

8. (c) For the decreasing speed of the disk, there are two accelerations a_n and $(-a_t)$ as shown.

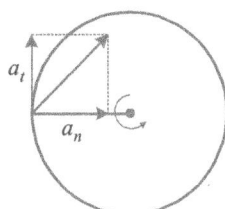

9. (c) $I_1 = 0 + md^2 + m(3d)^2 = 10md^2$

   $I_3 = 0 + m(2d)^2 + m(3d)^2 = 13md^2$

10. (c) For a body with constant angular velocity, there is only centripetal force, which passes through axis of rotation.

11. (b) As $\tau = F_2 r \sin\theta$; so if θ decreases, F_2 should be increased.

12. (c) The moment of arm of F_3 is greatest. So its torque will be greatest.

13. (b) The body with non-uniform speed, has two forces; normal force and tangential force, so there resultant will not pass through axis of rotation.

14. (d) In this case, the acceleration of each object will be $g\sin\theta$.

15. (d) $\tau = F \times$ moment arm; About both the ends, moment arm remains constant.

16. (b) Acceleration of sphere will be greatest and so its speed will be greatest at the bottom.

17. (b) Clearly, $I_2 > I_1$ and $I_1\omega_1 = I_2\omega_2$, so $\omega_2 < \omega_1$.

18. (d) $L_1 = L_3 = 0$; $L_2 = mv \times 3$ and $L_4 = mv \times 2$.

19. (a) $L_a = 2mv \times \ell$; $L_b = mv \times \ell$

    $L_c = 0$; $L_d = mv \times \ell$

20. (a) In accelerated car the net force along the inclined becomes zero.
    Also no torque is acting on the sphere, so it will continue pure rolling.

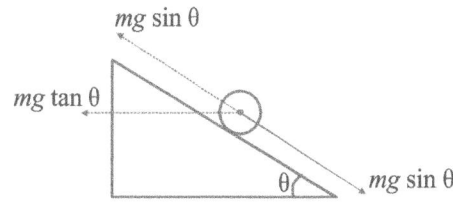

21. (a) If y is the distance from x-axis, then
    $L = mvy$. As y is constant, so L is constant.

22. (b) $I = 2\left[\dfrac{2}{5}Mr^2\right] + 2\left[\dfrac{2}{5}Mr^2 + M\ell^2\right]$

    $= M\left[\dfrac{8}{5}r^2 + 2\ell^2\right]$

23. (c) $I = 0 + 0 + mr^2$

    $= \dfrac{3}{4}m\ell^2$

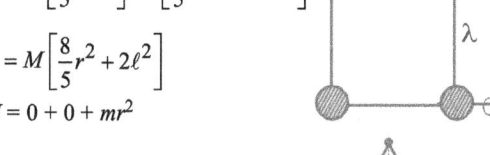

24. (c) In case of sliding, $v = \sqrt{2gh}$.
    In case of rolling of ring,

    $v' = \sqrt{\dfrac{2gh}{1+\dfrac{I}{mR^2}}} = \sqrt{gh} = \dfrac{v}{\sqrt{2}}$.

25. (d) $f = \dfrac{\dfrac{1}{2}mv^2 + \dfrac{1}{2}I\omega^2}{\dfrac{1}{2}I\omega^2} = \dfrac{\dfrac{1}{2}mv^2 + \dfrac{1}{2}(mR^2)\left(\dfrac{v}{R}\right)^2}{\dfrac{1}{2}(mR^2)\left(\dfrac{v}{R}\right)^2} = 2$

26. (b) $v = \sqrt{\dfrac{2gh}{1+\dfrac{I}{mR^2}}} = \sqrt{\dfrac{2gh}{1+\dfrac{mR^2/2}{mR^2}}} = \sqrt{\dfrac{4}{3}gh}$

27. (d) Moment arm $= \dfrac{|\tau|}{|F|} = \dfrac{|(2\hat{i}+\hat{j})\times(3\hat{i}+4\hat{j})|}{5}$

    $= \dfrac{5}{5} = 1$ m

28. (c) $\tau = Fr\sin\theta = 10 \times 1 \times \sin 30°$
    $= 5$ N-m

29. (b) $r_1 = \dfrac{m_2 r}{m_1 + m_2}$ and $r_2 = \dfrac{m_1 r}{m_1 + m_2}$

    Moment of inertia, $I = m_1 r_1^2 + m_2 r_2^2$

    $= \left(\dfrac{m_1 m_2}{m_1 + m_2}\right) r^2$

30. (b) $\dfrac{MR^2}{2} = \dfrac{M\ell^2}{12} + \dfrac{MR^2}{4}$

$\Rightarrow \ell = \sqrt{3}R$.

31. (a) $I = \dfrac{\dfrac{m}{2}\left(\dfrac{\ell}{2}\right)^2}{3} + \dfrac{m}{2}\left(\dfrac{\ell}{2}\right)^2$

$= \dfrac{m\ell^2}{6}$

32. (c) $\dfrac{1}{2}mv^2 + \dfrac{1}{2}I\omega^2 = mgh$

or $\dfrac{1}{2}mv^2 + \dfrac{1}{2}\left(\dfrac{2mR^2}{5}\right)\left(\dfrac{v}{R}\right)^2 = mgh$

Clearly h becomes free from mass of the sphere.

33. (d) Angular momentum

$L = mvd$ (constant)

As d constant

34. (a) The angular momentum,

$L = mvr \sin(180° - 30°)$

$= 2 \times 4 \times 3 \times \dfrac{1}{2} = 12$ kg m²/s

35. (b) $\vec{v}_A = \omega r(-\hat{j})$

$= 10 \times 1(-\hat{j}) = -10\hat{j}$ m/s

36. (c) In the process, $I_i\omega_i = I_f\omega_f$

or $(MR^2)\omega = (MR^2 + 2mR^2)\omega_f$

$\therefore \omega_f = \left[\dfrac{M\omega}{M+2m}\right]$

37. (c) As side AB > BC, so $I_{BC} > I_{AB}$

38. (d) $I_A = I_{cm} + mx^2$, so (d) is the correct option.

39. (a) $v_P = v_c - \omega r$ and $v_Q = v_c + \omega r$,

so $v_Q > v_c > v_P$

40. (b) In the process $\vec{L}$ remains constant, so

$I\omega = (2I)\omega_2$

$\Rightarrow \omega_2 = \dfrac{\omega}{2}$

$\dfrac{K_1}{K_2} = \dfrac{\dfrac{1}{2}I\omega^2}{\dfrac{1}{2}I_2\omega_2^2} = \dfrac{\dfrac{1}{2}I\omega^2}{\dfrac{1}{2}(2I)(\omega/2)^2}$

$\therefore K_2 = \dfrac{K}{2}$

41. (a) Its moment of inertia will be equal to the moment of inertia of the disc. So $I = \dfrac{MR^2}{2}$.

42. (b) The sliding tendency of point of contact of cylinder in both the cases is downward, so friction will act in upward direction.

43. (b) As no torque acts about axis of rotation, so its angular momentum remains constant.

44. (b) $I = 2\dfrac{M\ell^2}{12} = \dfrac{m\ell^2}{6}$

45. (c) $I = I_{cm} + mR^2$

$= \dfrac{MR^2}{2} + MR^2 = \dfrac{3}{2}MR^2$

$\therefore L = I\omega = \dfrac{3}{2}MR^2\omega$

46. (c) $I = \dfrac{MR^2}{2}$

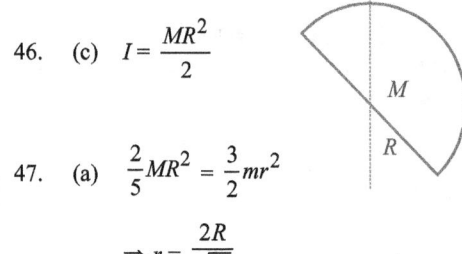

47. (a) $\dfrac{2}{5}MR^2 = \dfrac{3}{2}mr^2$

$\Rightarrow r = \dfrac{2R}{\sqrt{15}}$

48. (c) $I = 0 + 2m\left(\dfrac{\ell}{\sqrt{2}}\right)^2 + m(\sqrt{2}\ell)^2$

$= 3m\ell^2$

49. (b) As the fluid spread out, the moment of inertia of the platform increases and so angular velocity decreases ($I\omega$ = const). When fluid falls of the platform, its spread again increases.

50. (b) For smooth surface,

$\dfrac{1}{2}mv^2 = mgh$

$\therefore v = \sqrt{2gh}$

51. (c) The force on the cylinder changes periodically, so frictional force also changes periodically.

52. (d) The velocity of point of contact

$v_P = v - \omega R = v - v = 0$

centripetal acceleration, $a = v^2/R$

53. (c, d) For velocity to be vertical,

$v\cos\alpha = v$

or $\omega R\cos\alpha = v$

$\therefore \cos\alpha = \left(\dfrac{v}{\omega R}\right)$

54. (b) $L_i = -mvd\cos\theta$ and $L_f = +mvd\cos\theta$

$\therefore \Delta L = 2mvd\cos\theta$

55. (c) The tendency of sliding of point of contact is downward, so friction will act upward.

ROTATIONAL MECHANICS

56. (d) $mg\sin 60° - (T+f) = ma$ ... (i)

and $fR - TR = I\alpha$

or $f - T = \dfrac{Ia}{R^2}$ ... (ii)

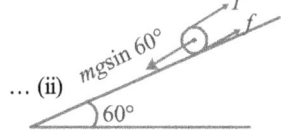

After simplifying, we get $f = mg/5$

57. (a) The sliding tendency of bottom most point of the spool is backward, so friction acts rightwards. Therefore centre of mass of spool moves rightwards.

58. (c) **For topple**

$F \times \ell \sin 60° \geq mg \times \ell/2$

$\Rightarrow F \geq mg/\sqrt{3}$

For translation

$F = \mu mg$

or $\dfrac{mg}{\sqrt{3}} = \mu mg$

$\therefore \mu = \dfrac{1}{\sqrt{3}}$

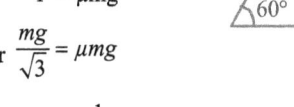

59. (c) $mg - T = ma_2$ ... (i)

and $TR = I\alpha_2$

or $T = \dfrac{I\alpha_2}{R}$

or $T = \dfrac{mR^2}{2}\dfrac{\alpha_2}{R}$ ... (ii)

or $\alpha_1 R = (a_2 - \alpha_2 R)$ ... (iii)

and $TR = \left(\dfrac{mR^2}{2}\right)\alpha_1$ ... (iv)

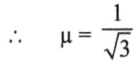
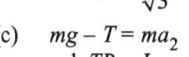

From equations, we get the answer.

60. (d) In the shown frame the particle appears to be at rest.
∴ Net force on it must be zero. Therefore pseudo force must be equal and opposite to the tension.

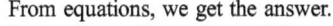

61. (c) Consider a situation when the bob A has fallen through an angle θ.

Loss in PE = Gain in KE

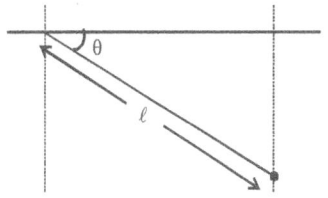

$\Rightarrow \dfrac{1}{2}I\omega^2 = mg\ell\sin\theta$

$\Rightarrow \omega_A = \sqrt{\dfrac{2mg\ell\sin\theta}{I}} = \sqrt{\dfrac{2mg\ell\sin\theta}{m\ell^2}}$

$\omega_A = \sqrt{\dfrac{2g\sin\theta}{\ell}}$

In the similar position

$\omega_B = \sqrt{\dfrac{4g\sin\theta}{\ell}} \Rightarrow \dfrac{\omega_A}{\omega_B} = \dfrac{t_B}{t_A} = \sqrt{\dfrac{1}{2}} \Rightarrow \dfrac{t_A}{t_B} = \sqrt{2}$

62. (d) The angular momentum of the system about O = 0
$\Rightarrow \omega = 0$.

63. (c) The position vector of the center of mass at the time t is

$\vec{r}_{cm} = \hat{i}(\cos 30°) + \hat{j}(\sin 30°) + \hat{k}(0.10)$

$= 0.866\,\hat{i} + 0.5\,\hat{j} + 0.10\,\hat{k}$

and the total momentum of the hoop is

$\vec{p} = m\vec{v}_{cm} = (0.50)(0.50\hat{j}) = 0.25\hat{j}$

Thus, $\vec{L}_{orb} = \vec{r}_{cm} \times \vec{p}$

$= (0.866\,\hat{i} + 0.5\,\hat{j} + 0.10\,\hat{k}) \times 0.25\hat{j}$

$= -0.025\,\hat{i} + 0.216\,\hat{k}$ kg m²/s

To find the spin angular momentum, note that every element of mass of the hoop is at the same distance from the centre of mass $r' = 0.10$ m, and every element rotates about the center of mass with a velocity $\vec{v}'$ (of magnitude 0.50 m/s) perpendicular to $\vec{r}'$. Thus,

$\vec{L}_{spin} = \int \vec{r}' \times \vec{v}'\, dm = \int r'v'(-\hat{i})\, dm$

$= -mr'v'\,\hat{i} = -0.025\,\hat{i}$ kg m²/s

Solutions EXERCISE 1.1 LEVEL-2

1. (d) For the equilibrium, $\Sigma\vec{F} = 0$ and $\Sigma\vec{\tau} = 0$
which is possible in A and C.

2. (c) In (c) the net force and net torque can be zero.

3. (a) Work done by gravitational force in both the cases is $W_1 = W_2 = mgh$.

4. (c) $v_1 = \sqrt{2gh}$ and $v_2 = \sqrt{\dfrac{2gh}{1 + \dfrac{I}{mR^2}}}$

Clearly, $v_1 > v_2$

5. (a) $E_1 = E_2 = mgh$

6. (c) $K_1 + 0 = mgh \Rightarrow K_1 = mgh$

and $K_2 + K_{rotational} = mgh \Rightarrow K_2 = mgh - K_{rotational}$

Clearly, $K_1 > K_2$

7. (d) $v = \sqrt{\dfrac{2gh}{1 + \dfrac{I}{mR^2}}} = \sqrt{\dfrac{2gh}{1 + \dfrac{2mR^2}{5mR^2}}} = \sqrt{\dfrac{10}{7}gh}$

Clearly velocity of c.m. does not depend on radius of the sphere.

$\omega_1 = \dfrac{v}{R}$ and $\omega_2 = \dfrac{v}{2R}$.

8. (d) In case (a) and (b), the sphere will move in pure rolling motion, while in (c), the sphere will not be in pure rolling. So some part of mechanical energy will convert into heat by friction.

9. (b) Taking moment of forces about O, and put $\Sigma \tau = 0$

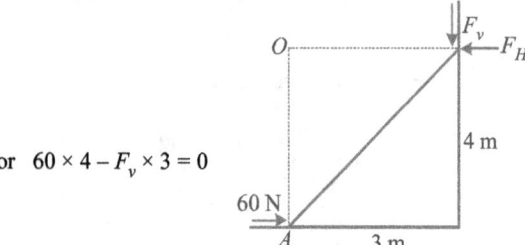

or $60 \times 4 - F_v \times 3 = 0$

∴ $F_v = 80$ N

10. (c) On inclined plane, the minimum friction needed for pure rolling, $f = \dfrac{Ia_m}{R^2}$.

For cylinder $a = \dfrac{2}{3} g \sin\theta$, $I = \dfrac{mR^2}{2}$

∴ $f = \dfrac{mg \sin\theta}{3}$.

Also $N = mg \cos\theta$

∴ $\mu = \dfrac{f}{N} = \dfrac{\tan\theta}{3}$.

11. (c) In the process,

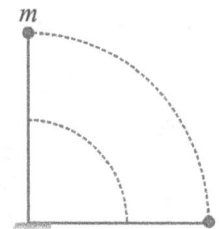

$mg\ell + mg\dfrac{\ell}{2} = \dfrac{1}{2} I\omega^2$

or $\dfrac{3}{2} mg\ell = \dfrac{1}{2}\left(\dfrac{m\ell^2}{3} + m\ell^2\right)\omega^2$

$\omega = \dfrac{3}{2}\sqrt{g/\ell}$

∴ $v = \omega\ell/2 = \dfrac{3}{4}\sqrt{g\ell}$

12. (c) $\omega = \dfrac{v}{r}$ and $\theta = \omega t = \dfrac{vt}{r}$.

The velocity of any point of the periphery is given by

$v = 2v \cos\dfrac{\theta}{2}$

or $v = 2v \cos\dfrac{vt}{2r}$.

13. (a) For m to be stationary
$T = mg$

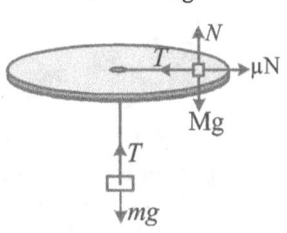

For M: $T - \mu N = M\omega^2 r$
or $mg - \mu Mg = M\omega^2 r$

∴ $r = \dfrac{mg - \mu Mg}{M\omega^2}$

14. (c) Given $I = \dfrac{MR^2}{4}$

$I_{tangent} = \dfrac{MR^2}{2} + MR^2 = \dfrac{3}{2} MR^2$

$= \dfrac{3}{2}[4I] = 6I$.

15. (c) By conservation of energy, we have

$mgh = \dfrac{1}{2} mv^2 + \dfrac{1}{2} I_{pulley}\omega_1^2 + \dfrac{1}{2} I_{shell}\omega_2^2$

$= \dfrac{1}{2} mv^2 + \dfrac{1}{2} I \left[\dfrac{v}{r}\right]^2 + \dfrac{1}{2}\left(\dfrac{2}{3} MR^2\right)\left(\dfrac{v}{R}\right)^2$

∴ $v^2 = \left[\dfrac{mgh}{\dfrac{m}{2} + \dfrac{I}{2r^2} + \dfrac{M}{3}}\right]$

16. (c) $\vec{\tau} = \dfrac{d\vec{J}}{dt} = \dfrac{d}{dt}(a\hat{i} + bt^2\hat{j}) = 2bt\hat{j}$

$\cos 45° = \dfrac{\vec{\tau}.\vec{J}}{\tau J}$

or $\dfrac{1}{\sqrt{2}} = \dfrac{(2b\hat{j}).(a\hat{i} + bt^2\hat{j})}{2bt \times \sqrt{a^2 + b^2 t^4}}$

or $t = \sqrt{\dfrac{a}{b}}$

and $\vec{\tau} = 2b \times \sqrt{\dfrac{a}{b}} \hat{j}$.

17. (d) At any instant,

$\omega = \dfrac{v_A}{x}$

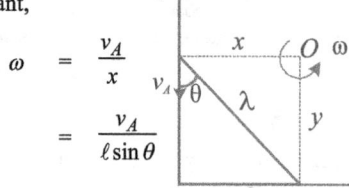

$= \dfrac{v_A}{\ell \sin\theta}$

18. (d) Area of the remaining disc $= \pi R^2 - \pi\left(\dfrac{R}{2}\right)^2 = \dfrac{3}{4}\pi R^2$

Mass of whole disc $M' = \dfrac{M \times \pi R^2}{\dfrac{3}{4}\pi R^2} = \dfrac{4M}{3}$

∴ Mass of the removed disc,
$$m = \frac{M}{3}.$$
Moment of inertia
$$I = I_{\text{whole disc}} - I_{\text{round disc}}$$
$$= \left(\frac{4M}{3}\right)\frac{R^2}{2} - \left[\frac{M}{3}\frac{(R/2)^2}{2} + \frac{M}{3}\left(\frac{R}{2}\right)^2\right]$$
$$= \frac{13}{24}MR^2.$$

19. (b) (A) $\alpha = \frac{\tau}{I} = \frac{5R}{I}$; and $a_t = \alpha R = \frac{5R^2}{I}$

(B) $\alpha = \frac{\tau'}{I} = \frac{TR}{I}$; and $a_t' = \alpha R = \frac{TR^2}{I}$

As $T < 5N$, so $a_t' < a_t$.

20. (c) $a = \frac{F}{M}$; $s = \frac{1}{2}at^2 = \frac{1}{2}\frac{F}{M}t^2$

$\alpha = \frac{\tau}{I} = \frac{FR}{\frac{MR^2}{2}} = \frac{2F}{MR}$

∴ $\theta = \frac{1}{2}\alpha t^2 = \frac{1}{2} \times \frac{2F}{MR} \times t^2 = \frac{Ft^2}{MR}$.

21. (b) We know that, $\vec{J} = m(\vec{v}_f - \vec{v}_i)$
or $7.5 = 15(v_f - 0)$
∴ $v_f = 0.5$ m/s
Energy transferred, $E = \frac{1}{2}mv_t^2 = \frac{1}{2} \times 15 \times (0.5)^2$
$= 1.9$ J

22. (c) By conservation of angular momentum about C.M, we have
$$Mv\frac{L}{2} = I\omega$$
$$= \frac{2M(2L)^2}{12}\omega$$
or $\omega = \frac{3v}{4L}$, counterclockwise

23. (b) By conservation of angular momentum about C.M.

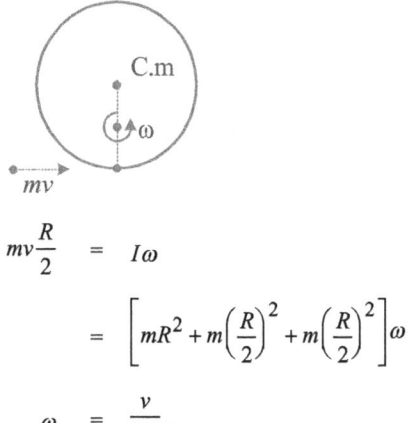

$mv\frac{R}{2} = I\omega$
$= \left[mR^2 + m\left(\frac{R}{2}\right)^2 + m\left(\frac{R}{2}\right)^2\right]\omega$

or $\omega = \frac{v}{3R}$.

24. (d) $\alpha = \frac{\tau}{I} = \frac{mgL/2}{\frac{mL^2}{3}} = \frac{3g}{2L}$

25. (a)

$J = I\omega$
or $Mv\frac{L}{2} = \left[2M\left(\frac{L}{2}\right)^2\right]\omega$
∴ $\omega = \frac{v}{L}$.

26. (c)

$I\omega = L$ (constant)
or $\omega = \frac{L}{I}$
$= \frac{L}{\left(\frac{MR^2}{2} + mx^2\right)}$

When tortoise moves along a chord, x decreases and then increases. So ω first increases and then decreases.

27. (d) $I_{AB} = I_{cm} + Md^2$
$= \frac{1.6Ma^2}{2} + M(2a)^2$
$= 4.8\,Ma^2$.

28. (b) The mass of the hole removed $= 9m \times \frac{\pi(R/3)^2}{\pi R^2} = m$
$I = I_{\text{whole disc}} - I_{\text{removed disc}}$
$= \frac{(9m)R^2}{2} - \left[\frac{m(R/3)^2}{2} + m\left(\frac{2R}{3}\right)^2\right]$
$= 4\,mR^2$

29. (d) $\frac{I_x}{I_y} = \frac{m_1R^2/2}{m_2(4R)^2/2} = \frac{\rho(\pi R^2)tR^2}{\rho\pi(4R)^2\frac{t}{4}\times(4R)^2}$
$= \frac{1}{64}$

30. (d) $L = 2\pi R \rightarrow R = \frac{L}{2\pi}$
$I = \left(\frac{mR^2}{2} + mR^2\right)$
$= \frac{3}{2}mR^2 = \frac{3}{2}(\rho L)\left(\frac{L}{2\pi}\right)^2$
$= \frac{3}{8}\frac{\rho L^3}{\pi^2}$

31. (c) $v_{block} = v_{tangent} = v_{cm} + \omega R$
$= \omega \times 2R + \omega R = 3\omega R$

32. (c) Taking moment O, we get

$$Fa = Mg \times \frac{a}{2}$$

or $\quad F = \dfrac{Mg}{2}$

33. (b)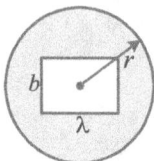

The mass of the rectangular piece

$$m' = \frac{m(\ell b)}{\pi r^2}$$

Moment of inertia, $I = \dfrac{mr^2}{2} - \dfrac{m'}{12}[\ell^2 + b^2]$

$$= \frac{mr^2}{2} - \frac{m\ell b}{12\pi r^2}(\ell^2 + b^2)$$

$$= \frac{m}{2}\left[r^2 - \frac{\ell b}{6\pi r^2}(\ell^2 + b^2)\right]$$

34. (c) $r = r_0 - a\theta$.
In the process v remains constant, so

$$\omega_0 r_0 = \omega r$$

or $\quad \omega = \dfrac{\omega_0 r_0}{r_0 - a\theta} = \dfrac{\omega_0}{\left(1 - \dfrac{a\theta}{r}\right)}$.

35. (a)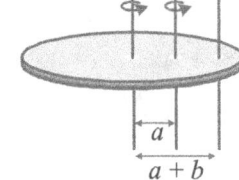

$$I_a = I_{cm} + ma^2$$

or $\quad mk^2 = I_{cm} + ma^2$

$\therefore \quad I_{cm} = mk^2 - ma^2$

Now $\quad I_{(a+b)} = I_{cm} + m(a+b)^2$

$= mk^2 - ma^2 + m(a+b)^2$.

36. (b) Velocity of plank will be $2v$.
Kinetic energy of plank,

$$K_{plank} = \frac{1}{2}M(2v)^2 = 2Mv^2$$

Kinetic energy of hollow cylinder,

$$K_{cylinder} = \frac{1}{2}Mv^2 + \frac{1}{2}I\omega^2$$

$$= \frac{1}{2}Mv^2 + \frac{1}{2}(MR^2)\left(\frac{v}{R}\right)^2$$

$$= Mv^2$$

$\therefore \quad \dfrac{K_{plank}}{K_{cylinder}} = 2$

37. (c)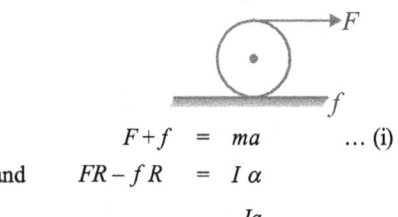

Acceleration of sphere

$$a = \frac{f}{m} = \mu g$$

Acceleration of plank

$$a' = \frac{f}{m} = \mu g$$

Acceleration of sphere relative to plank

$$= a + a' = 2\mu g.$$

38. (d)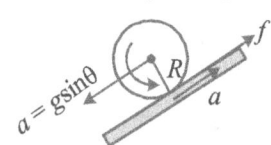

$F + f = ma$ ... (i)
and $FR - fR = I\alpha$

or $\quad F - f = \dfrac{Ia}{R^2}$

$$= \frac{mR^2 a}{R^2}$$

or $\quad F - f = ma$ ... (ii)
From above equations, $f = 0$.

39. (d)

$mg\sin\theta - f = m \times 0$
$f = mg\sin\theta$ ... (i)
Also $\quad fR = I\alpha$

or $\quad fR = \dfrac{mR^2}{2} \times \dfrac{a}{R}$

or $\quad f = \dfrac{ma}{2}$ ... (ii)

From equations (i) and (ii), we get
$a = 2g\sin\theta$.

40. (c) Torque about bottom most point is
$\tau = F(R+r) = 2t(R+r)$.
Angular momentum

$$L = \int_0^t \tau dt = \int_0^t 2t(R+r)$$

$$= t^2(R+r)$$

41. (a)
$$mvr = I\omega$$
or $$mv\frac{a}{2} = \left[\frac{ma^2}{6} + m\left(\frac{a}{\sqrt{2}}\right)^2\right]\omega$$
$$\therefore \omega = \frac{3v}{4a}$$

42. (a)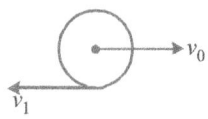

With respect to ground it has only rotation, so
$$v_1 = \omega r$$
Now using conservation of angular momentum about a fixed point at the level of bottom of the sphere,
$$mv_0 r = I\omega$$
$$= \frac{2}{5}mr^2 \times \frac{v_1}{r}$$
$$\therefore v_0 = \frac{2}{5}v_1.$$

43. (b)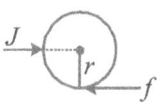

Using conservation of angular momentum about a fixed point at the level of contact point of the ring, we have
$$J \times r = I\omega$$
$$= (2mr^2)\omega$$
or $$\omega = \frac{J}{2mr}$$
$$\therefore v = \omega r = \frac{J}{2m}.$$

44. (c) Velocity of the particle perpendicular to z-axis is $\vec{v} = 2(\hat{i} - \hat{j})$. Angular momentum about z-axis,
$$\vec{L} = m(\vec{r} \times \vec{v})$$
$$= 1[(\hat{i} + \hat{j}) \times (2\hat{i} - 2\hat{j})]$$
or $$\vec{L} = -2\hat{k} - 2\hat{k} = -4\hat{k} \text{ kg-m}^2/\text{s}$$

45. (b) For spool to be stationary, $\Sigma F = 0$
or $F\cos\theta - f = 0$ ...(i)
Also, $\Sigma\tau = 0$,
or $Fr - fR = 0$ ... (ii)
From above equations,
$$\cos\theta = \frac{r}{R}.$$

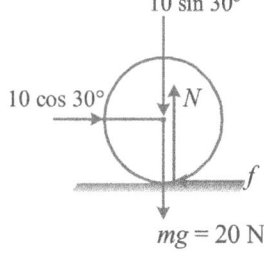

46. (b)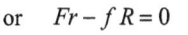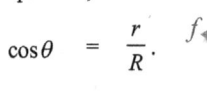

$$10\cos 30° - f = ma \qquad ...(i)$$
$$= 2a$$
Also $$fR = I\alpha$$
or $$f = \frac{Ia}{R^2}$$
$$= \frac{2}{3}mR^2\frac{a}{R^2} = \frac{2}{3} \times 2a = \frac{4a}{3} \quad ...(ii)$$
From above equations, we get
$$f = 2\sqrt{3} \text{ N}$$
Normal reaction, $N = 20 + 5 = 25$ N
$$\therefore \mu = \frac{f}{N} = 0.08\sqrt{3}$$

47. (d) Given, $I = 2x^2 - 12x + 15$
As moment of inertia is minimum about C.M. so $\frac{dI}{dx} = 0$,
or $\frac{d}{dx}(2x^2 - 12x + 15) = 0$
or $4x - 12 = 0$
or $x = 3$

48. (a) Angular impulse, $\vec{J} = I(\vec{\omega}_f - \vec{\omega}_i)$
or $$10 \times 1 = \frac{m\ell^2}{3}(\omega_f - 0)$$
$$= \frac{2 \times 1^2}{3} \times \omega_f$$
or $\omega_f = 15$ rad/s
$$\therefore K = \frac{1}{2}I\omega^2$$
$$= \frac{1}{2}\left(\frac{m\ell^2}{3}\right)\omega^2$$
$$= \frac{1}{2}\left[\frac{2 \times 1^2}{3}\right] \times 15^2$$
$$= 75 \text{ J}.$$

49. (b) $$mv \times \frac{\ell}{2} = I\omega$$
$$= \frac{M\ell^2}{3}\left[\frac{v}{\ell/2}\right]$$
$$\therefore \frac{M}{m} = \frac{3}{4}.$$

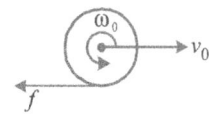

50. (c)

$$a = \frac{f}{m} = \mu g$$
and $$\alpha = \frac{\tau}{I} = \frac{fR}{I} = \frac{\mu mg \times R}{\frac{2}{5}mR^2}$$
$$= \frac{5\mu g}{2R}.$$

Using equation of motion, we have
$$0 = v_0 - at \quad \ldots (i)$$
and
$$0 = \omega_0 - \alpha t \quad \ldots (ii)$$
From above equations, we get
$$\frac{v_0}{\omega_0} = \frac{a}{\alpha}$$
$$= \frac{\mu g}{5\mu g/2R} = \frac{2R}{5}$$
or $\quad 5v_0 = 2\omega_0 R$.

51. (a) The tendency of sliding of contact point is rightward, so frictional force acts leftward.

52. (b)

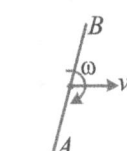

$$mv_0 + 0 = m \times 0 + mv$$
$$v = v_0$$

Also $\quad mv_0 x = I\omega = \frac{m\ell^2}{12}\omega$

or $\quad \omega = \dfrac{12 v_0 x}{\ell^2}$

For end A to be stationary
$$v_A = v_0 - \omega \frac{\ell}{2}$$
or $\quad 0 = v_0 - 12\dfrac{v_0 x}{\ell^2} \times \dfrac{\ell}{2}$
or $\quad x = \dfrac{\ell}{6}$.

53. (c) $\quad d = \sqrt{\ell^2 + (\ell/2)^2}$

$$I = \frac{m\ell^2}{3} + \left[\frac{m\ell^2}{12} + md^2\right]$$
$$= \frac{5}{3}m\ell^2$$

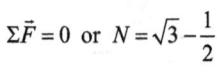

54. (b) For equilibrium of the block

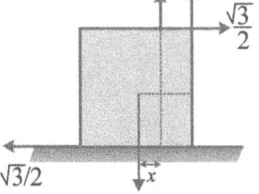

$\Sigma \vec{F} = 0$ or $N = \sqrt{3} - \dfrac{1}{2}$

Torque of all the force except N about A is found equal to zero.

55. (a) By conservation of linear momentum, we have
$$mv - mv = (m + m + m)v_{cm}$$
or $\quad v_{cm} = 0$
Now using conservation of angular momentum, we get
$$mv\ell = I\omega$$
$$= \left[\frac{m\ell^2}{12} + 2m(\ell/2)^2\right]\omega$$
$\therefore \quad \omega = \dfrac{12v}{7\ell}$

56. (d)

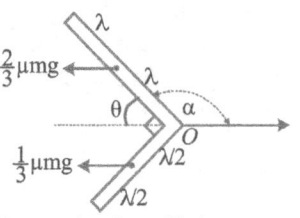

For rotational equilibrium,
$$\Sigma \tau_0 = 0$$
or $\quad \dfrac{2}{3}\mu mg \times (l\sin\theta) - \dfrac{1}{3}\mu mg \times \dfrac{1}{2}\cos\theta = 0$

or $\quad \tan\theta = \dfrac{1}{4}$

57. (c) $\quad K = K_{ring} + K_{particles}$
$$= \left[\frac{1}{2}mv_0^2 + \frac{1}{2}I\omega^2\right] + \left[\frac{1}{2}m(\sqrt{2}v_0)^2 + \frac{1}{2}m(2v_0)^2 + \frac{1}{2}m(\sqrt{2}v_0)^2 + 0\right]$$

Also $\omega = \dfrac{v_0}{R}$, $I = mR^2$

$\therefore \quad K = 5\, mv_0^2$

58. $\quad mvR = I\omega + mv'R$

or $\quad mvR = \dfrac{mR^2}{2}\left(\dfrac{v'}{R}\right) + mv'R$

$\therefore \quad v' = 2v/3$

59. (b) Vertical line from hinge A must pass through C.M. of rod system.

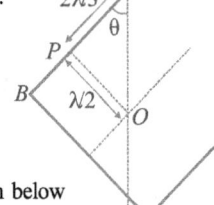

$$\tan\theta = \frac{OP}{AP} = \frac{\ell/2}{2\ell/3}$$

$\tan\theta = \dfrac{3}{4} \Rightarrow \theta = \tan^{-1}\left(\dfrac{3}{4}\right)$

60. (a) FBD of rod will be as shown below

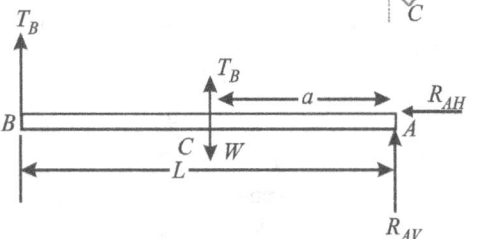

Summation of moments about A should be zero
$\Sigma M_A = 0 = -T_B \times L - (T_B - W) \times a = 0$

$\therefore \quad T_B = \dfrac{Wa}{(L+a)}$

Summation of moments about B should be zero
$\Sigma M_B = 0 = (T_B - W) \times (L - a) + R_{AV} \times L = 0$

$\left(\dfrac{Wa}{(L+a)} - W\right) \times (L - a) + R_{AV} \times L = 0$

$R_{AV} \times L = -\left(\dfrac{Wa - WL - Wa}{(L+a)}\right) \times (L - a)$

$\therefore \quad R_{AV} = \dfrac{WL(L-a)}{(L+a) \times L} = W\dfrac{(L-a)}{(L+a)}$

Solutions Exercise 1.2

1. (b, c) A body can be rotated about infinite axes.
2. (a, b, c) Mass and its distribution and axis of rotation
3. (a, b, c) In these cases, the torque about axis of rotation is zero and so angular momentum is constant.
4. (a, c) In the process, angular momentum
   $I\omega$ = constant
   As man moves away from axis of rotation, moment of inertia increase, and so ω decreases.
5. (a, b, d) $\vec{\tau}$ is perpendicular to $\vec{r}$ and $\vec{F}$.
6. (a, b, c, d) The moment of inertia of ring can have any value greater than $MR^2/2$.
7. (b, c) $\tau_0 = F_1 r_1 \sin\theta_1 - F_2 r_2 \sin\theta_2$ out of plane of the page
   or $\tau_0 = F_2 r_2 \sin\theta_2 - F_1 r_1 \sin\theta$, into the plane of the page.
8. (b, c) In this case $I_A = I_{cm} + md^2$ and $I_A + I_B = I$
   $\Rightarrow I_A < I_B$ or $I_A \leq I_B$
9. (c, d)

   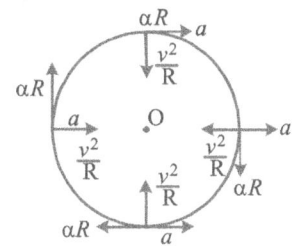

   In this case friction acts in backward direction of v_0. So v_0 decreases to v. The angular velocity will be
   $\omega = \left(\dfrac{v}{R} < \dfrac{v_0}{R}\right)$.
10. (a, b, c) The frictional force acts opposite to the sliding tendency of point of contact.
11. (a, b, d)

    Frictional force opposes the linear velocity, while its torque increases angular velocity (see fig)
12. (a, d) Normal acceleration is $a_n = \dfrac{v^2}{r}$. As r increases, v also increases to keep a_n constant.
13. (a, b, c, d) The acceleration is shown in figure.

14. (c, d) $a = \dfrac{f}{m} = \mu g$, and $\alpha = \dfrac{\tau}{I} = \dfrac{fR}{I} = \dfrac{\mu mgR}{mR^2/2} = \dfrac{2\mu g}{R}$
    $v = 0 + at$ and $\omega = \omega_0 - \alpha t$
    From above equations, we get
    $$v = \dfrac{a}{\alpha}(\omega_0 - \omega)$$
    Here $\dfrac{a}{\alpha}$ becomes free from μ.

$W = \Delta K = \left(\dfrac{1}{2}mv^2 + \dfrac{1}{2}I\omega^2\right) - \left(\dfrac{1}{2}I\omega_0^2\right)$ = constant

15. (a, b) $a_t = \alpha r = k\sin\theta \times \ell = k\ell\sin\theta$
    Also $\dfrac{dv}{dt} = k\ell\sin\theta$
    or $v\dfrac{dv}{ds} = k\ell\sin\theta$
    or $v\dfrac{dv}{Rd\theta} = k\ell\sin\theta$
    or $\displaystyle\int_0^v \dfrac{vdv}{R} = k\ell\int_0^\theta \sin\theta d\theta$
    or $\dfrac{v^2}{R} = 2k\ell(1-\cos\theta)$

16. (b, d) Velocity of the particle at the highest point $v = \sqrt{2gh}$.

    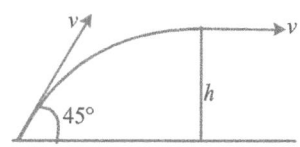

    Angular momentum
    $L = mv \times h$
    $= m\sqrt{2gh} \times h = m\sqrt{2gh^3}$
    Also $h = \dfrac{v^2 \sin^2 45°}{2g}$; then $L = \dfrac{mv^3}{4\sqrt{2g}}$

17. (b, c) Given $\vec{v}_{cm} = \vec{v}_B$
    $\vec{v}_C = \vec{v}_B + \vec{\omega}R$
    $\vec{v}_A = \vec{v}_B - \vec{\omega}R$
    From above equations, we get
    $\vec{v}_B = \dfrac{\vec{v}_A + \vec{v}_C}{2}$.

18. (b, c) If v_{cm} is the velocity of C. M, then
    $v = v_{cm} + \omega R$
    For no slipping, $v = \omega R$, $\therefore v_{cm} = 0$.

19. (a, c) If sufficient length of rough inclined plane is available, then cylinder will start rolling.

20. (a, c, d) $I_0 = I_1 + I_2 = I_3 + I_4$
    Also $I_1 = I_2$ and $I_3 = I_4$

21. (a, d) $\dfrac{1}{2}m(2g\ell) = mgh \Rightarrow h = \ell$
    The velocity of the ball is enough to complete the circle.

22. (a, b, c) Given $\vec{\tau} = \vec{A} \times \vec{L}$, Clearly $\vec{\tau}$ is perpendicular to $\vec{L}$. As $\vec{\tau}$ is perpendicular to $\vec{L}$ and $\vec{A}$, so it will cause no change in $\vec{L}$ or $\vec{A}$

Solutions EXERCISE-1.3

1. (a) Torque = F × moment arm.
    If force is applied close to hinge, moment arm will be small, so torque will be small.

2. (b) $\tau = \dfrac{dL}{dt}$ and $L = I\omega$.

3. (a) $Mk^2 = MR^2 \Rightarrow k = R$.

4. (a) In the process $I\omega$ = constant. As the person folds the hands, I decreases and so ω increases.

5. (d) $I = mr^2$, it depends on m and r both.

6. (c) α and a are different quantities, so they cannot be added. Similarly ω and v.

7. (a) $\tau = \omega \times$ moment arm. In this case $r = 0$, so $\tau = 0$.

8. (c) The body may not be in rotational equilibrium.

9. (b) If rod is in stable equilibrium, then net torque about any axis must be zero.

10. (a) In this process, $I\omega$ = constant. When buildings are constructed, I will increase, ω will decrease and T will increase.

11. (c) As ice melt, it spread towards the periphery, so moment of inertia increases. But $\vec{L}$ remains constant, because $\vec{\tau} = 0$.

12. (c) $K = K_{translational} + K_{rotation}$
    $= \dfrac{1}{2}mv^2 + \dfrac{1}{2}I\omega^2$
    $= \dfrac{1}{2}mv^2 + \dfrac{1}{2}(mR^2)\left(\dfrac{v}{R}\right)^2 = \dfrac{1}{2}mv^2 + \dfrac{1}{2}mv^2$
    As I is different for different objects, so the result is not same for all objects.

13. (a) $K = \dfrac{1}{2}mv^2 + \dfrac{1}{2}mv^2$
    $= 2K_{translational}$

14. (b) On smooth inclined plane, torque about geometric axis is zero. So rolling is not possible.

Solutions EXERCISE-1.4

Passage (Q. 1 - 3):

1. (c) $\dfrac{1}{2}kx_1^2 = \dfrac{1}{2}I(2\omega)^2$
    and $\dfrac{1}{2}kx_2^2 = \dfrac{1}{2}(2I)\omega^2$
    $\therefore \dfrac{x_1}{x_2} = \sqrt{2}$

2. (a) If ω' is the final angular velocity, then
    $I(2\omega) + 2I(\omega) = (I + 2I)\omega'$
    or $\omega' = \dfrac{4\omega}{3}$
    Thus $J_B = (L_f - L_i)/t$
    $= [(2I)\omega' - 2I\omega]/t$
    $= [2I \times \dfrac{4\omega}{3} - 2I\omega]/t$
    $= \dfrac{2I\omega}{3t}$

3. (b) Loss $= k_i - k_f$
    $= \left[\dfrac{1}{2}I(2\omega)^2 + \dfrac{1}{2}(2I)\omega^2\right] - \left[\dfrac{1}{2}(I+2I)\omega'^2\right]$
    $= \dfrac{1}{3}I\omega^2$.

Passage (Q. 4 - 6):

4. (d)

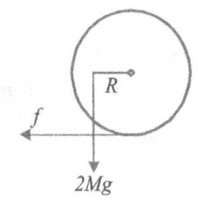

$f = (2M)a_{cm}$
and $2MgR - f(2R) = I\alpha$
or $2MgR - f(2R) = (4MR^2)\dfrac{a_{cm}}{(2R)}$
or $2MgR - 4Ma_{cm}R = 2MRa_{cm}$
$\Rightarrow a_{cm} = \dfrac{g}{3}$
so $\alpha = \dfrac{a_{cm}}{(2R)} = \dfrac{g}{6R}$.

5. (c) $f = 2M \times g/3 = \dfrac{2Mg}{3}$.

6. (a) $\dfrac{1}{2}I\omega^2 = (2M)gR$
    or $\dfrac{1}{2}(4MR^2)\omega^2 = 2MgR$
    $\omega = \sqrt{\dfrac{g}{R}}$

Passage (Q. 7 - 9):
7. (b); 8. (a); 9. (c)
    Drawing the F.B.D of the plank and the cylinder.

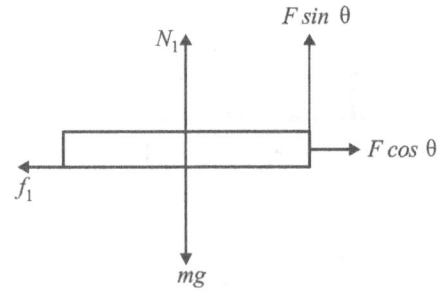

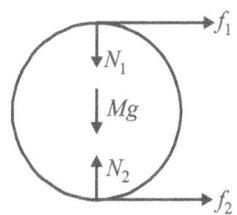

Equations of motion are
$F \cos\theta - f_1 = ma$ ....(1)
$F \sin\theta + N_1 = mg$ ....(2)
$f_1 + f_2 = MA$ .....(3)
$f_1 R - f_2 R = I\alpha$ .....(4)
$A = R\alpha$ .....(5)

$$a = \frac{4F\cos\theta}{3M + 8m} = \frac{4 \times 55 \times \frac{1}{2}}{[(3 \times 1) + (8 \times 1)]} = 10 \text{ m/s}^2$$

$$f_1 = \frac{3MF\cos\theta}{3M + 8m} = \frac{3 \times 1 \times 55 \times \frac{1}{2}}{3 \times 1 + 8 \times 1} = 7.5 \text{ N}$$

and $f_2 = \dfrac{MF\cos\theta}{3M + 8m} = \dfrac{1 \times 55 \times \frac{1}{2}}{3 \times 1 + 8 \times 1} = 2.5 \text{ N}$

Passage (Q. 10 - 12):

10. **(a)** Let linear velocity of the disc will become zero after a time t_1. Then it starts moving in backward direction and at time t_2 it comes in pure rolling. When disc starts pure rolling its linear and angular velocities will become constant and friction will be zero.

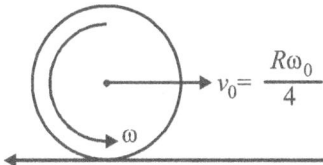

At time t_1,
$$0 = \frac{R\omega_0}{4} - \mu g t_1$$

$$t_1 = \left[\frac{R\omega_0}{4\mu g}\right] \quad \ldots \text{(i)}$$

At time t_2,
$v = \mu g t_2$
$\mu g t_2 = R\omega$

$$t_2 = \left[\frac{R\omega}{\mu g}\right] \quad \ldots \text{(ii)}$$

$\omega = \omega_0 - \dfrac{2\mu g}{R}(t_1 + t_2)$

$\omega = \omega_0 - \dfrac{2\mu g}{R}\left[\dfrac{R\omega_0}{4\mu g} + \dfrac{R\omega}{\mu g}\right]$

$\omega = \omega_0 - \dfrac{\omega_0}{2} - 2\omega$

$3\omega = \dfrac{\omega_0}{2}$ or, $\omega = \left[\dfrac{\omega_0}{6}\right]$

Now from (ii), $t_2 = \dfrac{R\omega_0}{6\mu g}$

Maximum displacement of the disc in forward direction,

$$S = \frac{R\omega_0}{4} \times \frac{R\omega_0}{4\mu g} - \frac{1}{2}\left(\frac{R\omega_0}{4\mu g}\right)^2 \mu g$$

$$= \frac{R^2\omega_0^2}{\mu g}\left[\frac{1}{16} - \frac{1}{32}\right] = \frac{R^2\omega_0^2}{32\mu g}$$

The displacement of the disc when it starts pure rolling

$$= \frac{1}{32}\frac{R^2\omega_0^2}{\mu g} - \frac{1}{2}\mu g\left(\frac{R\omega_0}{6\mu g}\right)^2 = \frac{5}{32 \times 9}\frac{(R\omega_0)^2}{\mu g}$$

$$\therefore \frac{\omega_0 R}{6} \times t_3 = \frac{5}{32 \times 9}\frac{(\omega_0 R)^2}{\mu g}$$

or, $t_3 = \dfrac{5}{48}\left(\dfrac{\omega_0 R}{\mu g}\right)$

Total time $= t_1 + t_2 + t_3 = \dfrac{25}{48}\dfrac{\omega_0 R}{\mu g}$.

11. **(b)** Time after which disc starts pure rolling.

$$t = t_1 + t_2 = \frac{R\omega_0}{4\mu g} + \frac{R\omega_0}{6\mu g} = \frac{5R\omega_0}{12\mu g}$$

12. **(c)** Angular momentum of disc after it starts pure rolling,
$L = MvR + I\omega$

$$= \left[\frac{MR\omega_0 R}{6} + \frac{MR^2}{2}\frac{\omega_0}{6}\right]$$

$$= MR^2\omega_0\left[\frac{1}{6} + \frac{1}{12}\right] = \left(\frac{MR^2\omega_0}{4}\right)$$

Passage (Q.13 -15):

13. **(b)** The force of impact at A is vertically upward.
14. **(d)**

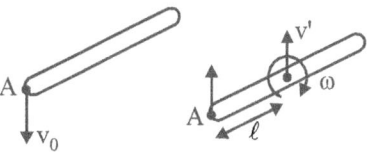

$v_A = v' + \ell\omega\cos\theta$
$\because$ collision is elastic
$\therefore v_0 = v' + \ell\omega\cos\theta$

15. **(b)** Angular momentum $\vec{L} = \vec{r} \times m\vec{v}$

$|\vec{L}| = mv_0\ell\cos\theta.$

Passage for (Q. 16 - 18) :

Suppose cylinder gets rotated through an angle before leaving contact. In the process

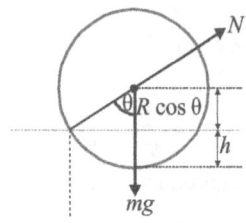

$$mgh = \frac{1}{2}Mv^2 + \frac{1}{2}I\omega^2$$

$$mgR(1 - \cos\theta) = \frac{1}{2}Mv^2 + \frac{1}{2}\left(\frac{MR^2}{2}\right)\left(\frac{v}{R}\right)^2$$

$$= \frac{3}{4}Mv^2$$

$$\therefore \quad v = \sqrt{\frac{4}{3}gR(1-\cos\theta)} \quad .....(i)$$

For the motion of the cylinder, we have

$$mg\cos\theta - N = \frac{mv^2}{R}$$

To leave the contact, $N = 0$,

$$\therefore \quad mg\cos\theta = \frac{mv^2}{R}$$

or $\quad \cos\theta = \dfrac{v^2}{gR}$ ...(ii)

16. (b) After solving equations (i) and (ii), we get

$$\cos\theta = \frac{4}{7}.$$

17. (c) From equation (i), we get

$$v = \sqrt{\frac{4gR}{7}}.$$

18. (b) We have $mgR\left(1 - \dfrac{4}{7}\right) = \dfrac{1}{2}mv^2 + \dfrac{1}{4}mv^2$

$$\therefore \quad \frac{1}{4}mv^2 = \frac{mgR}{7}$$

or $\quad K_{rot} = \dfrac{mgR}{7}$

Total decrease in potential energy
$= mgR$

$$\therefore \quad K_{trans} = mgR - \frac{mgR}{7}$$

$$= \frac{6}{7}mgR.$$

$$\therefore \quad \frac{K_{trans}}{K_{rot}} = 6.$$

Passage for (Q. 19 - 21) :

19. (a) Kinetic energy of the disc

$$k = \frac{1}{2}I\omega_0^2$$

$$= \frac{1}{2}\left(\frac{MR^2}{2}\right)\omega_0^2 = \frac{1}{4}MR^2\omega_0^2.$$

Angular momentum
$$L = I\omega_0$$
$$= \frac{MR^2}{2}\omega_0$$

20. (c) In the process, mechanical energy remains constant and so

$$\frac{1}{2}mv^2 = mgh$$

$$\therefore \quad h = \frac{v^2}{2g}$$

$$= \frac{(\omega_0 R)^2}{2g} = \frac{\omega_0^2 R^2}{2g}.$$

21. (d) Final angular momentum of the broken disc

$$L' = I'\omega_0$$

$$= \left(\frac{MR^2}{2} - mR^2\right)\omega_0$$

$$= \left(\frac{M}{2} - m\right)R^2\omega_0$$

Kinetic energy $K' = \dfrac{1}{2}I'\omega_0^2$

$$= \frac{1}{2}\left(\frac{M}{2} - m\right)R^2\omega_0^2 \quad \text{Ans.}$$

Passage for (Q. 22 - 24) :

22. (a) Let v_c and ω are the velocity of C.M. and angular velocity just after collision.

Using conservation of linear momentum, we have

$$mv_0 = 0 + Mv_c \quad ...(i)$$

and by conservation of angular momentum

$$mv_0 \frac{L}{2} = I\omega$$

or $\quad mv_0 \dfrac{L}{2} = \left(\dfrac{ML^2}{12}\right)\omega$ ... (ii)

From equations (i) and (ii)

$$v_c = \frac{mv_0}{M} \quad \text{and} \quad \omega = \frac{6mv_0}{ML}$$

Since collision is completely elastic, therefore K.E. before collision is equal to after collision

or $\quad \dfrac{1}{2}mv_0^2 + 0 = \dfrac{1}{2}Mv_c^2 + \dfrac{1}{2}I\omega^2$

or $\quad \dfrac{1}{2}mv_0^2 = \dfrac{1}{2}M\left(\dfrac{mv_0}{M}\right)v_c^2$

$$+ \frac{1}{2}\left(\frac{ML^2}{12}\right)\left(\frac{6mv_0}{ML}\right)^2$$

which gives $\quad \dfrac{m}{M} = \dfrac{1}{4}$ and $v_c = \dfrac{v_0}{4}$

23. (b)

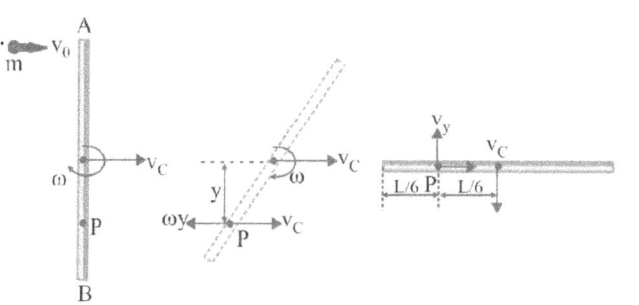

Velocity of point P immediately after collision be zero, let it is at a distance y from C.M.

$$\therefore \quad v_c - \omega y = 0$$

or $\quad \dfrac{mv_0}{M} - \left(\dfrac{6mv_0}{ML}\right)y = 0$

which gives $\quad y = \dfrac{L}{6}$

$\therefore \quad AP = \dfrac{L}{2} + \dfrac{L}{6} = \dfrac{2L}{3}$

24. (d) Angle rotated by rod in time $\dfrac{\pi L}{3v_0}$

$$\theta = \omega t = \dfrac{6mv_0}{ML} \times \dfrac{\pi L}{3v_0}$$

$$= \dfrac{\pi}{2}$$

The rod turns through $\dfrac{\pi}{2}$, in this interval of time. The velocity of point P in y-direction will be

$$v_y = \omega y = \dfrac{6mv_0}{ML} \times \dfrac{L}{6}$$

$$= \dfrac{v_0}{4}$$

The resultant velocity of point P

$$v = \sqrt{v_c^2 + v_y^2}$$

$$= \sqrt{\left(\dfrac{v_0}{4}\right)^2 + \left(\dfrac{v_0}{4}\right)^2}$$

$$= \dfrac{v_0}{2\sqrt{2}}$$

Passage for (Q. 25 - 27) :

25. (c) If $\quad \sqrt{2}\, v_{cm} = v$

$\therefore \quad v_{cm} = \dfrac{v}{\sqrt{2}}$

Angular velocity, $\omega = \dfrac{v_{cm}}{R} = \dfrac{v}{\sqrt{2}R}$.

26. (a) $K = \dfrac{1}{2}mv_{cm}^2 + \dfrac{1}{2}I\omega^2 = mv_{cm}^2$

$= m\left(\dfrac{v}{\sqrt{2}}\right)^2 = \dfrac{mv^2}{2}$

27. (c) In pure rolling, $W = f \times s = 0$

Passage for (Q. 28 - 30) :

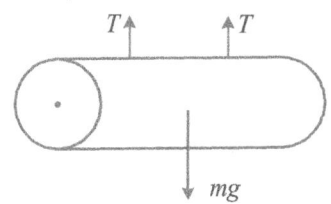

28. (a) $\quad mg - 2T = ma_{cm}$ ... (i)

and $\quad 2TR = I\alpha = \dfrac{mR^2}{2}\left(\dfrac{a_{cm}}{R}\right)$

or $\quad 2T = \dfrac{ma_{cm}}{2}$ ... (ii)

From above equations, we get

$$a_{cm} = \dfrac{2g}{3} = \dfrac{20}{3}\, m/s^2$$

29. (c) $\quad T = \dfrac{ma_{cm}}{4} = \dfrac{6 \times \dfrac{20}{3}}{4} = 10N$

30. (b) $\quad mg \times 7.5 = \dfrac{1}{2}mv^2 + \dfrac{1}{2}\left(\dfrac{mR^2}{2}\right)\left(\dfrac{v}{R}\right)^2$

$\Rightarrow \quad v = 10\, m/s$

Passage for (Q. 31 - 33) :

31. (c) $\quad v_{P_1} = v - \omega R/2$ and $v_{P_2} = v + \omega R/2$

32. (b) $\quad \tau = I\alpha = \left(\dfrac{mR^2}{2}\right)\alpha$

33. (d) $\quad a = \dfrac{v^2}{R}$.

34. $A \to (p);\ B \to (s);\ C \to (r);\ D \to (q)$
    Impulse, $\vec{J} = \Delta \vec{P} = m\Delta \vec{v}$

35. $A \to (q, r, s);\ B \to (q, r, s);\ C \to (p, q, r, s);\ D \to (p, q, r, s)$

(A) Moment of inertia of ring $\geq \dfrac{MR^2}{2}$

(B) Moment of inertia of sphere $\geq \dfrac{2}{5}MR^2$

(C) Moment of inertia of disc of cylinder $\geq \dfrac{MR^2}{4}$

36. Solution is given in the theory

37. $A \to (p, r);\ B \to (p, s);\ C \to (p, s);\ D \to (q, r)$

(A) A planet around sun in circular orbit; its angular momentum remains constant ($\tau = 0$). As its distance from sun is same, so speed is also same.

(B) A planet in elliptical orbit, $\tau = 0$, so angular momentum is zero. But its distance from sun changes, so speed changes.

(C) $\tau = F \times r = F \times 0 = 0$
In the process $\vec{L}$ is constant.

(D) In this case $\tau = Fr$,
so angular momentum does not remain constant.

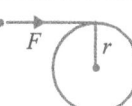

MECHANICS, HEAT, THERMODYNAMICS & WAVES

38. A → (s); B → (p); C → (p); D → (q, r)
    (A) In pure rolling on horizontal surface, friction is zero.
    (B) (C) On inclined plane, the point of contact has the tendency of sliding downward, so friction acts in upward direction.
    (D) In case of slipping $v_{cm} > \omega R$.

39. A → (p, s, r); B → (q, r, s); C → (q, r, s); D → (p, r, s)
    (A, D) The sliding tendency of point of contact of the disc may be forward or backward depending on relative value of F and Fh.
    (B,C) Sliding tendency of point of contact is forward so friction act in backward direction. The acceleration of C.M. will be in the direction of F.

40. A → s; B → r; C → q; D → t
    (A) MI of sphere $= \dfrac{2}{5} MR^2$
    (B) MI of shell about tangent $= \dfrac{2}{3} MR^2 + MR^2 = \dfrac{5}{3} MR^2$
    (C) MI of disc $= \dfrac{MR^2}{2}$
    (D) MI of disc about tangent in its plane
    $= \dfrac{MR^2}{4} + MR^2 = \dfrac{5}{4} MR^2$

41. A → p, q, r, s; B → p, s; C → p, q, r, s; D → q, r, s
    (A), (C) Dumbell experiences a force and net torque, so it has translation and rotation.
    Also $J = \Delta \vec{P}$, so linear momentum increase.
    $\vec{J}\ell = \Delta \vec{L}$, so angular momentum also increases.
    (B) $\tau = 0$, so it experiences translation and linear momentum increases
    (D) Due to hinge strip will not move.

42. Solution is given in the theory.

43. A → p, r; B → p, s, r; C → p, r, s; D → p, r, s
    Assume friction to be absent and horizontal force F is applied at a distance x above centre
    $$\therefore \quad a = \dfrac{F}{m} \quad \ldots\ldots(1)$$
    and $\quad Fx = \dfrac{mR^2}{2}\alpha$
    or $\quad R\alpha = \dfrac{2Fx}{mR} \quad \ldots\ldots(2)$
    If $a = R\alpha$ then from eq. (1) and (2) $\quad x = \dfrac{R}{2}$
    The friction force will be zero and $a = \dfrac{F}{m}$
    If $a > R\alpha$ or $x < \dfrac{R}{2}$, friction force is towards left and $a \neq \dfrac{F}{m}$
    If $a < R\alpha$ or $x > \dfrac{R}{2}$, friction force is towards right and $a \neq \dfrac{F}{m}$

Solutions EXERCISE-1.5

1. The rolling kinetic energy of the hoop is
   $$K = \dfrac{1}{2}mv^2 + \dfrac{1}{2}I\omega^2$$
   $$= \dfrac{1}{2}mv^2 + \dfrac{1}{2}(mR^2)\left(\dfrac{v}{R}\right)^2$$
   $$= mv^2$$
   $$= 100 \times (0.20)^2$$
   $$= 4 \text{ J}.$$
   Thus work done to stop the hoop $W = 4$ J. **Ans.**

2. The torque $= Fr$
   $= 25 \times 0.2 = 5$ N-m
   The moment of inertia $I = \dfrac{mR^2}{2}$
   $= \dfrac{20 \times (0.2)^2}{2} = 0.4$ kg-m^2
   (a) Angular acceleration, $\alpha = \dfrac{\tau}{I} = \dfrac{5}{0.4} = 12.5$ rad/s^2
   (b) Work done by the pull $W = F.s = 25 \times 2 = 50$ J
   (c) In case when there is no slipping between wheel and cord, friction does no work and so kinetic energy of the wheel
   K = work done
   $= 50$ J. **Ans.**

3. (a) In the device, $\omega_A r_A = \omega_B r_B$
   $$\therefore \quad \dfrac{\omega_A}{\omega_B} = \dfrac{r_B}{r_A}.$$

   For equal angular momentum, we have
   $I_A \omega_A = I_B \omega_B$
   $$\therefore \quad \dfrac{I_A}{I_B} = \dfrac{\omega_B}{\omega_A}$$
   $$= \dfrac{r_A}{r_B} = \dfrac{1}{3} \quad \textbf{Ans.}$$
   (b) For equal rotational kinetic energy, we have
   $$\dfrac{1}{2}I_A \omega_A^2 = \dfrac{1}{2}I_B \omega_B^2$$
   $$\therefore \quad \dfrac{I_A}{I_B} = \dfrac{\omega_B^2}{\omega_A^2}$$
   $$= \left[\dfrac{r_A}{r_B}\right]^2$$
   $$= \dfrac{1}{9}. \quad \textbf{Ans.}$$

4. The moment of inertia of the body,
   $I = 2[2Ma^2] + M[b^2 - a^2]$
   $= M(3a^2 + b^2)$.
   Thus work done in the process,
   $$W = \dfrac{1}{2}I\omega^2$$
   $$= \dfrac{1}{2}M(3a^2 + b^2)\omega^2$$
   $$= 2.6 \text{ J}. \quad \textbf{Ans.}$$

5. (a) If I_B be the moment of inertia of the wheel B, then by conservation of angular momentum.
$$I_A \omega_A + I_B \omega_B = (I_A + I_B)\omega$$
or $\quad 8 \times 600 + 0 = (8 + I_B) \times 400$
$\therefore \quad I_B = 4$ kg-m^2 **Ans.**

(b) The energy lost in the process
$$= k_i - k_f$$
$$= \frac{1}{2}I_A\omega_A^2 - \frac{1}{2}(I_A + I_B)\omega^2$$
$$= 5200 \text{ J} \quad \textbf{Ans.}$$

6. By Newton's second law
$$F_2 - F_1 = ma$$
$\therefore \quad F_1 = F_2 - ma$
$\quad\quad\quad = 5 - 1 \times 2 = 3$ N.

For rotational equilibrium, taking moment of forces about centre of mass, we get
$$F_1 \times \frac{l}{2} - F_2\left(\frac{l}{2} - y\right) = 0$$
$$3 \times \frac{l}{2} - 5\left(\frac{l}{2} - 0.2\right) = 0$$
$\therefore \quad l = 1$ m. **Ans.**

7. Given $\quad -\tau \propto \sqrt{\omega}$

As $\quad \alpha = \dfrac{\tau}{I}$

$\therefore \quad -\alpha \propto \sqrt{\omega}$

or $\quad \dfrac{d\omega}{dt} = -k\sqrt{\omega}$

or $\quad \displaystyle\int_{\omega_0}^{\omega} \dfrac{d\omega}{\sqrt{\omega}} = -k\int_0^t dt$

$\quad 2|\sqrt{\omega}|_{\omega_0}^{\omega} = -kt$

or $\quad \sqrt{\omega} = \sqrt{\omega_0} - \dfrac{kt}{2}$

or $\quad \omega = \left[\sqrt{\omega_0} - \dfrac{kt}{2}\right]^2 \quad$ ....(i)

For ω to be zero,
$$0 = \sqrt{\omega_0} - \frac{kt}{2}$$
$$t = \frac{2\sqrt{\omega_0}}{k} \quad ....(ii)$$

Average angular velocity
$$\omega_{av} = \frac{\int_0^t \omega dt}{t} \quad ....(iii)$$

After simplifying equations (i), (ii) and (iii), we get
$$\omega_{av} = \frac{\omega_0}{3} \quad \textbf{Ans.}$$

8. For the translation motion of the cylinder, we have
$$mg - 2T = ma \quad ...(i)$$

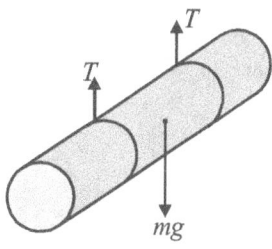

For rotation about axis of the cylinder
$$2TR = I\alpha \quad ....(ii)$$
where $\quad I = \dfrac{MR^2}{2}$
and $\quad \alpha = \dfrac{a}{R}$

On solving above equations, we get

(a) $\quad T = \dfrac{mg}{6}$

and $\quad \alpha = \dfrac{2g}{3R}$

(b) The velocity of centre of mass
$$v = at$$
$$= \frac{2gt}{3}$$

The average power generated by gravitational force
$$P = Fv$$
$$= mg \times \frac{2gt}{3}$$
$$= \frac{2}{3}mg^2 t \quad \textbf{Ans.}$$

9. $p \times \dfrac{L}{2} = \left(\dfrac{mL^2}{12}\right)\omega \Rightarrow \omega = \dfrac{6p}{mL}$

Rod will rotate about its c.m., one half exerts centrifugal force on the other half, therefore $F = \dfrac{m\omega^2}{2} \times \dfrac{L}{4}$

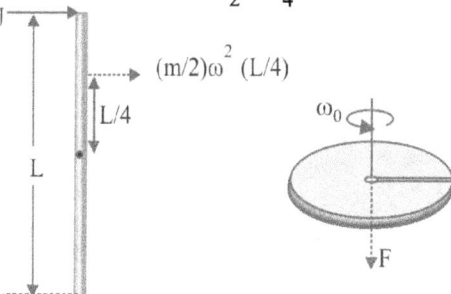

10 Given, diameter = 6 cm
$$\frac{20}{6-y} = \frac{10}{y}$$
or $\quad 20y = 10(6-y)$
or $\quad 20y + 10y = 60$
or $\quad 30y = 60$
or $\quad y = 2$

Solutions Exercise-1.6

1. (a) If h is the height reached by the cylinder, then

$$\frac{1}{2}mv^2 + \frac{1}{2}I\omega^2 = mgh$$

or $\frac{1}{2}mv^2 + \frac{1}{2}\left(\frac{mR^2}{2}\right)\left(\frac{v}{R}\right)^2 = mgh$

or $\frac{3}{4}mv^2 = mgh$

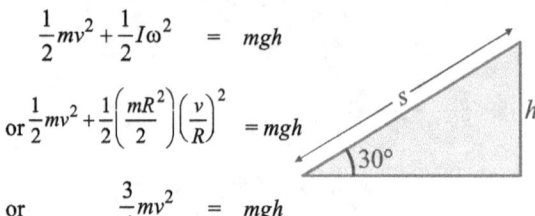

∴ $h = \frac{3v^2}{4g} = \frac{3 \times 5^2}{4 \times 9.8} = 1.9\ m$

The distance $s = \frac{h}{\sin 30°} = \frac{1.9}{1/2} = 3.8\ m$

(b) Acceleration of the cylinder $= \frac{2}{3}g \sin 30°$

or $a = \frac{2}{3} \times 9.8 \times \frac{1}{2} = 3.27\ m/s^2$

The time taken to move the distance of 3.8 m

$3.8 = \frac{1}{2}at^2$

∴ $t \simeq 1.5\ s$

Total time taken $T = 2t = 3\ s$ **Ans.**

2. If α be the necessary retardation, then

$0 = \omega_0 - \alpha t$

∴ $\alpha = \frac{\omega_0}{t} = \frac{\left(2\pi \times \frac{240}{60}\right)}{20}$

$= \frac{2\pi}{5}\ rad/s^2$.

The torque needed $(\tau)\ \tau = I\alpha$

$= \frac{mR^2}{2}\alpha$

$= \frac{25 \times 0.2^2}{2} \times \frac{2\pi}{5}$

$= \frac{\pi}{5}\ N\text{-}m$

If F is the required force, then $F = \frac{\tau}{R} = \frac{\pi/5}{0.2} = \pi\ N$ **Ans.**

3. Given $\omega_0 = 10\pi\ rad/s$.

The acceleration for translation $a = \frac{f}{m} = \frac{\mu mg}{m} = \mu g$

$= 0.2 \times 9.8$
$= 1.96\ m/s^2$.

Angular retardation, $\alpha = \frac{\tau}{I} = \frac{fR}{I} = \frac{\mu mg \times R}{I}$

For disc $I = \frac{mR^2}{2}$,

∴ $\alpha = \frac{\mu mgR}{\frac{mR^2}{2}}$

$= \frac{2\mu g}{R}$

$= \frac{2 \times 0.2 \times 9.8}{0.1} = 39.2\ rad/s^2$.

For ring $I = mR^2$,

∴ $\alpha = \frac{\mu mgR}{mR^2} = \frac{\mu g}{R} = 1.96\ rad/s^2$

If t is the time taken to start pure rolling, then

$\omega = \omega_0 - \alpha t$, ...(i)
$v = 0 + at$ ....(ii)
and $v = \omega R$ ....(iii)

After solving above equations, we get

$t = \frac{\omega_0}{\left(\alpha + \frac{a}{R}\right)}$

Thus $t_{disc} = \frac{10\pi}{\left(39.2 + \frac{1.96}{0.1}\right)} = 0.53\ s$

Similarly $t_{ring} = 0.80\ s$ **Ans.**

Obviously disc begins to roll earlier than the ring.

4. (a) In the process angular momentum remains constant, so

$I_i \omega_i = I_f \omega_f$

∴ $\omega_f = \frac{I_i \omega_i}{I_f}$

$= \frac{[7.6 + 2 \times 5(0.9)^2] \times (2\pi \times 30)}{[7.6 + 2 \times 5(0.2)^2]}$

$\simeq 59\ rpm$.

(b) Kinetic energy in the process does not remain constant. Workdone by the man using his muscle power will increase the kinetic energy. Thus

$\frac{k_f}{k_i} = \frac{\frac{1}{2}I_f \omega_f}{\frac{1}{2}I_i \omega_i}$

$= \frac{[7.6 + 2 \times 5(0.2)^2](59)^2}{[7.6 + 2 \times 5(0.9)^2](30)^2}$

$= 1.97$ **Ans.**

5. Given $\omega = a - bt$.
The time of zero velocity $0 = a - bt$,
∴ $t = a/b$

Again $\dfrac{d\theta}{dt} = (a - bt)$

or $\int_0^\theta d\theta = \int_0^{a/b}(a - bt)dt$

∴ $\theta = \dfrac{a^2}{2b}$. **Ans.**

6. In case of hollow structures, their masses are at the periphery. Therefore A has the smallest and D has the largest moment of inertia.

7. The moment of inertia about the given axis

$I = \dfrac{mR^2}{2} + \left[\dfrac{mR^2}{2} + m(2R)^2\right]$

$= 5\,mR^2$ **Ans.**

8. The restoring torque
$\tau_{rest} = f \times 0.5 + 5$

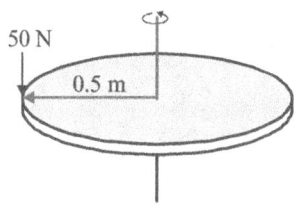

$= \mu N \times 0.5 + 5$
$= 0.6 \times 50 \times 0.5 + 5$
$= 20$ N-m

If τ is the required torque, then by Newton's second law, we have
$\tau - \tau_{rest} = I\alpha$
∴ $\tau = \tau_{rest} + I\alpha$

$= 20 + 3.75 \times \left(\dfrac{2\pi \times \dfrac{120}{60}}{9}\right)$

$= 25.23$ N-m.

The force applied $F = \dfrac{\tau}{r}$

$= \dfrac{25.23}{0.5}$

$\simeq 50$ N. **Ans.**

(b) To maintain the constant speed, the torque needed

$= \tau_{rest}$
$= 20$ N.

Thus force required $= \dfrac{\tau_{rest}}{r}$

$= \dfrac{20}{0.5}$
$= 40$ N. **Ans.**

(c) The angular retardation $\alpha = \dfrac{\tau}{I}$

$= \dfrac{5}{3.75} = 1.33$ rad/s^2.

If t is the required time, then
$0 = \omega_0 - \alpha t$

∴ $t = \dfrac{\omega_0}{\alpha}$

$= \left[\dfrac{2\pi \times \dfrac{120}{60}}{1.33}\right]$

$= 9.44$ s **Ans.**

9. If a be the acceleration of the bucket, then
$mg - T = ma$ ......(i)

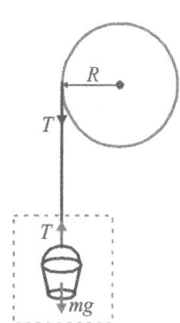

and $TR = I\alpha$
As $\alpha = a/R$
∴ $TR = Ia/R$ ......(ii)

After solving above equations, we get

$a = \dfrac{mg}{m + \dfrac{I}{R^2}}$

$= \dfrac{mg}{m + \dfrac{MR^2/2}{R^2}}$

$= \dfrac{mg}{m + \dfrac{M}{2}}$

or $a = \dfrac{20 \times 9.8}{20 + \dfrac{20}{2}}$

$= 6.53$ m/s^2

(a) Tension $T = \dfrac{Ia}{R^2}$

$= \dfrac{MR^2/2}{R^2} \times a$

$= \dfrac{Ma}{2}$

$= \dfrac{20 \times 6.53}{2}$

$= 65.3$ N. **Ans.**

(b) If v is the velocity of the bucket, then
$v^2 = 0 + 2al$
$= 2 \times 6.53 \times 20$
∴ $v = 16.2$ m/s **Ans.**

(c) If t be is the time of fall, then

$$l = \frac{1}{2}at^2$$

$$\therefore \quad t = \sqrt{\frac{2l}{a}}$$

$$= \sqrt{\frac{2 \times 20}{6.53}}$$

$$= 2.47 \text{ s} \quad \text{Ans.}$$

10. If ω is the final angular velocity of the system, then

$$I_{table}\omega - mvR = (I_{table} + I_{man})\omega'$$

or $\quad 400 \times 0.2 - 60 \times 1 \times 2 = (400 + 60 \times 2^2)\omega'$

$\therefore \quad \omega' = 0.0625 \text{ rad/s} \quad$ **Ans.**

11. Velocity of the particle just before striking the rod $v = \sqrt{(2gh)}$

In the process of collision the angular momentum of the system remain constant

$$mv\ell + 0 = I\omega \quad \ldots(i)$$

where $\quad I = \frac{M\ell^2}{3} + m\ell^2$

Substituting value of I in equation (i), we get

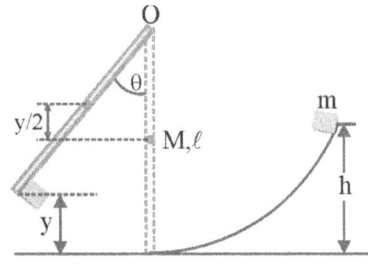

$$\omega = \frac{mv\ell}{(M\ell^2/3 + m\ell^2)}$$

Let rod deflects through an angle θ before momentarily stops. The rotational K. E. of the rod + particle is used to raise the particle as well as to raise the c.g. of the rod.

$$\therefore \quad \frac{1}{2}I\omega^2 = mgy + \frac{Mgy}{2} \quad \ldots \text{(ii)}$$

where $y = \ell(1 - \cos\theta)$.

Solve above equations to get the value of θ.

12. (a) If v is the min. velocity to complete the loop, then

$$mg + N = \frac{mv^2}{R} \quad (R \gg r).$$

As $\quad N = 0$,

$\therefore \quad v = \sqrt{gR}$.

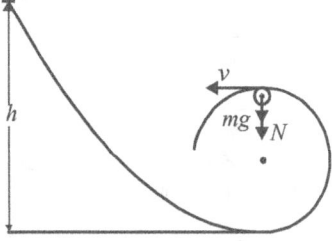

For the rolling marble, we can write

$$mg(h - 2R) = \frac{1}{2}mv^2 + \frac{1}{2}I\omega^2$$

$$= \frac{1}{2}mv^2 + \frac{1}{2} \times \frac{2}{5}mr^2 \times \left(\frac{v}{r}\right)^2$$

$$= \frac{7}{10}mv^2$$

$$= \frac{7}{10}m \times gR$$

$\therefore \quad h = 2.7 R.$ **Ans.**

(b) By using conservation of mechanical energy, we have

$$mgh = mgR + \frac{1}{2}mv_Q^2 + \frac{1}{2}I\omega^2$$

or $\quad mg(6R) = mgR + \frac{7}{10}mv_Q^2$

$\therefore \quad v_Q = \sqrt{\frac{50}{7}gR}$

The normal (horizontal) force at Q

$$F_Q = \frac{mv_Q^2}{R}$$

$$= \frac{50}{7}mg. \quad \text{Ans.}$$

13. Net torque, $\tau_{net} = mgl_2 - mgl_1$

If α is the angular accelerations, then

$$\alpha = \frac{\tau_{net}}{I}$$

$$= \frac{mg(l_2 - l_1)}{ml_1^2 + ml_2^2}$$

$$= \frac{g(l_2 - l_1)}{l_1^2 + l_2^2}$$

$$= \frac{9.8(0.8 - 0.2)}{0.2^2 + 0.8^2}$$

$$= 8.65 \text{ rad/s}^2$$

$\therefore \quad a_1 = \alpha l_1$

$$= 8.65 \times 0.2$$

$$= 1.73 \text{ m/s}^2$$

$a_2 = \alpha l_2$

$$= 8.65 \times 0.8$$

$$= 6.92 \text{ m/s}^2$$

14. Given, $\vec{v} = (30\hat{i} + 60\hat{j})$ m/s

$\vec{r} = (3\hat{i} - 4\hat{j})$ m

(a) The angular momentum, $\vec{L} = m(\vec{r} \times \vec{v})$

$$= 2[(3\hat{i} - 4\hat{j}) \times (30\hat{i} + 60\hat{j})]$$

$$= 600 \hat{k} \text{ kg-m}^2/\text{s} \quad \text{Ans.}$$

(b) Here $\vec{r} = [(3 - (-2)\hat{i} + \{(-4 - (-2)\hat{j}\}]$

$$= (5\hat{i} - 2\hat{j}) \text{ m}$$

The angular momentum,

$$\vec{L} = m(\vec{r} \times \vec{v})$$
$$= 2[(5\hat{i} - 2\hat{j}) \times (30\hat{i} + 60\hat{j})]$$
$$= 720\,\hat{k} \text{ kg-m}^2/\text{s}$$

15. (a) Moment of inertia of the sculpture

$$I = \frac{mR^2}{2} + mR^2 + \left[\frac{mL^2}{12} + m\left(\frac{L}{2} + R\right)^2\right]$$

$$= \frac{mR^2}{2} + mR^2 + \left[\frac{m(2R)^2}{12} + m(R+R)^2\right]$$

$$= 5.83\, mR^2$$

(b) In the process mechanical energy remains constant. Therefore

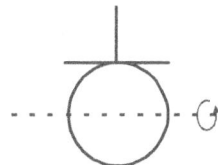

$$K_i + U_i = K_f + U_f$$

$$0 + [mgR + mg(R+R)] = \frac{1}{2}I\omega^2 + [-mgR - mg(R+R)]$$

After substituting the values and solving, we get

$$\omega = 12 \text{ rad/s}.$$

16. The mass of the carpet of radius $R/2$

$$m' = \frac{M(R/2)^2}{R^2}$$

$$= \frac{M}{4}.$$

Using conservation of mechanical energy, we have

$$MgR + 0 = \frac{M}{4}g\frac{R}{2} + \frac{1}{2}\left(\frac{M}{4}\right)v^2 + \frac{1}{2}I\omega^2$$

or $\quad \frac{7}{8}MgR = \frac{Mv^2}{8} + \frac{1}{2}\frac{\left(\frac{M}{4}\right)\left(\frac{R}{2}\right)^2}{2} \times \left(\frac{v}{\frac{R}{2}}\right)^2$

$$\frac{7}{8}MgR = \frac{3}{16}Mv^2$$

$\therefore \quad v = \sqrt{\frac{14}{3}gR}$. **Ans.**

17. Moment of force $\vec{N} = \vec{r} \times \vec{F}$

$$= (a\hat{i} + b\hat{j}) \times (A\hat{i} + B\hat{j})$$
$$= -bA\hat{k} + aB\hat{k}$$
$$= (aB - bA)\hat{k}.$$

Moment arm $\quad l = \dfrac{|\vec{r} \times \vec{F}|}{|\vec{F}|}$

$$= \frac{(aB - bA)}{\sqrt{A^2 + B^2}}. \quad \text{Ans.}$$

18. Resultant force $\vec{F} = A\hat{j} + B\hat{i}$.

Resultant torque $\vec{\tau} = \vec{r_1} \times \vec{F_1} + \vec{r_2} \times \vec{F_2}$

$$= (a\hat{i} \times A\hat{j}) + (b\hat{j} \times B\hat{i})$$
$$= aA\hat{k} + bB(-\hat{k})$$
$$= (aA - bB)\hat{k}$$

Moment arm $\quad l = \dfrac{|\vec{\tau}|}{|\vec{F}|}$

$$= \frac{(aA - bB)}{\sqrt{A^2 + B^2}} \quad \text{Ans.}$$

19. The given system of forces is like as shown in figure. Thus

$$F_x = F + F = 2F$$

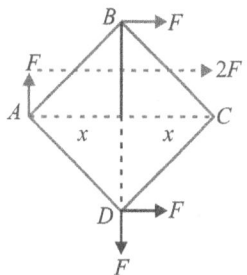

and $\quad F_y = F - F = 0$

Resultant of these, $R = \sqrt{F_x^2 + F_y^2} = 2F$

Suppose the resultant force R passes from a point, a distance y from A, then

$$Fx - 2Fy = 0$$

$$\Rightarrow \quad y = \frac{x}{2}$$

Thus the resultant is applied at the mid point of side BC.

20. Solution is given in the theory.
21. Solution is given in the theory.
22. For any angular position θ, the torque of the force F relation to A

$$\tau = F \times l \cos\theta$$

Thus $\int_0^\phi \tau d\theta = \frac{1}{2}I\omega^2$

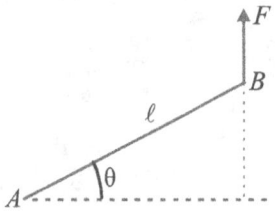

$\int_0^\phi Fl\cos\theta \, d\theta = \frac{1}{2}\frac{ml^2}{3}\omega^2$

or $Fl\sin\phi = \frac{ml^2}{6}\omega^2$

$\therefore \omega = \sqrt{6F\sin\phi/ml}$
Ans.

23. From FBD, we have $m_2 g - T_2 = m_2 a$ ...(i)

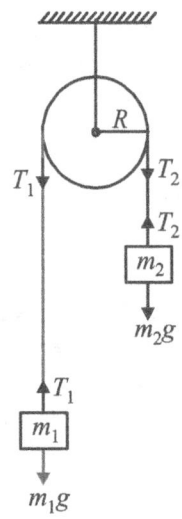

and $T_1 - m_1 g = m_1 a$ ...(ii)

For the rotation of the pulley
$T_2 R - T_1 R = I\alpha$ ...(iii)

Also $\alpha = \dfrac{a}{R}$ and

$I = \dfrac{mR^2}{2}$ ....(iv)

After simplifying above equations, we get

$\alpha = \dfrac{(m_2 - m_1)g}{\left[m_1 + m_2 + \dfrac{m}{2}\right]R}$ **Ans.**

24. To get frictional torque on the disc, take an element of width dr a distance r from the centre of the disc. The frictional torque

$d\tau = dF \, r$
$= \mu (dN) r$
$= \mu \left[\dfrac{mg}{\pi R^2} \times 2\pi r dr\right] r$
$= \dfrac{2\mu mg r^2 dr}{R^2}$

$\therefore \tau = \dfrac{2\mu mg}{R^2}\int_0^R r^2 dr$

$= \dfrac{2}{3}\mu mgR$

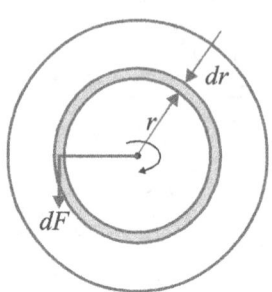

The angular retardation $\alpha = \dfrac{\tau}{I}$

$= \dfrac{\frac{2}{3}\mu mgR}{\dfrac{mR^2}{2}}$

$= \dfrac{4\mu g}{3R}$

Now from $\omega = \omega_0 - \alpha t$, we have

$t = \dfrac{\omega_0}{\alpha}$

$= \dfrac{\omega}{\dfrac{4\mu g}{3R}}$

$= \dfrac{3\omega R}{4\mu g}$. **Ans.**

25. The mass of the hanging part of the cord
$m' = \dfrac{mx}{R}$

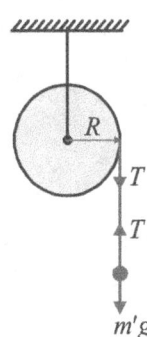

Thus $m'g - T = m'a$ ....(i)
and $TR = I\alpha$

or $T = \dfrac{Ia}{R^2}$ ...(ii)

On solving equations, we get

$$a = \frac{m'g}{m' + \frac{I}{R^2}}$$

Here $I = \frac{MR^2}{2} + \frac{m}{l}(l-x)R^2$

After simplifying, we get

$$\alpha = \frac{2mgx}{Rl(M+2m)} \quad \text{Ans.}$$

26. For translational motion of the cylinder, we have
$$mg\sin\alpha - T = ma_{cm} \quad \text{.......(i)}$$

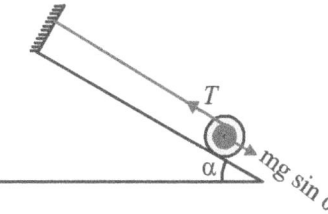

and for rotational motion
$$Tr = I\left(\frac{a_{cm}}{R}\right) \quad \text{.......(ii)}$$

On solving above equations, we get

$$a_{in} = \frac{g\sin\alpha}{\left[1 + \frac{I}{mR^2}\right]} \quad \text{Ans.}$$

27. From FBD, we have
$$N = F + mg$$
Frictional force
$$f = \mu N$$
$$= \mu(F + mg) \quad \text{.....(i)}$$

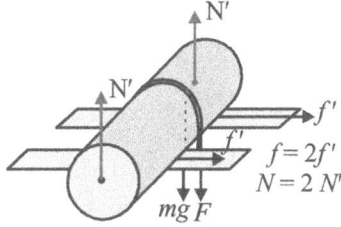

For translational motion of the cylinder
$$f = ma_{cm} \quad \text{.....(ii)}$$
For rotational motion of the cylinder
$$FR - fR = I\alpha \quad \text{.....(iii)}$$

Here $\alpha = \frac{a_{cm}}{R}$

and $I = \frac{MR^2}{2}$

After simplifying above equations, we get

$$a_{cm} = \left[\frac{2\mu g}{2 - 3\mu}\right]$$

and $$F_{max} = \left[\frac{3\mu mg}{2 - 3\mu}\right]$$

28. If a_x be the acceleration of the spool along x-axis, then
$$F\cos\alpha - f = ma_x \quad \text{.....(i)}$$
and $$fR - Fr = I\alpha \quad \text{.....(ii)}$$

where $\alpha = \frac{a_x}{R}$

and $I = \gamma mR^2$

(a) After simplifying above equations, we get

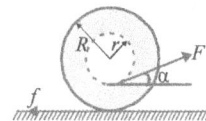

$$a_x = \frac{F(\cos\alpha - r/R)}{m(1 + \gamma)}$$

(b) The displacement of the spool in t second
$$s = \frac{1}{2}a_x t^2$$

Thus work done $W = Fs\cos\alpha$

$$= \frac{F^2 t^2 (\cos\alpha - r/R)^2}{2m(1+\gamma)}$$

Ans.

29. Acceleration for translation, $a = \frac{f}{m}$

$$= \frac{\mu mg}{m}$$

$$= \mu g$$

Retardation for rotation $\alpha = \frac{\tau}{I}$

$$= \frac{fR}{I}$$

$$= \frac{\mu mgR}{\frac{mR^2}{2}}$$

$$= 2\mu g / R$$

If t be the required time and v and ω are linear and angular velocities after pure rolling, then
$$\omega = \omega_0 - \alpha t$$
and $$v = 0 + at$$
After getting pure rolling, $v = \omega R$.
After solving equations, we get

(a) $$t = \frac{\omega_0 R}{3\mu g}$$

(b) Work done by frictions $W = k_i - k_f$

$$= \frac{1}{2}I\omega_0^2 - \left[\frac{1}{2}mv^2 + \frac{1}{2}I\omega^2\right]$$

$$= -\frac{m\omega_0^2 R^2}{6} \quad \text{Ans.}$$

30. By conservation of angular momentum, we have
$$Mv_1 R = I\omega + Mv_2 R$$

where $I = \frac{MR^2}{2}$

and $\omega = \dfrac{v_2}{R}$

Thus, $M v_1 R = I \times \dfrac{v_2}{R} + M v_2 R$

$\therefore v_2 = \dfrac{v_1}{\left[1 + \dfrac{I}{MR^2}\right]}$ **Ans**

31. Choose an element of the rod of width dx at a distance x from the hinge.

Mass of the element, $dm = \dfrac{m}{\ell} dx$. The centrifugal force on this element

$$dF = (dm)\,\omega^2\,(x\sin\theta).$$

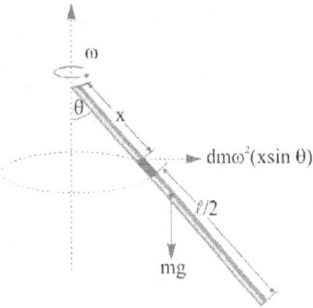

Fig. 6.44

Its moment of force about the hinge

$$d\tau = dF \times x\cos\theta$$
$$= (dm)\,\omega^2\,(x\sin\theta)(x\cos\theta)$$
$$= \left(\dfrac{m}{\ell}dx\right)\omega^2 x^2 \left(\dfrac{\sin 2\theta}{2}\right)$$
$$= \dfrac{m\omega^2}{2\ell}\sin 2\theta\; x^2\, dx \quad ....(i)$$

For the moment of force of whole length of rod, integrating (i)

$$\tau = \dfrac{m\omega^2}{2\ell}\sin 2\theta \int_0^\ell x^2 dx$$

$$= \dfrac{m\omega^2 \ell^2}{6}\sin 2\theta \quad ....(ii)$$

In the rotating frame, apart from other forces the centrifugal force also act. For rotational equilibrium of the rod, we have $\Sigma\vec{\tau} = 0$. Taking moment of all forces about hinge and putting their algebraic sum zero, we get

$$mg\dfrac{\ell}{2}\sin\theta = \dfrac{m\omega^2 \ell^2}{6}\sin 2\theta$$

or $\cos\theta = \dfrac{3g}{2\omega^2 \ell}$ **Ans.**

32. Hint : $\left(\dfrac{ML^2}{3}\right)\omega_0 = \left(\dfrac{ML^3}{3}\right)\omega + mr^2\omega$

$\dfrac{1}{2}\left(\dfrac{ML^2}{3}\right)\omega_0^2 = \dfrac{1}{2}\left(\dfrac{ML^2}{3}\right)\omega^2 + \left[\dfrac{1}{2}mv'^2 + \dfrac{1}{2}(mr^2)\omega^2\right]$

33. Hint : $\left(\dfrac{MR^2}{2}\right)\omega = \left(\dfrac{MR^2}{2}\right)\omega_0 + (mR^2)\omega$

W.d. = change in rotational K. E.

34. (a) In the process angular momentum remains constant. If ω be the final angular velocity, then
$$I_1\omega_1 + I_2\omega_2 = (I_1 + I_2)\omega$$
$\therefore \omega = \left[\dfrac{I_1\omega_1 + I_2\omega_2}{I_1 + I_2}\right]$ **Ans.**

(b) Work done by friction $W = K_i - K_f$
$$= \left[\dfrac{1}{2}I_1\omega_1^2 + \dfrac{1}{2}I_2\omega_2^2\right] - \dfrac{1}{2}\left[(I_1 + I_2)\omega^2\right]$$
$$= \dfrac{I_1 I_2(\omega_1 - \omega_2)^2}{2(I_1 + I_2)} \quad \textbf{Ans.}$$

35. Acceleration for translation

$$a = \dfrac{f}{m}$$
$$= \dfrac{\mu mg}{m}$$
$$= \mu g$$

Angular retardation $\alpha = \dfrac{\tau}{I}$
$$= \dfrac{fR}{I}$$
$$= \dfrac{\mu mg R}{\dfrac{2}{3}mR^2}$$
$$= \dfrac{3}{2}\dfrac{\mu g}{R}$$

For translational motion $v^2 = 0 + 2as$

For rotational motion $\omega^2 = \omega_0^2 + 2\alpha\theta$

where $\theta = s/R$

After getting pure rolling, $v = \omega R$

After solving above equations and substituting the values, we get
$$s = 0.58\, m. \quad \textbf{Ans.}$$

36. In the process of falling of rod

(a) decrease in P.E. = increase in rotational K.E.

or $Mg\dfrac{L}{2} = \dfrac{1}{2}I\omega^2$

or $Mg\dfrac{L}{2} = \dfrac{1}{2}\dfrac{(ML^2)}{3}\omega^2$

$\therefore \omega = \sqrt{\dfrac{3g}{L}}$

(b) Torque acting on the rod about left end

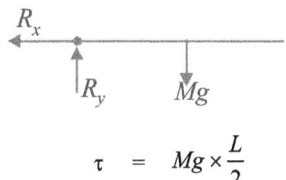

$$\tau = Mg \times \frac{L}{2}$$

By Newton's second law

$$Mg\frac{L}{2} = I\alpha$$

or $$Mg\frac{L}{2} = \left(\frac{ML^2}{3}\right)\alpha$$

∴ $$\alpha = \frac{3g}{2L}$$

(c) $$a_x = \omega^2 r$$

$$= \frac{3g}{L} \times \frac{L}{2}$$

$$= \frac{3g}{2}$$

and, $$a_y = \alpha r$$

$$= \frac{3g}{2L} \times \frac{L}{2}$$

$$= \frac{3g}{4}$$

Thus $$F_x = Ma_x$$

$$= \frac{3Mg}{2}$$

For the translation of centre of mass along y-axis, we have

$$Mg - R_y = Ma_y$$

$$R_y = M\left(\frac{3g}{4}\right)$$

∴ $$R_y = \frac{Mg}{4}.$$ **Ans.**

37. (a) The position of c.m.

$$y = \frac{6 \times 0 + 3 \times 1.5}{6+3}$$

$$= 0.5 \text{ m from top.}$$

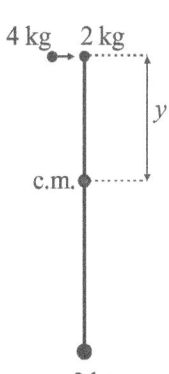

Velocity of combined mass (4 + 2) kg after collision:
$$4 \times 3 + 0 = (4+2)v$$
∴ $$v = 2 \text{ m/s}$$

The velocity of c.m. is given by

$$v_{cm} = \frac{m_1 v_1 + m_2 v_2}{m_1 + m_2}$$

$$= \left[\frac{6 \times 2 + 3 \times 0}{6+3}\right]$$

$$= \frac{4}{3} \text{ m/s} \quad \textbf{Ans.}$$

(b) Using conservation of angular momentum about c.m. we have
$$4 \times 3 \times y = I\omega$$
or $$4 \times 3 \times 0.5 = [6 \times 0.5^2 + 3 \times 1^2] \times \omega$$
∴ $$\omega = \frac{4}{3} \text{ m/s} \quad \textbf{Ans.}$$

38. (i) Suppose a is the acceleration of the block, then the tangential acceleration of the pulley will be a. Thus angular acceleration of the pulley

$$\alpha = \frac{a}{R}$$

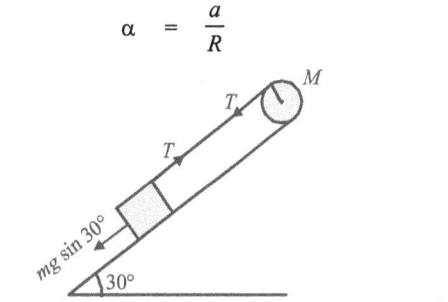

Thus $$mg\sin 30° - T = ma \quad .....(i)$$
and $$TR = I\alpha$$

or $$TR = \frac{MR^2}{2} \times \frac{a}{R}$$

∴ $$T = \frac{Ma}{2} \quad ....(ii)$$

From equations (i) and (ii), we get

$$a = \frac{mg\sin 30°}{m + \frac{M}{2}}$$

$$= \frac{mg}{2m + M}$$

$$= \frac{0.5 \times 9.8}{2 \times 0.5 + 2}$$

$$= 1.63 \text{ m/s}^2$$

and $$T = \frac{2 \times 1.63}{2}$$

$$= 1.63 \text{ N} \quad \textbf{Ans.}$$

(ii) In process the K.E. of the system will convert into potential energy of the block and so

$$\frac{1}{2}mv^2 + \frac{1}{2}I\omega^2 = mgh$$

or $$\frac{1}{2}m(\omega R)^2 + \frac{1}{2}\left(\frac{MR^2}{2}\right)\omega^2 = mg(s\sin 30°)$$

After simplifying, we get
$$s = 1.224 \text{ m} \quad \textbf{Ans.}$$

39. Similar to problem 34.

40. Retardation for translation $a = \dfrac{f}{m}$

$= \dfrac{\mu m g}{m}$

$= \mu g$

Angular acceleration $\alpha = \dfrac{\tau}{I}$

$= \dfrac{fR}{I}$

$= \dfrac{\mu mg \times R}{\dfrac{m}{2}R^2}$

$= \dfrac{2\mu g}{R}$

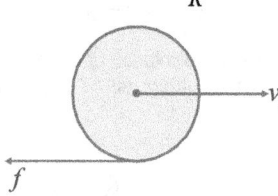

If v and ω are the linear and angular velocities after getting rolling, then

$v = v_0 - at$ ......(i)
$= v_0 - \mu g\, t_0$

and $\omega = 0 + \alpha t$

$= \dfrac{2\mu g}{R} t_0$ ......(ii)

Also $v = \omega R$ ......(iii)

(a) Thus $v_0 = \mu g t_0$

$= \dfrac{2\mu g t_0}{R} R$

$\therefore t_0 = \dfrac{v_0}{3\mu g}$

From equation (i),

$v = v_0 - \mu g \times \dfrac{v_0}{3\mu g}$

$= \dfrac{2v_0}{3}$ **Ans.**

(b) Work done by frictional force
$W = K_i - K_f$

$= \dfrac{1}{2}mv_0^2 - \left[\dfrac{1}{2}mv^2 + \dfrac{1}{2}I\omega^2\right]$

$= -\dfrac{1}{6}mv_0^2$

41. (a) Suppose the distance of c.m. of the laminer sheet from AB is x. The M.I. of the sheet about AB,

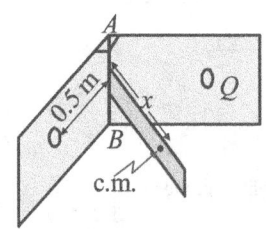

$I_{AB} = I_{cm} + mx^2$
$= 1.2 + 30\, x^2$.

If ω_i and ω_f are the inital and final angular velocities of the sheet about AB, then

angular impulse $=$ change in angular momentum
$J \times 0.5 = I_{AB}[\omega_f - (-\omega_i)]$

or $6 \times 0.5 = (1.2 + 30\, x^2)(\omega_i + \omega_f)$ ......(i)

Velocity of c.m. of the sheet
$v_i = \omega_i x$
and $v_f = \omega_f x$

(b) Also Impulse $=$ Change in momentum

or $J = m[v_f - (-v_i)]$

or $6 = 30[\omega_i + \omega_f] x$ ......(ii)

Given $\omega_i = 1$ rad/s

Solving equations (i) and (ii), we get
$x = 0.1$ m
and $\omega_f = 1$ rad/s

(c) As there is no friction between laminer sheet and obstacles, so sheet remains continually hitting the obstacles.

42. For the motion of the plank, we have
$F - f_1 = m_2 a_2$ .....(i)

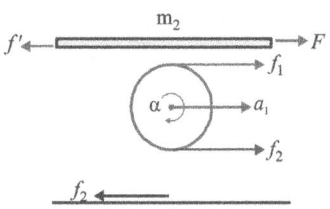

FBD

For the motion of the cylinder
$f_1 + f_2 = m_1 a_1$ .....(ii)

and $f_1 R - f_2 R = I\alpha$ .....(iii)

Also $a_2 = a_1 + \alpha R$ .....(iv)

For no slipping of cylinder, $a_1 = \alpha R$ .....(v)

Solving above equations, we get

$a_1 = \dfrac{4F}{3m_1 + 8m_2}$,

$a_2 = \dfrac{8F}{3m_1 + 8m_2}$

$f_1 = \dfrac{m_1 F}{3m_1 + 8m_2}$,

$f_2 = \dfrac{3m_1 F}{3m_1 + 8m_2}$ **Ans.**

43. In the process, frictional force at contact point consitutes torque, which causes change in angular momentum of the cylinders. If ω_1' and ω_2' are the final angular velocities of the cylinder then for no slipping

$\omega_1' r_1 = \omega_1' r_2$ .....(i)

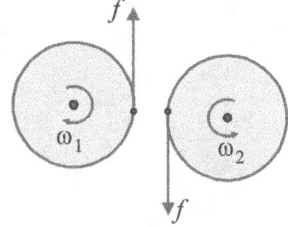

ROTATIONAL MECHANICS 119

For first cylinder
$$-fr_1 t = I_1(\omega_1' - \omega_1) \quad .....(ii)$$
For second cylinder
$$fr_2 t = I_2(\omega_2' - \omega_2) \quad .....(iii)$$
After solving above equations, we get
$$\omega_1' = \left[\frac{I_1\omega_1 r_2 + I_2\omega_2 r_1}{I_2 r_1^2 + I_1 r_2^2}\right] r_2$$
and
$$\omega_2' = \left[\frac{I_1\omega_1 r_2 + I_2\omega_2 r_1}{I_2 r_1^2 + I_1 r_2^2}\right] r_1 \quad \text{Ans.}$$

44. The velocity of the particle before collision
$$v = \sqrt{2gh}$$

(a) Angular momentum of the system after collision
= angular momentum before collision
$$= \vec{L}_{particle} + \vec{L}_{rod}$$
$$= mv\frac{L}{2} + 0$$
$$= m\sqrt{2gh}\frac{L}{2}$$
$$= \frac{mL\sqrt{gh}}{\sqrt{2}} \quad \text{Ans.}$$

By conservation of angular momentum, we have
$$mv\frac{L}{2} = I\omega$$
or
$$\frac{mL\sqrt{gh}}{\sqrt{2}} = \left[2mL^2 + m\left(\frac{L}{2}\right)^2\right]\omega$$
$$\therefore \quad \omega = \frac{\sqrt{8gh}}{3L} \quad \text{Ans.}$$

(b) The velocity of the particle + ball B after collision

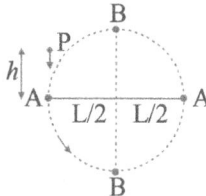

$$v' = \frac{m\sqrt{2gh} + 0}{m + m}$$
$$= \sqrt{\frac{gh}{2}}.$$

For the full rotation to occur, ball B will reach to the highest point, and so
$$K_i + U_i = K_f + U_f$$
$$\frac{1}{2}(m+m)v'^2 + 0 = 0 + \left[2mg\frac{L}{2} - mg\frac{L}{2}\right]$$
After substituting the value of v' and simplifying, we get
$$h = \frac{3L}{2} \quad \text{Ans.}$$

45. (a) If a_{cm} is the acceleration of the cm of the hollow sphere, then
$$mg\sin\theta - f = ma_{cm} \quad .....(i)$$
and
$$fR = I\alpha$$
or
$$fR = I\frac{a_{cm}}{R}$$
$$\therefore \quad f = I\frac{a_{cm}}{R^2} \quad .....(ii)$$
After solving equations, we get
$$a_{cm} = \left[\frac{g\sin\theta}{1 + \frac{I}{mR^2}}\right]$$

For hollow sphere, $I = \frac{2}{3}mR^2$

$$\therefore \quad a_{cm} = \frac{3}{5}g\sin\theta$$

Thus
$$f = \frac{Ia_{cm}}{R^2}$$
$$= \frac{\frac{2}{3}mR^2 \times \frac{3}{5}g\sin\theta}{R^2}$$
or
$$f = \frac{2}{5}mg\sin\theta$$
$$\therefore \quad \mu_{min} = \frac{f}{N}$$
$$= \frac{\frac{2}{5}mg\sin\theta}{mg\cos\theta}$$
$$= \frac{2}{5}\tan\theta \quad \text{Ans.}$$

(b) Given,
$$\mu = \frac{\mu_{min}}{2}$$
$$= \frac{\tan\theta}{5}$$

Now $mg\sin\theta - f = ma$
or $mg\sin\theta - \mu N = ma$
or $mg\sin\theta - \frac{\tan\theta}{5} \times mg\cos\theta = ma$

$$\therefore \quad a = \frac{4g\sin\theta}{5}$$

For rotational motion of the sphere
$$fR = I\alpha$$
or
$$\mu NR = \frac{2}{3}mR^2\alpha$$
or
$$\frac{\tan\theta}{5} \times mg\cos\theta R = \frac{2}{3}mR^2\alpha$$
$$\therefore \quad \alpha = \frac{3g\sin\theta}{10R}$$

The linear velocity after moving a distance ℓ

$v^2 = 0 + 2a\ell$

$= 2 \times \dfrac{4}{5} g \sin\theta \ell$

$= \dfrac{8}{5} g\ell \sin\theta$

Thus translational K.E.,

$K_{Trans} = \dfrac{1}{2} mv^2$

$= \dfrac{4}{5} mg\ell \sin\theta$.

We can write $\dfrac{\omega}{v} = \dfrac{\alpha}{a}$

$\therefore \quad \omega = v\left(\dfrac{\alpha}{a}\right)$

$= \sqrt{\dfrac{8}{5} g\ell \sin\theta} \times \left[\dfrac{3g \dfrac{\sin\theta}{10R}}{4g \dfrac{\sin\theta}{5}}\right]$

$= \dfrac{3}{8} R \sqrt{\dfrac{8}{5} g\ell \sin\theta}$

Rotational kinetic energy of the sphere

$K_{rot} = \dfrac{1}{2} I\omega^2$

$= \dfrac{1}{2} \times \dfrac{2MR^2}{3} \times \left[\dfrac{3}{8R}\sqrt{\dfrac{8g\ell\sin\theta}{5}}\right]^2$

$= \dfrac{3}{40} mg\ell \sin\theta$.

Total kinetic energy

$K = K_{Trans} + K_{rot}$

$= \dfrac{4}{5} mgl \sin\theta + \dfrac{3}{40} mgl \sin\theta$

$= \dfrac{7}{8} mg\ell \sin\theta$ **Ans.**

46. The force exerted by the particles = $2nmv$ per unit area

Total force exerted $F = 2nmv \times \left(\dfrac{a}{2} \times b\right)$

$= 2 \times 100 \times 0.01 \times v \times (0.3 \times 0.4)$

$= 0.24 v$

This force acts at a distance of $x = 0.3 + \dfrac{0.3}{2}$

$= 0.45$ m.

For the rotational equilibrium of the plate, we have

$\tau_{weight} = \tau_{force}$

$[3g] \times 0.3 = F \times 0.45$

$= 0.24 \times 0.45$

$\therefore \quad v = 83.3$ m/s **Ans.**

47. (a) The effective system is shown in figure. Here

$r = \ell \cos 30°$

$= \dfrac{\sqrt{3}}{2} \ell$.

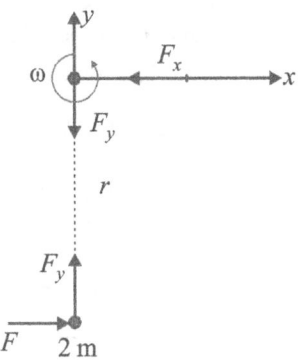

Thus, $F_y = M\omega^2 r$

$= (2m)\omega^2 \times \dfrac{\sqrt{3}}{2} \ell$

$= \sqrt{3} m\ell \omega^2$

(b) Suppose F_x be the horizontal force exerted by the hinge. If α is the angular acceleration, then

$Fr = I\alpha$

$\therefore \quad \alpha = \dfrac{Fr}{I}$

$= \dfrac{F \times \sqrt{3}\dfrac{\ell}{2}}{2m\ell^2}$

$= \dfrac{\sqrt{3} F}{4m\ell}$

$a_x = \alpha r$

$= \dfrac{\sqrt{3} F}{4m\ell} \times \dfrac{\sqrt{3}\ell}{2}$

$= \dfrac{3F}{8m}$

Now $F - F_x = (2m) a_x$

$= (2m) \times \dfrac{3F}{8m}$

$\therefore \quad F_x = \dfrac{F}{4}$ **Ans.**

www.ingramcontent.com/pod-product-compliance
Lightning Source LLC
LaVergne TN
LVHW061937070526
838199LV00060B/3857